MODERN GUERRILLA
INSURGENCY

Modern Guerrilla Insurgency

Anthony James Joes

PRAEGER

Westport, Connecticut
London

Library of Congress Cataloging-in-Publication Data

Joes, Anthony James.
    Modern guerrilla insurgency / Anthony James Joes.
        p.   cm.
    Includes bibliographical references and index.
    ISBN 0-275-94263-5 (alk. paper)
    1. Military history, Modern—20th century. 2. Insurgency—
History—20th century. 3. Guerrillas—History—20th century.
4. World politics—1945–   I. Title.
D431.J64   1992
355.02′18—dc20   91-46994

British Library Cataloguing in Publication Data is available.

Library of Congress Catalog Card Number: 91-46994
ISBN: 0-275-94263-5

First published in 1992

Praeger Publishers, 88 Post Road West, Westport, CT 06881
An imprint of Greenwood Publishing Group, Inc.

Printed in the United States of America

The paper used in this book complies with the
Permanent Paper Standard issued by the National
Information Standards Organization (Z39.48-1984).

10 9 8 7 6 5 4 3 2 1

For
My Students

Contents

Acknowledgments

I am deeply indebted to the following colleagues who very kindly consented to criticize parts of earlier drafts of this book: Douglas MacDonald of Colgate University, Gabriel Marcella of the U.S. Army War College, Richard Shultz of the Fletcher School of Law and Diplomacy, and Peter Woolley of Fairleigh Dickinson University. Dean Vincent McCarthy of Saint Joseph's University gave important assistance at a strategic moment. Barbara Lang of the Drexel Library of Saint Joseph's University was unfailingly helpful. My wife, Chris Calhoun Joes, has once again been a tower of strength. Any merit this work may possess is owing to all this good assistance. For the book's shortcomings I alone bear full responsibility.

MODERN GUERRILLA
INSURGENCY

Introduction

Insurgency and the Future

As this unhappy century draws to a close, two great phenomena dominate the global political landscape. The first is the moral and material bankruptcy of the Marxist-Leninist empire. The second, closely related, is the belief that a clash between major powers along the lines of World War II, or even Korea, is highly improbable.

The proclamations of a new era of world order are reminiscent of the days of the Congress of Vienna or the period immediately after the surrender of Japan.[1] Nevertheless, however unlikely direct great-power confrontations in the foreseeable future may seem to some observers, the world is not heading for universal peace. Far from it. Over large areas of the globe festering problems, including increasing population pressures, persistent inequalities between city and countryside, and—above all—unresolved ethnic and religious resentments and conflicts, have created or aggravated explosive situations. Large areas of Latin America, sub-Saharan Africa and the Middle East, China, and the former Soviet empire, all hover on or close to the brink of the abyss.

The nature of the societies afflicted with these problems makes it a certainty that when large-scale violence erupts, it will very often assume the form of a guerrilla insurgency, traditional weapon of the weak but determined. And the very disappearance of the tensions between the United States and the Soviet Union seems to have made it more likely that as volatile areas from the Balkans to the Andes burst into the flames of guerrilla war, one or another major power will be tempted to intervene to protect its perceived interests.

This circle of temptation includes the United States. Twice in this century—and before Americans learned to fear the Soviet Union—an apparently stable, even dormant Mexico erupted into guerrilla rebellion,
eventually drawing a U.S. response. How certain is anyone that something
like this will not happen again? Or, what if the continuing breakup of the
Soviet empire reaches the point where a clearly popular independence movement faces annihilation and appeals for assistance to the West?

For this country to adopt, a priori, a rigid rule against intervention in
any insurgency would almost certainly mean allowing others to create new
equations of power and commit new crimes against humanity. And, the
"Viet Nam Syndrome" notwithstanding, the United States has involved
itself in foreign insurgencies with much success in key areas. At any rate,
strategic calculations, ideological affinities, humanitarian impulses, and ethnic, racial, and/or religious sympathies will force American leaders to con-
template some sort of involvement in some of these future conflicts.

Yet for the United States to become involved in such struggles is patently
perilous. In the twentieth century, many of the world's great powers found
themselves enmeshed in guerrilla conflicts: the British in Ireland, the Japanese in China, the Germans in Yugoslavia, the French in Tonkin, the
Americans in South Viet Nam, the Russians in Afghanistan. In all of these
wars, the great power settled for something far removed from the classical
concept of victory and was widely perceived as having suffered a defeat.
This record suggests that translating commonly defined military might into
effective counterguerrilla strategy and tactics is very difficult. Years ago a
knowledgeable student of insurgency observed that "guerrilla warfare is
what regular armies always have most to dread, and when this is directed
by a leader with a genius for war, an effective campaign becomes well nigh
impossible."[2] With the spread of sophisticated yet relatively cheap weaponry
all around the globe, this comment is more cogent today than it was then.
All war involves risk; war against guerrillas on their home territory can be
a real throw of the dice.

The present volume examines guerrilla insurgency in five societies:
Greece, the Philippines, French Indochina, South Viet Nam, and Afghanistan. Although the United States was involved in all of these conflicts to
one degree or another, the configuration and consequences of each exhibits
great diversity. The basis for selecting each of these cases was its effect on
world affairs at the time and/or its instructive nature for us today. The
method of constructing this study has been historical and comparative; thus
it is largely a work of synthesis and interpretation. This book neither sets
up a grand theory of guerrilla insurgency nor throws down the gauntlet,
except in one or two instances, to expensively acquired conventional wisdom. Its principal thesis is quite venerable and still vital: the true sources
of any serious guerrilla insurgency lie in the political realm, and it is political
understanding and skill that ultimately determine whether the government

or the insurgents prevail. Sound military operations cannot compensate for bad political practices; in fact, the two are radically incompatible. From this conviction arises the book's concentration on the interplay between military strategy and political context.

Whatever else may be in dispute, it is clear that the American people face a world of difficult political and moral choices. They also have a notoriously short memory, and their historical experience is often jammed into such Procrustean ambiguities as "no more Munichs" or "no more Viet Nams." In light of the grim possibilities that lie ahead, therefore, any effort, however inadequate, to contribute to the clarification of the subject of guerrilla insurgency may find justification.

NOTES

1. See, for example, Stephen Van Evera, "Primed for Peace: Europe after the Cold War," *International Security*, vol. 15, no. 3 (Winter 1990–91); Robert J. Art, "A Defensible Defense: America's Grand Strategy after the Cold War," *International Security*, vol. 15, no. 4 (Spring 1991); Bruce Russett and J. S. Sutterlin, "The U.N. in a New World Order," *Foreign Affairs*, vol. 70, no. 2 (Spring 1991).

2. C. E. Callwell, *Small Wars: Their Principles and Practice* (Wakefield, England: EP Publishing, 1976 [orig. 1906]), p. 126.

Chapter 1

On the Nature of Guerrilla War

No major proposal required for war can be worked out in ignorance of political factors.

Carl von Clausewitz, *On War*

If historical experience teaches us anything about revolutionary guerrilla war, it is that military measures alone will not suffice.

Samuel B. Griffith, *Mao Tse-tung on Guerrilla Warfare*

For the past five decades, many Americans have associated the term "guerrilla warfare" with Communist revolutionary movements. But in fact, guerrilla warfare is only the name for a set of combat tactics; the decision to engage in a guerrilla struggle is an answer to the question How shall we fight against overwhelming odds? Guerrilla warfare is the option of those who confront an enemy greatly superior in numbers, equipment, and training: it is the weapon of the weak, whatever their political complexion. In itself therefore it is devoid of ideological content. Thus not only Communists, but also conservatives, nationalists, traditionalists, and monarchists have engaged in guerrilla warfare. The stubborn revolt in the Vendée against the First French Republic, the long struggle by Spanish partisans against Napoleonic France (where the name "guerrilla" comes from), anticommunist revolts in the Ukraine, Tibet, and most recently Afghanistan are a few examples of guerrilla war waged by conservative and/or nationalist popular movements.

HOW GUERRILLAS FIGHT

Since the guerrillas are by definition the weaker side, their first duty, and in the early stages their only duty, is to stay alive, to survive in the face of the numerical and technical superiority of their opponents. Both Clausewitz and Mao insist that for guerrillas there is no such thing as a decisive battle, no stake for which one may legitimately risk the survival of the guerrilla movement. Hence for guerrillas to retreat in the face of superior or merely equal forces is no disgrace; indeed, it is mandatory.

A successful guerrilla war therefore means a protracted conflict. If the struggle is not protracted but brief, it will be because the guerrillas have been killed or dispersed. On the other hand, an extended struggle means that the government forces are unable to defeat the guerrillas; hence, the continuation of the conflict will wear down both the morale of the army and civilian support for the government. The passage of time allows the guerrillas to train and test their members and identify natural leaders. And the longer the conflict persists, the greater the possibility of outside intervention on behalf of the guerrillas. Most of all, a protracted conflict gives the guerrillas time to accomplish their real purpose: to develop and build up their own conventional forces so that they can abandon guerrilla tactics and meet the enemy on its own terms. For guerrillas, ultimate success means that they cease to be guerrillas and become conventional (regular) troops.

Mao wrote that "the strategy of guerrilla warfare is to pit one man against ten, but the tactic is to pit ten men against one." This means that well-led guerrilla forces, although strategically on the defensive, will be tactically on the offensive: they will look for opportunities to fight the enemy with the certainty of victory or at least the certainty of doing serious damage. Such certainty requires that the guerrillas have greatly superior numbers at the point of combat; this in turn demands that the guerrillas be able to assemble, attack, withdraw, and disperse again very quickly. Well-led guerrillas will strive to attack the government forces at night, or in the rain, or when the latter are eating or are worn out from completing a difficult march.[1] The essence of all such operations must be speed, concealment, and deception.

Here the numerical and technological weaknesses of the guerrillas actually turn to their advantage: small and lightly armed bands of guerrillas can move much more quickly and quietly than conventional forces, especially over difficult terrain (the Roman word for the equipment and baggage of a regular army was *impedimenta*). That is why Clausewitz advises guerrillas to operate in rough country and away from the seacoast. The great disparity of equipment and speed between guerrilla and conventional forces accounts for the fact that the mining of roads is a universal and favorite guerrilla tactic.

WHAT GUERRILLAS NEED

Guerrillas are combatants who seek to wage a protracted conflict emphasizing speed, deception, and small victories through great superiority at the crucial point. In order to operate in this way, guerrillas need high morale, reliable intelligence, and, if possible, a secure base and foreign assistance.

On the surface, the life of the guerrilla seems romantic and exciting; that is why it is usually easy for guerrilla bands to recruit youngsters. But in fact guerrilla existence is filled with hardships: inadequate and irregularly available food, exposure to the elements, little or no medical care, the danger of injury, capture, or death.[2] Guerrillas also have to kill people and destroy property. After the initial excitement wears off, morale declines, and many members of a guerrilla band will want to go home. Some guerrilla leaders in the past tried to prevent desertion by forcing members of their band to commit some heinous act in public, thus cutting them off from normal society; but such practices further undermine unit morale.

The key to waging a protracted guerrilla campaign is to sustain high morale. One way to do this is to limit recruitment to volunteers; another is to maintain complete (and visible) equality between officers and men with regard to food and living conditions. But the best sustenance for morale among guerrillas is their belief in both the rightness of what they are doing and in its eventual triumph. In short, guerrillas need a cause. Well-led guerrilla units will therefore systematically and frequently discuss the political genesis and foundations of their movement.

The leaders of a guerrilla war will usually be urban and educated and hence comfortable with abstractions, such as national independence, or the dictatorship of the proletariat. But since by definition protracted guerrilla warfare takes place in rural areas, the cause must be a concrete one that appeals to country folk. Such a cause will normally be based on one of the following: (1) the elimination of a group of persons, such as landlords, government officials, or soldiers, whom peasants perceive as inflicting injustice on them, or (2) the defense of the peasants' religion.

The sometimes quite well-founded perception of injustice among the peasantry is that source of support for a guerrilla rebellion that should be most easy for the government to eliminate or modify. In fact, however, it is very often the aspect of the conflict that governments are least aware of or willing to address.

Where religion is the basis of the insurgency, a difference of religion between guerrillas and their enemies will often also entail a difference of nationality, as in Spain under Napoleonic occupation or Afghanistan under the Soviets (but not always, as in the Catholic Vendée during the French Revolution). And where there are differences neither of religion nor nationality between the contending forces, as in the Philippine Huk rebellion, the ability of the government to decide the course of the struggle through political means is greatly enhanced (see Chapter 3).

If the guerrillas are to fight successfully—indeed, if they are to survive—they must have information about the numbers, equipment, and morale of the enemy forces in the places chosen for attack and also the safest routes of escape. This invaluable information and analysis is intelligence, and can come from penetration of the police, the army, and/or the bureaucracy, but most of all from sympathizers among the rural folk. Each guerrilla band should recruit at least some of its members from the particular geographical area in which it plans to operate. This ought to guarantee both knowledge of the physical layout of the countryside and rapport with the local peasantry. Such rapport provides the basis for building the guerrilla movement's political infrastructure, the supporters in every village or hamlet who can supply the guerrillas with information, food, and new recruits. The fighting guerrillas operate outside the villages, the infrastructure inside. A good infrastructure makes it possible for guerrillas to take heavy losses and yet survive and even grow. As Mao observed, "the guerrillas move among the people as fish move through the water." Conversely, guerrillas who mistreat the civilians among whom they operate are making a big mistake (see Chapter 2).

The absolute necessity that guerrillas have a morale-building cause and timely intelligence is clear. But many students of guerrilla war believe that in order to wage a protracted conflict, guerrillas also need a base area, a part of the country so remote, in terms of distance, difficulty of terrain, or lack of communications that the government forces cannot or will not attack it, or at least cannot enter it in strength without the guerrillas perceiving such a move in plenty of time to get out of their way. Within this base area the guerrillas can rest themselves, grow food, train recruits, make weapons, stock supplies, and tend their sick and wounded. To the degree that this kind of base is truly necessary, it follows that protracted guerrilla war (as opposed to urban terrorism) would be close to impossible in highly developed regions where there are no inaccessible areas, such as Belgium or Honshu.

Even in underdeveloped countries, it may be that guerrillas can no longer count on having a truly secure base. The contemporary concept of the secure base grew out of Mao's struggles against the armed forces of Nationalist China and Imperial Japan. Neither of those governments possessed massive troop-carrying helicopters or powerful long-range bombers like the B–52. Today the existence of such weapons extends the government's offensive capability to every part of even a large and underdeveloped country like Afghanistan. But if they lack a true base area inside their country, the guerrillas may be able to substitute for it a sanctuary across the national frontier, in the manner of the Greek Communists, the Viet Cong, and the Mujahideen.

HELP FROM OUTSIDE

The question of cross-border sanctuaries raises the issue of outside assistance to the guerrillas. To sustain themselves, well-led guerrillas can almost always get enough supplies, including weapons, from government forces and the markets. But to win their war, guerrillas usually have to develop at least to some degree into conventional forces; that means they have to acquire substantial amounts of artillery, armored vehicles, and fuel. Under normal circumstances, guerrillas can obtain adequate supplies of that kind only from outside, from or through a government friendly to them. In the years since World War II it would be very difficult to identify a single clear-cut case of a guerrilla insurgency that achieved victory while relying completely on domestic resources.[3]

Events in the wider world are always important and sometimes decisive for the guerrillas. The Chinese Communists, to take one monumental example, were not doing at all well against the Nationalist forces of Chiang Kai-shek until the Japanese invaded China. The Japanese army mauled and ruined Chiang's forces; when it then turned to deal with the Communists, the progress of American campaigns in the Pacific caused Tokyo to withdraw many divisions from North China. Both the Japanese invasion of China and the American defeat of Japan were the equivalent of massive outside intervention against Mao's opponents. Without these circumstances, it is very difficult to imagine how the Communists would have won.

Similarly, the Japanese invasion of French Indochina and later Chinese assistance to the Viet Minh were essential to the Communist victory in Tonkin (see Chapter 4). Whether or not American assistance to the Afghan guerrillas was indispensable in bringing about the withdrawal of the Soviets, it certainly made the conduct of that struggle vastly more difficult and costly for them.

Minimally, experience suggests that it will be exceedingly difficult for a government to defeat guerrillas who possess both an attractive cause and foreign assistance. Conversely, guerrilla movements that have neither a secure base nor a transfrontier sanctuary are in serious trouble. It is also extremely rare for guerrillas to succeed unless they can fly the banners of national independence or religious vindication; but neither of these causes, nor even their combination, guarantees victory, as Algeria, Cambodia, Tibet, and the Vendée testify.

MILITARY RESPONSES TO INSURGENCY

To the casual observer, the inability of the government to destroy the guerrillas or at least disrupt their operations with ease may present a puzzle. After all, the government will have a preponderance of troops and a superiority of weapons (if the guerrillas were numerous and well armed, they would not be guerrillas, but conventional forces).

The government's superiority of numbers is not always what it seems. Guerrillas have only to fight; they do not have to hold territory. The government has to do both; it needs sufficient forces not only to go out looking for guerrillas, but also to safeguard the normal functioning of society by maintaining order and protecting vital installations and communications systems. Besides, since guerrillas need not hold territory, they only fight when they choose; the remainder of the time they can rest. Government forces must be on the alert everywhere all the time. This is why many authorities on guerrilla warfare maintain that a government needs at least a 10-to-1 ratio of troops to guerrillas in order to win. Often a government will not be able to reach such a favorable ratio, and even if it does, the accumulation may be at ruinous expense to the economy and to other vital security forces, such as the police.

The superiority of weapons and technology available to a government also can be very deceptive. "The greatest victories that have been won in war do not depend on a simple superiority of technology, but rather on a careful meshing of one side's advantages with the other's side's weaknesses so as to produce the greatest possible gap between the two."[4] In many circumstances guerrillas are relatively immune to modern weapons. Where the enemy's technical superiority is too great, they can simply decline to fight. Guerrillas are normally dispersed and thus are poor targets for either artillery or aircraft. They can also keep government forces from using these weapons by fighting very close to them or by operating in the midst of a civilian population (but this last did not work against the Soviets in Afghanistan).

To say the least, bringing the government's superior military resources to bear against the guerrillas in an effective way is not easy. Neither is it an object that can be achieved in itself: a successful military response by the government needs to be closely linked to a sound political program, as the following case studies will constantly suggest to the reader.[5]

NOTES

1. Although not leading a guerrilla movement properly so called, George Washington employed basic guerrilla tactics for most of the American Revolutionary War. Convinced that the preservation of his army was the supreme strategic object, Washington rarely hesitated to retreat before superior enemy forces. He normally fought the British only when his intelligence network gave him moral certitude that because of overwhelming numerical superiority he would win. See Russell F. Weigley, *The American Way of War: A Military History of United States Military Strategy and Policy* (Bloomington: Indiana University Press, 1973), Chapter 1.

2. Taruc, in *Born of the People* (Westport, CT: Greenwood Press, 1973 [orig. 1953]), wrote:

Sickness was our worst enemy and accounted for many times the casualties inflicted by the Japanese and puppets. It was the one problem we were never quite able to overcome. Malaria was the worst cause of death. Our squadrons were often forced to live in the swamps, which were thickly infested by malarial mosquitos. . . . Dysentery and stomach ulcers, from inadequate food, were other serious afflictions. (p. 139)

3. In a number of recent instances, most notably in Colombia, guerrilla insurgents financed themselves through sales of illegal drugs.

4. Martin Van Creveld, *Technology and War* (New York: Free Press, 1989), p. 90.

5. A brief list of studies of guerrilla warfare for the interested reader would include R. Asprey, *War in the Shadows* (London: Macdonald, 1976); C. E. Callwell, *Small Wars: Their Principles and Practice* (Wakefield, England: EP Publishing, 1976 [original 1906]); J. E. Cross, *Conflict in the Shadows* (New York: Doubleday, 1963); John Ellis, *A Short History of Guerrilla Warfare* (London: Ian Allen, 1975); Geoffrey Fairbairn, *Revolutionary Guerrilla Warfare* (Harmondsworth, England: Penguin, 1974); L. H. Gann, *Guerrillas in History* (Stanford, CA: Hoover Institution, 1971); Samuel B. Griffith, *Mao Tse-tung on Guerrilla Warfare* (New York: Praeger, 1961); Walter Laqueur, *Guerrilla: A Historical and Critical Study* (Boulder, CO: Westview, 1984); Peter Paret and John Shy, *Guerrillas in the 1960s*, rev. ed. (New York: Praeger, 1962).

Chapter 2

A Greek Drama

WHAT WAS THE GREEK CIVIL WAR?

The Cold War turned hot in several countries: Afghanistan, Viet Nam, Korea, and elsewhere, but first of all in Greece. Greece was the only state in which the efforts of the United States to rebuild war-shattered Europe encountered armed Communist resistance. The first military confrontation between the Communist East and the democratic West, the Greek insurgency called forth the proclamation of the Truman Doctrine and thus served as a major catalyst of the Cold War.

Since the dawn of history, Greece has been too poor in material resources to support all her numerous progeny. But the Greek conflict was not in its essence a conflict of classes; both sides drew supporters from all social strata.[1] The war was at base an ideological struggle.[2] It was a symbol and microcosm of the great global confrontation that, from the mountains of Greece to the mountains of Afghanistan, from Berlin and Budapest to Seoul and Saigon, would overshadow the human race for forty years. It seems profoundly fitting that the contest that would strain the power and wisdom of the democracies to their limits should find its first battleground in Greece, the birthplace of democracy.[3]

Mountains cover two thirds of Greece, and in the post–World War II period the road network was quite poor. Thus the country was ideal for the waging of guerrilla warfare. Nevertheless, in the late 1940s, a serious and well-armed Communist guerrilla movement suffered an unequivocal defeat at the hands of the Greek national government advised and supported by the United States. But the simultaneous victory of Mao Tse-tung in faraway China completely stole the attention of the world, including that of Washington itself, away from these auspicious Hellenic events. Consequently, the Americans ignored or quickly forgot certain valuable lessons that could have saved blood, tears, and treasure a decade and a half later in Viet Nam.

POVERTY AND TURBULENCE

The Greece of today is about 51,000 square miles, the size of Alabama, or of Virginia and Maryland combined. When the Greek Communists began their attempt at armed conquest, Greece had been an independent state for only a little more than a century. Much of the territory comprising Greece had been under her control only since the end of the Second Balkan War in 1913. Until fairly recent times, many Greeks still looked toward "Constantinople" rather than Athens as the true capital of Greek civilization.

In her great days, Greece wrote a record of incomparable glory. But since well before the Christian era Greece had been reduced to being part of someone else's empire. After centuries as a backwater of the Roman Empire, Greece formed part of the Byzantine Empire, centered at Constantinople. After 1453 arrived the Turkish Empire, although the island of Crete did not fall until 1669. Their Turkish overlords allowed the Greeks religious freedom, but otherwise the Turks were oppressive and obscurantist, and under their domination Greece sank slowly and deeply into economic and cultural depression. Many consider the civil war of the 1940s as an effort to reduce Greece to a province of yet another empire, Stalin's.

The events of the French Revolution, Russian victories over the Turks, and the sympathy of the Russian crown for Greek aspirations all greatly stimulated Greek nationalism. A war of independence against the Turks began in 1821, largely a guerrilla war. The Greeks enjoyed the moral support of all Europe. Many volunteers came to fight for free Greece, including George Gordon Lord Byron, who died there. In 1828 Russia declared war against Turkey. The conflict concluded the following year when the Turks recognized the independence of the Peloponnesus and the southern mainland.[4]

Victorious participation in the Balkan Wars of 1912 (against Turkey) and 1913 (against Bulgaria) more than doubled Greece's territory. Turkey was the protégé of the German Empire; by suggesting Turkey's true weakness, these Balkan clashes were a stimulus to World War I. In 1917 Greece entered that conflict on the side of the Allies under Prime Minister Eleutherios Venizelos, after the pro-German King Constantine had been forced to abdicate in favor of his son. Venizelos had been born a Turkish subject in Crete in 1864. A staunch antimonarchist, he headed the Liberal Party for many years, served as prime minister several times between 1910 and 1933, and led Greece into the Balkan and the world wars. Frequently an exile, often by choice, he died in Paris in 1936.

At the end of World War I, Greece obtained most of Thrace (including Bulgaria's southern coastline) and laid claim to a substantial area in Asia Minor. The Greeks invaded the Turkish mainland, but Turkish forces under the celebrated Kemal Ataturk repulsed them with great loss of life in 1922. Greece had to accept the repatriation of 1.5 million Greeks from Turkish territory. In the wake of this double catastrophe, virtual civil war engulfed the country; in 1924 King George's enemies sent him into exile and proclaimed a republic. After many convulsions and coups, the monarchy was restored in 1935. None of these turbulent proceedings strengthened the prestige of parliamentary government.

THE GREEK COMMUNISTS

For the first decade and a half of its existence, the Greek Communist Party (KKE) was a marginal force in the life of the country. Many looked upon it as the agent of a foreign power. Its advocacy of independence for Greek Macedonia, so recently acquired in the Balkan Wars, further damaged its electoral prospects.[5] After World War I and the calamitous defeat at the hands of the Turks in 1922, economic conditions in the country were terrible. Despite this, membership in the party during the 1920s never exceeded 2,500.[6] At the dawn of the 1930s, there were only about 1,700 Greek Communists, with fewer than two hundred in Athens, the country's only large city.

From 1936 to 1941, General Ioannis Metaxas, a staunch monarchist and a great opponent of Venizelos, exercised dictatorial powers under King George II. Metaxas nearly extinguished the Greek Communist Party. He offered amnesty to party members who would publicly testify about their subversive activities. In response to these lurid revelations other members also recanted their errors. The government then organized its "own" Communist Party; the resulting confusion and dissension wreaked havoc inside what was left of Greek Communism.[7] Because Hitler and Stalin were partners in 1940, the party was about to administer the coup de grace to itself by stupidly choosing to collaborate with the Italian and German invaders of Greece. Hitler saved the Communists (and not only in Greece) from that miserable fate when he attacked Stalin's Russia on June 22, 1941. In the end, the German invasions of Greece and the Soviet Union were to transform the numerically tiny, intellectually sterile and morally bankrupt Greek Communist Party into a body capable of attempting to take over the country by armed force.

THE GERMAN OCCUPATION AND THE EAM

During World War II, Greece was a major conduit of supplies from Germany to Field Marshal Erwin Rommel's North African army. The Germans kept large forces in the country in order to protect these supply routes, and also because Hitler was sure that Greece, and not Italy, would be the scene of the Allied invasion of southern Europe. By 1944, there were 180,000 Axis troops inside Greece: about 100,000 Germans, the rest Bulgarians, Italians, and others.[8]

In response to the German occupation, the Communists took the lead in organizing the National Liberation Front (EAM) in September 1941. The Front was a variation on standard Communist tactics all over the world. Fronts were a device by which Communists could come into contact with, organize, and manipulate people who would not otherwise have joined any group known to be under the domination of Communists. To that end, the platform of EAM said absolutely nothing about any proletarian revolution or dictatorship; its purpose, according to its leaders, was strictly and simply to organize the population for resistance to the Axis occupation. The king and cabinet had retreated in the face of the German invasion, first to the island of Crete and then to Egypt, under British protection. Thus EAM came into existence at a time when there was a real vacuum of national leadership. Meticulously avoiding any allusions to class struggle or internal divisions, EAM became for many a real beacon of leadership at a time of deep national suffering. It also exposed numerous republican and socialist elements in the country to KKE infiltration.[9]

EAM did not get around to creating a serious fighting arm for quite a while. In December 1942, EAM leaders announced the formation of the National Liberation Army ELAS (very close to "Hellas," the national name for Greece).[10] When Leon Trotsky built the first Red Army during the Russian Civil War, he imposed on every unit a double-headed command structure: the orders of the military commander were subject to veto by the political officer representing the Communist leadership. ELAS units were organized along the same lines.

EAM/ELAS did not have a monopoly on anti-German resistance. Notable among the non-ELAS guerrilla forces was EDES, the Greek National Republican League, led by the dashing Colonel Napoleon Zervas. The Communists feared and hated EDES.

The first priority of ELAS was to procure weapons. This was not a difficult task. Before its disintegration in the face of the Nazi invasion in 1941, the Greek army hid stocks of small arms, many of which were revealed to ELAS. With little attention to possible postwar consequences, the British also began to supply weapons to the various guerrilla formations, including ELAS. In fact, British insistence that all guerrilla forces unite under a single overarching command often meant that non- and anti-Communist guerrilla bands had to subordinate themselves to regional ELAS forces, or even become integrated with them.

When the Italian government surrendered to the Allies in September 1943, ELAS persuaded the British to order Italian forces in Greece to break up into small units. These ELAS then proceeded to disarm. In this way ELAS came into possession of large stores of weapons both heavy and light; it thus became independent of its British suppliers. And when in 1944 the German Army decided to abandon Greece, it left behind many weapons and much ammunition, probably with the intention that ELAS would use these to resist the Allies.[11]

"Topographically, [Greece] provides almost optimum conditions for waging guerrilla warfare."[12] In a poor country, the most attractive and important target for guerrilla forces is almost always the transportation system, because almost any disruption in it is a major disruption. In Greece, land communications had been poor from ancient times, owing in part to the ease of coastal sailing in small craft. With few paved roads and only one main railroad line, the Greek communications network was exquisitely vulnerable to guerrilla action, and so were the Germans who used it. By January 1944, ELAS had control over almost 25,000 full-time fighters with perhaps another 40,000 reserves.[13] In spite of these numbers, ELAS accomplished rather little: its most spectacular action was the blowing up, under British supervision, of the Gorgopotamos railway viaduct.

The Communist leadership of ELAS was much less concerned with the conflict at hand than with the power vacuum that must surely come into existence at war's end. Survival, expansion, and the elimination of rival resistance groups were the main objectives; fighting the Axis came in fourth on this list of priorities.[14] ELAS tried to keep direct engagement with German forces to a minimum, so that "only a small fraction of the armed manpower of ELAS was ever in action against the Germans. The rest were reserved for purposes of political control."[15] ELAS units kept pretty much to the mountains and were obviously reluctant to confront German forces on any large scale. The Germans employed with some success specially trained guerrilla–hunting units that operated in guerrilla dress. But their principal tactic against guerrillas was the wide encirclement, an operation requiring secrecy and a great deal of time and manpower to make sure there were no gaps in the circle.[16] Besides, the Germans cared less about guerrillas in the mountains than transit through the valleys; German troops in Greece therefore did not pursue ELAS units with much energy.[17] Their energies were turned elsewhere.

Greece suffered more from World War II than did most other countries in Europe. Deaths alone amounted to 8 percent of the population; the destruction of the already quite limited material wealth of the country was hard to calculate.

Much of this destruction was the result of German policy. The Germans did not commit enough strength in Greece to pursue guerrillas systematically, so they resorted to reprisals against civilians as the main counter-guerrilla method (as the Soviets would do 40 years later in Afghanistan).[18] ELAS units would carry out an operation in full knowledge that the German authorities would hold responsible the entire community in whose neighborhood the act occurred. The Germans destroyed over 2,000 villages in whole or in part. They machine-gunned civilian prisoners by the hundreds. In July 1944 in one unfortunate town they locked hundreds of women and children in a building and then set it on fire. The savagery of their reprisals, the indiscriminate killing of civilians and burning of dwellings, turned men loose from their destroyed villages to become new recruits for ELAS.[19] In areas where guerrillas might operate, German obliteration of the line between pro- and antiguerrilla Greeks made it safer to be a guerrilla than a peaceful civilian.[20] But many who suffered loss of loved ones or property, or both, from German reprisals blamed these losses on ELAS policies.[21]

In addition to German reprisals, the peasants were subject to depradations by ELAS itself. The guerrillas forcibly requisitioned food from the barely surviving villagers and compelled boys and girls to join their ranks. Throughout the war ELAS employed terror tactics, including murder, against their Greek opponents or suspected sympathizers of their opponents. In the autumn of 1943, with the war in Europe reaching a crescendo, ELAS chose to launch major attacks against EDES and other nonsubmissive guerrilla forces.[22] Some view this campaign to destroy EDES as the real beginning of the Greek Civil War.

Many Greeks watched with dismay the growth of this Communist-dominated armed force, so circumspect toward the Germans and so violent toward fellow Greeks. They wondered whether the clearly doomed German occupation would give way to a permanent Stalinist dictatorship before Allied troops were able to establish themselves.

These lawless and violent conditions help explain the appearance, in the summer of 1943, of armed citizens' units called Security Battalions. The main function of these units was to try to maintain order in their local areas with the acquiescence of German military authorities. Membership in these Security Battalions was never very large, perhaps around 15,000. Some joined the Security Battalions in reaction to excesses committed by ELAS. Some recruits were former members of EDES and other guerrilla formations that ELAS had attacked and dispersed.[23] Some joined out of fear of or sympathy for the Germans. For others—large numbers, in fact—whether one joined ELAS or EDES or a Security Battalion had to do with little more than the accident of who was in control of the area in which one happened to live.[24] And for still others, joining a Security Battalion was a conscious choice with regard to the question of what kind of Greece should emerge from the war. By mid-1943 it was clear that Germany was headed for defeat. Many Greeks found temporary collaboration with the Germans preferable to permanent subordination to the EAM.

In the eyes of ELAS and EAM, of course, Security Battalion members and their families and friends were nothing but collaborators and fascists, and hence legitimate targets for assassination. When German troops began their pullout from the Peloponnesus, ELAS units there murdered many civilians.[25] Soon ferocious encounters between Communists and anticommunists were blazing all over the country.

THE CIVIL WAR: THE STRUGGLE FOR ATHENS

In October 1944, the Germans and the other Axis forces withdrew from Greece. They did this not as a response to pressure from the guerrillas, but in order to avoid being cut off by military developments elsewhere in Europe. Greece, in other words, was not liberated; it was evacuated.

These events opened the way for the return of the royal government from Cairo to Athens. Throughout the war, Communist agents had fostered dissent and mutinies inside the armed forces of the Greek government-in-exile. Their agitation was so successful that the British authorities in Egypt were forced to disband most of the units of the Royal Greek Army, so that by April 1944 "the Greek armed forces in the Middle East were a thing of the past."[26] The Communist plan was simple: at the end of the war, with the Germans gone, rival guerrilla forces destroyed, and the exile government lacking prestige or significant military resources, ELAS would face no serious rivals for power. When the royal government landed at Athens on October 18, 1944 (without the king, George II, who said he would return if a plebiscite called him), it brought with it only about 3,000 troops, a large proportion of them officers. At that point, ELAS controlled something like three-quarters of the territory and about one-third of the population of Greece.[27]

A few weeks later a brigade of soldiers loyal to the newly returned royal government marched through Athens. They received a tumultuous welcome from the inhabitants of that city, a welcome attributed to widespread popular fear of ELAS.[28] These Greek soldiers were eventually backed up by British forces, but only a small proportion of the latter were combat troops.[29]

In what may have been the most fatal mistake of the entire civil war, ELAS did not offer any resistance when the first small detachments of British troops landed in the Athens area in the fall of 1944. Anti-Communist forces would never again be so weak as they were in those days. EAM nevertheless went ahead with preparations for an uprising. It ordered general strikes throughout the country to prevent distribution of United Nations Relief and Rehabilitation Administration (UNRRA) relief and thus increase the level of economic misery. ELAS units moved close to Athens.[30]

The attempted seizure of power began in the first days of December 1944. The Communists lost the conflict from the very first day. They failed to storm central Athens, contenting themselves instead with numerous minor successes in outlying areas, overcoming police posts, or annihilating surviving pockets of EDES supporters in Epirus.[31] During most of the fighting, major ELAS forces were in Thessaly, several days' march away from Athens. Thus the British were granted precious time in which to reinforce the capital. Besides, the very concept of confronting the British was a flawed one. ELAS was in essence a hit-and-run guerrilla force that had seen little action against regular troops in its two years of existence. In ordering the uprising, the Greek Communist leadership was in effect demanding that ELAS turn itself overnight into a regular combat force, prepared to take and hold territory and expel British and Greek national forces from Athens and Salonika. This was not to be the last time the Greek Communist leadership made such a fateful error.

On December 11, 1944, after a week of serious fighting, Field Marshal Harold Alexander, Supreme Allied Commander in the Mediterranean Theater, came to Athens to inspect the situation. A few days later ELAS mounted new attacks on the city. The British repulsed these attacks, even though a couple of days later ELAS managed to overrun a Royal Air Force (RAF) detachment outside the main British defense perimeter. On Christmas, Prime Minister Winston Churchill and Foreign Secretary Anthony Eden arrived in beleaguered Athens. Churchill met with leaders of the Greek government and with ELAS, but nothing came of these talks and the fighting went on.[32] There were by then 60,000 British troops in the Athens area; Britain eventually committed 75,000 soldiers to the battle, of whom 2,100 became casualties. By mid-January, ELAS was in full retreat, and agreed to a truce starting January 15.

While the fight was raging around Athens, ELAS units in other parts of Greece were busy attacking rival guerrilla bands. A lack of ammunition particularly handicapped EDES, and ELAS destroyed it as a fighting force.[33]

During the weeks of combat ELAS had rounded up thousands of hostages in Athens. Before abandoning the outskirts of the city, ELAS units began killing these hostages. British forces found many mutilated bodies, victims of Communist "People's Courts."[34] Much of the deep popular animosity toward ELAS, especially in the Athens area, home in those days to one Greek out of every seven, dates from these savage events. Some of those whom ELAS killed were non–Communist trade union leaders; their murders caused prominent Socialist politicians to abandon the EAM. Sympathy for EAM also precipitously decreased in British left-wing circles. The hostage killings caused numerous non- and anti-Communist members of the middle classes in Greece to seek insurance against a Communist victory through cash payments and other services to the guerrillas.[35] In later years the Athens Communist Party organization expressed the view that the killing of the hostages had been one of the main tactical errors of the entire civil war.[36]

By the Varkiza Agreement of February 1945, all fighting in Greece came to a halt. The Greek Communist Party (KKE) was recognized as a legal entity and allowed to publish newspapers freely and continue to operate EAM. In return, ELAS agreed to hand over a large quantity of arms, and did so. Most of the weapons it surrendered, however, were old Italian pieces. ELAS kept hidden against future need the good weapons left behind by German army units.

No one will ever be sure of the extent of Soviet involvement in the EAM uprising until or unless the secret records of the Kremlin are opened, if they still exist. It nevertheless seems doubtful that Stalin instigated the Greek Civil War. Stalin apparently neither knew nor cared very much about Greece. A small Soviet military mission that visited Greece in 1944 seems to have been unimpressed with what it saw of ELAS, because no aid was forthcoming from Stalin.[37] At the Tehran Conference in November 1943, Churchill, Roosevelt, and Stalin had decided against any large-scale operations in the Balkans. In October 1944, with tacit American approval, the British and the Soviets had divided up that area: Rumania and Bulgaria were to come under Soviet control, and Greece would remain under British influence.[38] Even after EAM had gone into open rebellion, the Soviets sent an ambassador to Athens, thus recognizing the royal government's legitimacy and signaling something less than enthusiasm for the Greek Communists and their uprising.

THE CIVIL WAR: THE MAIN EVENT

In March 1946, national elections were held to choose a new parliament. In spite of serious and mounting problems of postwar adjustment, and despite (or perhaps because of) the presence of hundreds of election observers from France, Britain, and elsewhere, the Communists decided to boycott these elections. (There were no observers from the Soviet Union; Moscow did not want to set a precedent for outside observers of elections in its newly acquired East European empire.) There were at least two reasons for this electoral boycott. First, the KKE did not wish to reveal to the world how low its electoral appeal actually was.[39] Second, the Communists had decided that they would try again to come to power by force. To this end, KKE had already established a guerrilla training base at Boulkes, northwest of Belgrade in Tito's Yugoslavia, at that time the Communist state most vociferously loyal to Stalin. It was also counting on support from Communist regimes in neighboring Albania and Bulgaria.

Thus, just as conservative and moderate parties were winning an overwhelming victory at the polls, Communist forces attacked the village of

Litokhoron, on the slope of Mount Olympus, an assault generally taken to be the beginning of the second phase of the revolution.

The Communists waged a guerrilla campaign. It began with the murders of local officials and civilians known to be friendly to the government. Then came attacks on small police stations, forcing their consolidation into larger and fewer positions. The guerrillas would then begin raiding the villages where the police posts had just been abandoned, seeking supplies and recruits. Finally came attacks on larger police posts (30 to 40 men), forcing these also to be consolidated. By the late autumn of 1946 only the large towns, as a rule, were under government control. Vast areas of the countryside were wide open to guerrilla activities. When at length the Greek National Army was called in, the guerrillas employed the same general tactics against it: attacks on small army posts along the frontier with Yugoslavia and Albania forced their consolidation into ever larger, ever fewer positions, leaving wide gaps along the border areas through which the guerrillas could freely pass back and forth.

Many students of guerrilla warfare have maintained that a 10-to-1 ratio of government troops to guerrillas is necessary for the thorough defeat of an insurgency. By the end of 1946, the guerrillas, newly renaming themselves the Democratic Army, had 13,000 members operating inside Greece, with another 12,000 across the three borders. Against them the National Army could muster 90,000, with the national police (gendarmerie) adding another 30,000.[40] By the autumn of 1947, the National Army had grown to about 135,000 men, while the Democratic Army counted perhaps 23,000, not including reserves and units across the frontiers.[41] Thus the numbers of the Greek government forces were clearly inadequate, especially to impede the passage of guerrilla units across Greece's more than 600 miles of frontier with her Communist neighbors.

The main areas of guerrilla operations were in the mountains along the northern borders. This was so not only for the obvious strategic reasons. Further south, in Athens and the Peloponnesus fear and hatred of the guerrillas prevailed, rooted in ELAS provocations and atrocities during the German occupation and above all in the killing of numerous hostages in the Athens area in the first period of armed conflict (from December 1944 to January 1945).[42]

THE INSURGENTS

Where did the members of the Democratic Army come from? Who joined the guerrillas to take up arms against the parliamentary government in Athens?

The insurgency gathered its strength from four principal sources. First there were members of the KKE and their sympathizers. These were mainly urban, above average in education, and quite often fanatically devoted to the party's cause, the New Greece of which they of course would be the rulers.

There was also a large group of Macedonian separatists. Macedonia had been misruled by the Turks until the Balkan Wars of 1912–1913. At the outbreak of the civil war Greece possessed 13,000 square miles of Macedonia, while Bulgaria and Yugoslavia divided another 12,000. The KKE pledged that in the event of a Communist military victory, Greek Macedonia would be allowed to go its separate way, presumably to become the nucleus of a united and independent Macedonian state that would include territories in Yugoslavia and Bulgaria. Only a minority of the Macedonians in the Democratic Army appear to have been Communists, or even knowledgeable about Marxism in general.[43]

A third key group in the Democratic Army consisted of former members of ELAS. Greece had too many people. Thus for large numbers of Greeks the main aspects of village life were omnipresent poverty, class tensions, and a bleak future.[44] To many villagers, therefore, the wartime resistance experience had represented both a welcome escape from all this and the opportunity to display heroism, all under the rubric of struggling for justice and a better life. For these persons the end of World War II had been a real letdown, a return to an uneventful, unrewarding existence. When in the spring of 1946 the Communists began widespread recruiting of guerrillas again, many former resistance fighters welcomed the chance to abandon drudgery and discontent and turn back the clock to more fulfilling days.

The fourth element of the guerrilla ranks, and the largest, was composed of forced recruits and abductees, often teenagers of both sexes. As the conflict ground on, the Communists came to rely more and more on forced recruitment and kidnappings. After the insurgency had been defeated, the principal military leader of the Democratic Army wrote that from the middle of 1947, almost all new guerrillas had been brought into the ranks by compulsion.[45]

The reader may immediately suspect that recruits obtained in this manner would make poor fighters. Sometimes this was the case, but any generalization would be hasty. The normal way the Democratic Army obtained the services of such persons was to threaten them and their family members with death if they refused to serve or tried to desert. These forced recruits were always well aware of how vulnerable they and their families were to reprisals. The dangerous life of the guerrillas often forced them, especially very young ones who had never lived outside their parents' houses before, to turn to each other for support and loyalty. Besides, the KKE placed great stress on the political indoctrination of all Democratic Army members, and this was not without effect. All these powerful pressures produced Democratic Army units that, either from conviction or desperation, often fought well.[46]

Although the Democratic Army was unable to attract great numbers of volunteers, many factors operated in its favor. The Greek tradition of guerrilla warfare went deep into history, into the long night of Turkish occupation. The general poverty of the rural areas and the great devastation wrought by World War II had created a population capable of withstanding the physical hardships of guerrilla life. The EAM still basked in the afterglow of the resistance to the detested Germans, while in contrast the royal Greek government had spent most of those bitter years outside the country. The Greek National Army had superior equipment, but the country's difficult terrain and primitive transportation system favored the lightly armed and tactically flexible guerrillas. The guerrillas had no responsibility for holding or defending particular territory. If pressed by government troops, even if surrounded, they simply broke up into smaller units and (usually) escaped their enemies.

Greece was especially suited to that main guerrilla tactic, the mining of roads. By 1947, mines had become "the most effective single weapon in the guerrilla arsenal."[47] They greatly hampered the movement of the National Army, with conversely little effect on the guerrillas, who possessed no tanks and few trucks.

The Communists also derived strength from the fact that they had a cause, a vision of a Bright New Greece in which everyone's desires would find fulfillment. In contrast, the government seemed to offer only a dreary status quo. There was no charismatic hero to offer a shining vision of a non-Communist Greece. In fact, the government seemed incapable of dealing even with the most pressing and mundane economic and social problems, problems greatly aggravated by the fact that the fighting in the mountains produced a flood of 700,000 refugees, a tenth of the nation, pouring into the cities and swamping the government's slender resources.[48]

The contrast between the bleak today offered by the government and the bright tomorrow offered by the Communists and their fellow travelers was able to win for them, at least in the early stages of the civil war, the support of roughly a fifth of the population.[49] In most parts of Greece the KKE was able to operate a well-articulated underground organization called the Yiafaka, built upon the reliable infrastructure EAM had created in many parts of the country during the German occupation. By 1947, Yiafaka had perhaps 50,000 active members. This network of agents and sympathizers helped provide food for the guerrillas. Above all, it supplied intelligence. Yiafaka had penetrated both the National Army and the civil service fairly thoroughly, so that the Democratic Army always had a good idea of the plans of its enemies.[50]

Finally, assistance to the guerrillas from Greece's Communist neighbors had become quite open by July 1946; even the skeptical Soviets eventually sent a supply of 105mm howitzers.[51] During 1947, the guerrillas greatly benefited from the arrival of men trained in military institutions in Albania, Bulgaria, and Yugoslavia.[52] The Yugoslavs also attached a general and a small staff to the headquarters of the Democratic Army.[53] The efforts of the National Army to intercept supplies for the insurgents coming from the northern neighbors were only partially effective.

The existence of these sanctuaries across the rugged frontiers was the most serious tactical challenge with which the insurgents confronted the national government and army. Time after time, the National Army would corner insurgent units in the north, only to watch in frustration as they escaped over the border into a Communist state.

For example, the guerrillas maintained a major stronghold in the Grammos mountain area, along the Greek-Albanian border. In June 1948, the Greek National Army launched the major operation of the entire war against this Grammos base. After a tremendous battle, in which eventually perhaps half of the total number of guerrillas in the entire country participated (12,000), the National Army was able to occupy Mount Grammos. Guerrilla losses were severe: those killed or captured alone amounted to almost 4,000.[54] Most of the guerrilla forces on Grammos, however, retreated into Albania, and after a march through southern Yugoslavia, they appeared again on Greek soil in Macedonia. This proximity to any Democratic Army unit of sanctuary inside one of the three Communist neighbor states meant that for the most part the guerrillas fought only when and where they chose. The constant appeals of the Greek government to the United Nations to remedy the constant violation of its borders produced hardly more than a waterfall of words. It was little wonder, then, that the morale in the Greek National army was low.

THE GREEK NATIONAL ARMY

The Athens government held in the beginning very few good cards. Anti-Communist forces suffered from deep political fissures and grave military weaknesses.

From Plato to Brinton, students of revolution have identified divisions within the governing class as a prime condition for revolution. Bitter hostility between monarchists and republicans had been poisoning Greek political life for more than a generation before the German invasion. After World War II, in the midst of devastation and insurgency, this hostility reasserted itself as if nothing had changed. With at least one eye on electoral considerations, many leftist and liberal politicians in Greece showed themselves more susceptible to offers of compromise from the EAM than to exhortations to pursue victory over the Communist-led insurrection. On the other side, elements on the extreme right of the majority populist (monarchist) party had discredited themselves by committing atrocities against Communists and other enemies as bad as any the guerrillas had ever perpetrated. Dwight Griswold, the Nebraska Republican who headed the U.S. aid mission to Greece, cabled Washington: "You cannot build a government on the rightist parties and [expect to] establish peace and quiet in Greece. There is too much of a tendency in those groups to carry on a blood feud against all Greeks who do not agree with them politically."[55]

The partisanship, selfishness, nepotism, and "inveterate pettiness" of Greek politicians discredited the parliamentary system, increased the attractiveness of the insurgency, exasperated the Americans, and generally hampered a successful anticommunist effort.[56]

As for the armed forces, when the Communists launched the major phase of the civil war in 1946, the Greek National Army was in real trouble. During the Axis occupation of Greece (from 1941 to 1944) the army, except for some units in Egypt, did not exist. Soldiers and officers alike lost their skills and their traditions. The new army that came into existence after 1945 was poorly trained. There was little time for training in the midst of civil war, and so basic deficiencies in operations remained uncorrected almost until the end. The equipment of the GNA was inadequate, with a pronounced shortage of mountain artillery. The Royal Hellenic Air Force dominated the skies of Greece, but in the early years of the civil war this was of little benefit to the government because there were so few planes and trained pilots.

Napoleon said that in war, the proportion of moral factors to material factors is three to one. In the GNA of 1947, if equipment was poor and training was sketchy, morale was close to disastrous. This dangerous situation arose from problems in the officer corps, inattention to the requirements of enlisted men, and faulty disposition of military resources.

First and foremost, the GNA faced an acute problem of officer quality. The German conquest of Greece, the government's flight into exile, and the political divisions within it and the army demoralized and disintegrated the officer corps. In the reconstituted army, professional training was low. For attracting the attention of one's superiors and obtaining promotion, skill or bravery counted less than political connections. Political interference led to the promotion of unsuitable officers and encouraged insubordination. Incompetence or fear of making mistakes inhibited the aggressiveness of many officers toward the enemy. Yet it was extremely difficult to remove poor or insubordinate officers because of this same plague of political interference with army personnel matters that had led to their promotions in the first place.[57] Not surprisingly, the army had three different chiefs of staff during 1947 alone. (Nevertheless, the number of GNA officers who defected to the Democratic Army was extremely small—perhaps as few as 27.)[58]

Among the ranks of the enlisted, poor morale derived from a perception of multiple inequities. The first classes of draftees into the new National Army were veterans of the Albanian War; they could not understand why they were called to the colors while younger men were left at home. Most of these draftees were family men, and army pay was so low and government services so poor that their families were often in a state of real want.[59] The rich and the politically well connected were able to obtain exemptions from military service. Those few high-ranking officers who bothered to listen to the problems of their men knew that poor morale also resulted from too few decorations for bravery, an inadequate promotion policy, haphazard punishment for those who tried to avoid military service, and the failure to distribute arms to loyal but defenseless villagers.[60]

The way the National Army conducted its operations did nothing for morale either. The frontiers of Greece with her Communist neighbors extended for several hundreds of miles, very long in comparison to the total area of the country. Under the best of circumstances the GNA would have found it extremely difficult to control the length of these borders, as well as to protect major urban centers, patrol important highways, guard essential crops, guarantee public services, and pursue guerrilla bands. What in fact rendered the performance of these tasks quite impossible was that influential politicians demanded the stationing of troops in their constituencies.[61]

The GNA responded to these many pressures by adopting a posture of static defense: an attempt to occupy every place of any potential value to the government or to the insurgents. This was the worst possible posture for fighting guerrillas. It enabled the guerrillas, by assembling units from several different districts, to attain numerical superiority over the government troops at any particular point of attack. In the meantime, the GNA could not take the offensive against the guerrillas because it lacked sufficient manpower to simultaneously protect every point in the country and maintain mobile, offensive units.

In April 1947 the army temporarily broke out of its static defense posture to attempt a major clean-up of Central Greece, with the idea of forcing guerrilla units toward the northern frontiers. The campaign failed for several revealing reasons. First was the insufficiency of competent officers. Another was the self-imposed time limit on these clearing operations: since there were not enough troops to both garrison all sensitive places, including important politicians' bailiwicks, and at the same time carry out aggressive mobile clearing operations, only a limited amount of time—a few days or a few weeks, depending on its size—was allocated to the "cleaning" of any particular area. When the allotted time had expired, army units in that area moved on to some other designated place, whether all the guerrillas in the first area had been driven out or not.[62]

The guerrilla practice of killing local officials and unfriendly civilians, both in the mountains and in the large towns, undercut their support; so did the kidnapping of thousands of children to be sent to Soviet satellites, there to be trained to be good citizens of a new, Communist Europe. But these were weaknesses of the insurgency rather than strengths of the government, and they paled when compared to the enormous advantages enjoyed by the guerrillas. Thus, during 1946 and 1947, the Communists were able to make great physical and psychological gains, while belief in the victory, or even the survival, of the government was steadily evaporating.

To summarize the first eighteen months of the conflict, although there was never a real danger that Democratic Army forces would successfully attack Athens, the government's inability to defeat the guerrillas meant that time was working against it. Without some unforeseeable, drastic alteration in the struggle, a Communist victory, and consequently the Stalinization of Greece, seemed inevitable to many.

But in fact, as 1947 drew to a close, the beleaguered government in Athens was about to see the scales of war tip undramatically but definitely in its favor. A new national defense corps was coming into existence, to prevent the reinfiltration of areas that had been cleared of guerrillas. And the morale of both the GNA and the government received a tremendous boost from the arrival of liaison officers of the United States Army.[63]

THE TRUMAN DOCTRINE

During the truce period between the end of the first phase of the civil war and the beginning of the second, the British Labour government under Clement Attlee took responsibility for training the new Greek National Army. This force, including National Guard units, grew from 30,000 in February 1945 to 75,000 by the end of the year.[64] Until the spring of 1947, Britain also maintained 143,000 of her own troops in Greece, not counting 1,400 officers and enlisted men involved in training the National Army.[65]

But on February 21, 1947, the Attlee government informed the Truman Administration that Britain could no longer afford to support her clients in Greece, nor in Turkey either. This information reached Washington at a crucial point in the reassessment of United States foreign policy that had been under way since the surrender of Japan.[66] The Administration had been fairly well informed about events in Greece during World War II, but Secretaries of State Cordell Hull and E. R. Stettinius, Jr., had no wish to become embroiled in what they judged to be unpalatable controversies of old-world imperialist politics. Thus, up to the very eve of the Cold War, the United States government did not develop a serious or even a consistent policy regarding Greece.[67] Nevertheless, late in February 1947, General George Marshall gave President Truman a blunt message: while no one could guarantee that U.S. aid would definitely save Greece, he could guarantee that the refusal of U.S. aid would definitely lose Greece.[68] At the same time, Dean Acheson wrote a memorandum in which he stated his belief that the loss of Greece would eventually result in the Communization of all the Near East (the Balkans), and most of the Middle East and North Africa as well.[69] Reflecting on the fermentation of thought in that crucial late winter and early spring of 1947, George Kennan wrote:

People in Western Europe did not, by and large, want Communist control. But this did not mean that they would not trim their sails and even abet its coming if they gained the impression that it was inevitable. This was why the shock of a Communist success in Greece could not be risked.[70]

The Truman Administration became interested in Greece because of its conviction that the Soviets were involved in the insurgency. The degree of such Soviet involvement will probably never be known.[71] And it is not necessary to thrash out here the question of whether Soviet foreign policy was prompted by a desire for expansion or a quest for security: from Stalin through Brezhnev the results were the same. A distinguished historian of U.S. foreign policy has elaborated and summarized the view from Washington:

The United States had no choice but to act in this situation. The results of inaction were only too clear: the collapse of Europe's flank in the Eastern Mediterranean, establishment of Communist dominance in the Middle East, and a Soviet break-through into South Asia and North Africa. The psychological impact upon Europe of such a tremendous Soviet victory over the West would have been disastrous. For Europeans already psychologically demoralized by their sufferings and fall from power and prestige, this would have been the final blow. In short, what was at stake in Greece was America's survival itself.[72]

There was considerable opposition in Washington to any overt U.S. participation in Greek affairs. Many felt that such an involvement would be nothing more than Americans "pulling British chestnuts out of the fire."[73] Nevertheless, three weeks after being informed by the British that they would have to abandon their commitments in Greece, President Truman went before a joint session of Congress and delivered one of the most important speeches in the history of the United States. In that address he laid the foundations of American policy for what would become known ever after as the Cold War:

I believe that it must be the policy of the United States to support free peoples who are resisting attempted subjugation by armed minorities or by outside pressures.

I believe that we must assist free peoples to work out their own destinies in their own way.

I believe that our help should be primarily through economic and financial aid which is essential to economic stability and orderly political processes. . . . Should we fail to aid Greece and Turkey in this fateful hour, the effect will be far-reaching to the West as well as to the East.

The terse sentences of the March presidential message, soon to be universally known as the Truman Doctrine, received a beautifully expressed elaboration some weeks later in a highly influential article by Kennan in the prestigious journal *Foreign Affairs.* Kennan saw Soviet policy as "a fluid stream which moves constantly, wherever it is permitted to move, toward a given goal. Its main concern is to make sure that it has filled every nook and cranny available to it in the basin of world power." He therefore recommended to the American people "a policy of firm containment, designed to confront the Russians with unalterable counterforce at every point where they show signs of encroaching upon the interest of a peaceful and stable world." Such a policy of containment would both defend the territory of the West and "promote tendencies which must eventually find their outlet in either the breakup or the gradual mellowing of Soviet power."[74]

Also in July 1947, Secretary of State George Marshall identified U.S. objectives in Greece more specifically. American assistance must be addressed to maintaining the independence and territorial integrity of that nation; to this end it was necessary to develop the Greek economy and raise general living standards, distribute the tax burden more equitably, and eliminate corruption as far as possible.[75]

The course pursued by the Truman Administration during those fateful months between March and July 1947 has come in for some well-after-the-fact criticism. "By presenting aid to Greece and Turkey," writes one influential scholar, "in terms of an ideological conflict between two ways of life, Washington officials encouraged a simplistic view of the Cold War which was, in time, to imprison American diplomacy in an ideological straitjacket almost as confining as that which restricted Soviet foreign policy."[76]

How valid it is to criticize one administration for (alleged) shortcomings and errors of those that followed is a thorny question. Much of the later academic discussion of the Truman Doctrine ignores the fact that the president, in his message to Congress, never mentioned the Soviet Union by name. The decision to assist the Greek government against the Communist-led guerrillas is perhaps best understood in the light of the circumstances in which it was taken. Under that rubric,

an impartial observer could well conclude in the autumn of 1947 that the Americans and their representatives were displaying amazing maturity and boldness in restructuring their foreign policy. He could also add that in their enlightened self-interest they were striking the right balance between the extremes of bellicosity toward the Soviet Union and supine acquiescence in the face of Communist encroachment. The judgment . . . still stands.[77]

U.S. ASSISTANCE

After the austere cadences of President Truman's March address to Congress had died away, Americans began to confront the enormity of the task they had undertaken. In his report to the National Security Council in January 1948, former Director of Central Intelligence Sidney Souers stated:

The Greek government rests on a weak foundation and Greece is in a deplorable economic state. There are general fear and a feeling of insecurity among the people, friction among short-sighted political factions, selfishness and corruption in government, and a dearth of effective leaders. The Armed Forces of Greece are hampered in their efforts to eliminate Communist guerrillas by lack of offensive spirit, by political interference, by disposition of units as static forces and by poor leadership.[78]

Nevertheless, the United States had to make the effort. The Souers report continued:

The defeat of Soviet efforts to destroy the political independence and territorial integrity of Greece is necessary in order to preserve the security of the whole Eastern Mediterranean and Middle East, which is vital to the security of the United States.[79]

And Loy Henderson, director of the State Department's Office of Near Eastern and African Affairs, cautioned that the Kremlin undoubtedly planned to wear down U.S. willpower in Greece:

If it should be decided that we are not capable as a country of dogged determination we should review our whole foreign policy in order to make sure that, in view of our inherent psychological weakness, it might be better for us to return to isolationism and abandon a policy in world affairs which we are not capable of carrying out.[80]

A few weeks after the Souers report, the urgency of Greek affairs received a heavy underlining when Communists in Czechoslovakia destroyed the democratic institutions of that country in a brutal takeover. And soon after that, in an attempt to push the West yet further back toward the English Channel, the Soviets imposed the Berlin Blockade. The Cold War was really on, and Greece was emerging as a major battleground.

As Secretary of State Marshall noted, the reestablishment of order in Greece did not require the destruction of all the guerrillas, which in any case would be close to impossible.[81] What was required was a well-led, aggressive army capable of pushing the guerrillas back from the centers of Greek life and keeping them away—a tall order.

By the end of 1947, the United States had shipped 174,000 tons of military supplies to Greece, but the guerrilla movement was not suffering visible defeat; on the contrary, the overextended GNA, penetrated by Communist agents, was effectively in control of only about a fifth of the territory of the country.[82] American military leaders such as Major General Stephen Chamberlin, director of army intelligence, believed that the problem with the GNA was not its size but its leadership and tactics. The Americans asked the British to provide direct operational guidance to Greek units; but the British were unwilling to comply, suggesting that the Americans take on the task.[83]

The Americans thus established the Joint United States Military Advisory and Planning Group (JUSMAPG) to assist the Greek National Army with planning and leadership development. Marshall chose General James Van Fleet to be the director of this Group. No desk-bound commander, Van Fleet was often on the front lines observing the good and bad features of the GNA's antiguerrilla campaigns. He also kept up a constant barrage of requests for more American help for the Greek army. By the spring of 1948, a year after the proclamation of the Truman Doctrine, there were about 250 U.S. officers in Greece with JUSMAPG. Some of them participated in a joint Greek–U.S. staff formed to plan and supply operations (combat missions). This joint staff had a bracing effect on the Greek army: because the Americans were less knowledgeable and less sensitive to the nuances of Greek politics, they were thus able to bring more strictly military considerations to bear on operational planning than Greek officers had been accustomed to.

By mid–1948, the United States was expending something like $10,000 to eliminate one guerrilla.[84] American assistance to Greece, even purely economic aid, was always controversial. Certain elements in the press and several members of President Truman's own party in Congress took the position that the Greek Civil War was nothing more than an uprising by an oppressed and impoverished people. The corrupt and harsh government was hardly better than a thieving clique of Nazi collaborators and had justly earned the hatred of its suffering countrymen; in supporting the Athens government, therefore, the United States was fighting not Communism but democracy. Certainly those Americans who opposed, for whatever reasons, the effort to defeat the Greek Communist insurgency could find plenty of opportunities to criticize the government in Athens over the rivalry and hostility between the major Greek political parties.

Key American officials in Greece disliked and distrusted the leader of the conservative Populists, Constantine Tsaldaris. They wanted to avoid having the United States become too dependent on his party even though it had won a majority of parliamentary seats in the 1946 elections. At the same time, in order to gather as much support as possible for the anticommunist effort, Secretary of State Marshall from the beginning wanted Greece to be governed by a broad coalition.[85] Such a coalition proved difficult both to construct and to preserve.

That Greek politicians felt that they could continue in their old partisan ways, scheming in the corridors and cafés of Athens while an armed revolutionary challenge crackled all around them, may seem paradoxical. But many Greeks, not just politicians but citizens and soldiers as well, were apathetic in the face of the mortal challenges facing them, believing that outside factors in the civil war were so massive that their own efforts were puny and inconsequential in comparison.[86] In the view of most Greek politicians, assistance from the United States guaranteed ultimate victory; hence they seem to have felt absolved from having to mute their internal squabbles and give serious and sustained attention to painful decisions about reforming the government and the economy.[87]

Impatience with the shortcomings of Greek politicians made itself felt within the Truman Administration. A Policy Planning Staff report of November 1948 suggested that the secretary of state make it clear that there were limits to U.S. aid and that if the Greek government was not willing to carry out certain economic and military changes, the United States might conclude that it had better places to spend its money.[88]

The U.S. Embassy in Athens, on the other hand, pointed out that the Greek government was being severely damaged by propaganda emanating from the Soviet Union and eagerly repeated by Communist and sympathizer elements in the United States and Western Europe, propaganda magnifying Greece's admittedly serious problems and the shortcomings of the government. Many of these problems and shortcomings, indeed, stemmed from the existence of foreign-fueled civil war.[89] (Two decades later, similar arguments would rage around the issue of helping the South Vietnamese. The rough edges of the electoral processes in a country with no democratic tradition, torn by civil war and subversion, and the widespread corruption in a poor country inundated by American troops with plenty of cash received extensive attention by the news media that had the run of the South and no access at all to the North.)

Clearly, in the grave crisis confronting the country "a parochial, narrow-minded leadership, with anti-Communism its only credential, [could] not possibly provide the required foundations for a successful war against a Communist guerrilla offensive."[90] Seeming to realize this, many national party leaders did eventually manage to put aside, for the most part, the worst of their partisan belligerence. The leader of the minority Liberal party, Themistocles Sophoulis, agreed to preside over a coalition cabinet consisting mainly of his old enemies, the Populists. Constantine Tsaldaris, although the leader of the majority party and therefore the parliamentarian with the most right to be prime minister, agreed to accept a subordinate post in the Sophoulis cabinet. It was this coalition that guided the nation through the worst days of the civil war to victory, from September 1947 to June 1949, when Sophoulis, close to ninety, passed away. Indeed, in a sense the civil war had gone into its most serious phase in July 1947, after Sophoulis rejected feelers from the EAM to include them in a coalition cabinet of "peace and reconciliation."

TO SEND AMERICAN TROOPS TO GREECE

In the beginning the Truman Administration was fairly optimistic about the prospects for success in Greece and wished to short-circuit any potential opposition to its project for assistance to the Athens government.

It therefore emphasized from the beginning that any U.S. military personnel sent to Greece would be there solely in an advisory, and not a combat, role.[91]

Nevertheless, from the early days of open United States involvement in the conflict, pressures began to build toward commitment of American ground combat forces. "Greek officials," noted a State Department internal memorandum, "are obsessed with the idea of getting the United States so deeply committed in Greece that it will be unable to withdraw if the Greeks themselves lie down on the job."[92] Constantine Tsaldaris, head of the Populist Party and eventually foreign minister, suggested throughout 1947 that the United States send a small number of combat troops to his country, in order to bolster the morale of the National Army.[93]

During the winter of 1947–1948, with the situation in Greece dark and foreboding, the Administration contemplated the advisability of expanding the U.S. military role. The State Department's Loy Henderson expressed his belief in December 1947 that if Greece's Communist neighbors should recognize a guerrilla counterstate within Greece and send assistance to it, or if they should introduce their own troops into the fighting, then the United States should at the least call on the United Nations to authorize the sending of armed forces to assist the legitimate government.[94] In a top-secret memorandum, Major General A. V. Arnold declared that the sending of two United States army divisions to Thrace might make a major contribution to ending the war. Arnold and the State Department's Robert Lovett discussed this possibility, among others, with George Kennan. Kennan appeared not to oppose the idea of U.S. troops as part of a United Nations force to seal the northern borders but seemed to think that if American soldiers went to Greece to fight, the Peloponnesus might be an easier place to defend. (This conversation is not found in Kennan's *Memoirs*.)[95] It was General Marshall's view that the Greek Army was tired from fighting, that it had no time to train its soldiers adequately, and that there was no end in sight as long as the guerrillas could escape over the frontiers.[96]

Nevertheless, scenarios and proposals to send U.S. ground combat units to Greece stirred up opposition so strong that a real debate never developed. John Foster Dulles was the principal Republican spokesman on foreign affairs. He was almost a certainty to become secretary of state in the event of a Republican capture of the White House. In August 1947, while serving as a member of the U.S. delegation to the United Nations, Dulles expressed himself forcefully against sending U.S. combat troops for the purpose of closing the northern frontier (which of course would have been, next to preventing the fall of Athens itself, the most serious justification for the deployment of American troops).[97] U.S. Ambassador to Greece Lincoln MacVeagh, described by Dean Acheson as "wise and first-rate,"[98] believed that the GNA could achieve control of the situation with better tactics and leadership.[99] And Dwight Griswold also came out vigorously against the use of U.S. combat units. "Defeat of Communism," he wrote, "is not solely a question of military action as demonstrated in Germany, France and elsewhere. In Greece, the military and economic fronts are of equal importance." Therefore he "would oppose the use of even a single American officer or soldier against the Greek bandits [guerrillas]."[100]

A Department of State draft report to the National Security Council in the fall of 1948 warned that the introduction of American combat units might serve the Kremlin as an excuse to send Soviet forces into formerly subservient and now rebellious Yugoslavia.[101] During the winter of 1948–1949, when many in Washington were gloomy about the course of the war, General Marshall flew to Athens to get a better grasp of the situation. He returned home echoing the view of the U.S. ambassador that what was needed was not an increase in the size of the Greek Army but improvement in the use of it.[102]

Surprisingly (but in fact, *not* surprisingly), powerful opposition to American troop deployment in Greece came from the United States military. In September 1947, Undersecretary of War Kenneth Royall told Marshall that the introduction of U.S. combat units into Greece would be "disturbing and provocative."[103] About a month later, Major General Stephen Chamberlin, who had headed a special military mission to Greece, expressed his conviction that the Greek army should be able to cope with the guerrillas, provided there was no overt intervention from the north.[104] General Marshall feared that the dispatch of U.S. combat troops to Greece would result either in a buildup of forces there larger than the United States should commit to one place or their withdrawal under unpropitious and unheroic circumstances.[105] Major General A. M. Harper compared the sending of American forces to Greece to putting them in a strategic "mousetrap."[106] The Joint Chiefs went on record against such a deployment unless it was preceded by national mobilization. This was hardly a likelihood in 1947 with the vast postwar demobilization still going on and in the wake of the election of an economy-minded Republican Congress, the first in eighteen years. In mid-1945, the United States armed forces totalled 12 million men and women; by mid-1947 they were less than 1.6 million.[107]

Those high-ranking military leaders who publicly expressed themselves on this question were almost unanimously opposed to sending U.S. combat forces to Greece. They believed that the Greek Army was big enough to do the job, that there were other important demands on slender U.S. forces, and that U.S. troops would find themselves in an untenable position in the event of a Soviet invasion of Greece. Taking account of and reflecting these points of view, Souers told the National Security Council in May 1948 that "the United States should not now send armed forces to Greece as token forces or for military operations."[108] Thus it was that in September 1948, almost a year and a half after the enunciation of the Truman Doctrine, there were no more than 450 U.S. military personnel in Greece providing operational advice, and this only down to the division level. (Of these, three American officers were to lose their lives.)[109]

DEVELOPMENT OF THE GREEK NATIONAL ARMY

The Greek and American governments did not know or even suspect the gravity of the problems confronting the insurgents. On the contrary, as the year 1948 wore on, a feeling of despondency began to envelop the Greek government and army and their supporters in Washington. In a major change of tactics, the GNA had launched massive assaults against guerrilla base areas on Grammos and Vitsi mountains, cutting off insurgent supply routes. The attacks were costly, and in the end the guerrillas escaped into Albania and eventually returned to Grammos. The GNA was suffering 1,800 casualties a month, yet nothing much seemed to be getting accomplished: "two years of hard and bloody effort seemed to have ended in failure."[110]

In November 1948, the Policy Planning Staff of the State Department produced an analysis of the military situation in Greece. The inefficiency of the Greek National Army, it stated, was partly the result of physical and mental exhaustion. Conventional combat, military occupation, and insurgency had been battering Greece ever since 1940. For the Greek soldier, there was no end in sight to the fighting in which he was called upon to engage, because the enemy had the ability to escape across the borders. The guerrillas, in contrast, could find rest and supplies on non-Greek territory whenever necessary. Additionally, the proportion of their troops who were in combat units was very high compared to that of the GNA, because medical care, supply and training facilities, and personnel were to a large degree furnished to the guerrillas by the neighboring Soviet satellites. The report stressed the need to improve training in the GNA and to weed out incompetent officers.[111]

The American ambassador in Greece, Henry F. Grady, also contributed some trenchant observations on the disappointing course of the conflict. He disagreed strongly with General Van Fleet's requests for more men, more money, and more arms for the GNA. Both Greek and American army officers always wanted more of everything, but for Grady the real solution lay elsewhere. He pointed out that "the bandit [Democratic] land army is not backed by a single airplane, heavy gun or naval vessel."[112] The Greek army was in his view already too big, draining the economy of manpower and money. Greece required not a bigger and bigger army, but a stronger, more united, and more efficient government in Athens. Victory demanded "spirit and leadership," and the Americans could not provide these things to the Greeks. An army smaller in size but better trained, better fed, stripped of its old worn-out soldiers and political officers could wage a more aggressive campaign against the guerrillas, especially in winter, which in a country like Greece was really an ally of the government.[113]

Grady had put his finger on a number of important, if sensitive, spots. The leaders of the Greek National Army were slow to grasp the fact that one of their allies was the weather. Most guerrillas operated in the mountain areas. During the winter they suffered from cold and lack of supplies. Many died of exposure. Besides, the guerrillas could be tracked in the snow. True, the winter also impeded the National Army's use of trucks and heavy equipment, but with its regular supply lines and relatively unlimited food and medicine, the individual GNA soldier suffered much less than the guerrilla. In countries with harsh winters, the government needs to appreciate the tactical possibilities of winter campaigning.[114]

During 1948, substantial changes did in fact occur in the organization and tactics of the Greek National Army. The government began deploying the National Defense Corps, civilians organized into 100 battalions of 500 men each. The original plan was for these battalions to act as minutemen in support of the GNA, but eventually they were turned into full-time soldiers. In addition, the army established, with American aid, commando units specially trained for difficult counterguerrilla operations.[115]

The government also abandoned the policy of inducting only politically reliable young men into the ranks of the GNA. This policy of selective recruitment had left politically disloyal elements free to engage in subversion or even join the guerrillas. Under the new system all eligibles were drafted, with the unreliable stationed in nonvital posts. The worst cases were sent to the island of Makronisos for political education.

In addition, the National Army also began the practice of removing civilians from the vicinity of an insurgent stronghold that was targeted for attack. This imposed a temporary hardship on the villagers involved, but it also deprived the Communists of intelligence and food.[116] One keen student of the war has identified the removal of the population from around guerrilla-controlled areas as a secret of the success of the Greek government.[117]

The GNA became more attentive to the fact that it was not enough to clear armed guerrillas out of an area; the civilian infrastructure also had to be uprooted if government success was to be lasting.[118] Thanks to improved intelligence, the government found it easier to infiltrate its agents into Yiafaka.

These were all important changes, and American assistance was helping to bring the Greek National Army into good material shape. From mid-1948, therefore, the GNA's real need was not to increase its numbers and equipment; it was to have its numbers and equipment used with greater efficiency and determination. What the army required above all, in other words, was skilled and aggressive leadership: "all depended on leadership and morale."[119] Improvement in that crucial sphere was on the way. In

January 1949, the king appointed General Alexander Papagos as commander in chief of the Greek armed forces.

Papagos had led Greek forces to victory in the Albanian war in 1940. He thus had sufficient seniority and prestige to overcome the habitual lack of discipline among Greek Army commanders, and indeed he had refused to accept appointment as commander in chief unless he was given supreme power to remove incompetent or disobedient officers. Papagos had no great new ideas nor even any new plans. What was new was his self-confidence and spirit of aggressiveness, an attention to detail and a determination to have strict compliance with his orders. He gave operations a unity they had lacked before.

Papagos was determined to clear systematically both the guerrillas and the Yiafaka infrastructure from southern and central Greece. A good beginning had been made before Papagos took over supreme command: holding the bulk of the guerrilla fighting units at bay in the mountainous northern strongholds with minimal forces, the GNA concentrated on the final clearing of the Peloponnesus. This was strategically a sound choice, owing to the distance of that region from the Communist borders and the relative strength of monarchist and conservative republican sympathies there. Once he had chased out the guerrillas and broken the Yiafaka in the south, Papagos repeated the operation in other regions. (The clearing and holding of guerrilla-dominated areas receives more extensive attention in the concluding chapter.) His intention was to pin the Democratic Army against the northern borders while depriving it of its network of civilian sympathizers and agents, so that it would become like a great tree with withered roots.

Papagos received some good advice from the British and American military missions, because they could speak to him not from the point of view of domestic Greek politics (the plague of the GNA), but as detached professionals. But in essence, General (later Field Marshal) Papagos simply forced the Greek Army to do what it had the capability to do, and that was enough.[120] His task was made very much easier by some mistakes of his opponents, on both sides of the frontiers.

As 1948 became 1949, no one in Athens or Washington could know it for sure, but the Democratic Army was on the verge of defeat. American assistance, the unification of non-Communist political forces, and the leadership of General Papagos all played essential roles in this denouement. Even more important, however, were two disastrous decisions on the part of the insurgent leadership: to terrorize the peasantry and to adopt conventional war tactics.

THE COMMUNISTS AND THE PEOPLE

Between the end of the German occupation and the height of the insurgency, the relationship between the Greek peasantry and the guerrillas underwent a profound change. During the occupation, ELAS had stressed national resistance to the Germans. Many peasants had responded, providing food, shelter, and information. But during the civil war, the Democratic Army received supplies from across the frontiers and was thus less dependent on peasant goodwill. At the same time, peasants who had been willing to give some help against the Germans were reluctant to participate in an uprising against a legitimate Greek government. Under these circumstances, the fact that Communists composed most of the leadership of the Democratic Army became crucial.

That segment of the population attracted by the Communist Party was not only numerically slender; it was sociologically unrepresentative as well. Leadership was drawn from lower-middle-class urban intellectuals. Membership consisted overwhelmingly of those who lived in areas only recently acquired by Greece, and socially marginal groups like students, tobacco workers, and seamen, in a predominantly peasant country.[121] As the conflict wore on, Communist behavior toward the peasants worsened. Supplied with information about the identities of nationalist sympathizers and the location of their homes, Democratic Army units would swoop down upon a village or small town and kill these suspects and their families. Then they would carry off scarce foodstuffs, forced recruits, and hostages.[122] Further, the insurgents often deliberately destroyed whole villages for no other purpose than to create hungry refugees that the government would be hard pressed to feed and house. Sometimes they committed atrocities with no discernible explanation at all. Thousands of young children, moreover, some no more than 14 years old, were taken from their homes and sent to be trained as guerrillas or Communist functionaries in Eastern Europe. As many as 28,000 children were thus removed from Greece. Only about half of them were ever repatriated.[123] Efforts of the International Red Cross to obtain information on the missing children met with little success.

By antagonizing the mountain people in these various ways, the guerrillas undercut themselves in their own immediate theater of operations, destroying their last chance to build up a reliable base populated with supportive civilians. As the year 1948 wore on, it became evident that the insurgency had few followers in the cities. In Athens, scene of many grisly hostage murders in 1945, even the small proletariat was apathetic. The purging of the entire Communist leadership group in the capital city produced no beneficial change. And in the Peloponnesus, guerrilla activity had never been very successful, both because of the relatively good transportation system and the widespread monarchist sentiment in the area.

The original objectives of the insurgents had been to bring the Greek economy crashing down and to break the Greek National Army. American assistance meant that neither of these objectives had any serious chance of attainment, while Communist economic warfare had filled all Greece with fear of a Communist victory and alienated large numbers of originally neutral civilians.[124] One ominous consequence of these serious and largely self-created political weaknesses was that the insurgents were becoming ever more dependent on help from Communist states across the northern borders.

THE SWITCH TO CONVENTIONAL WARFARE

About a year after the outbreak of the second phase of the civil war, the Communist leadership decided to set up a counterstate, a "Free Greece." Because a state needs permanent territory and a capital city to receive accredited foreign diplomats, the Democratic Army sought to capture the town of Florina, near the Albanian border, in late May 1947. After severe fighting the insurgents withdrew, defeated. Nevertheless, the desire to set up a counterstate endured, and the insurgents proclaimed the birth of this state on December 24, 1947. This was a mistake. Neither the Soviets nor any satellite state recognized the existence of Free Greece, a grave moral setback. And to get themselves a capital, the insurgents decided to abandon their largely successful guerrilla tactics and launch a major conventional attack on a suitably large town. They chose Konitsa, only five miles from the Albanian border. On December 25, 1947, about 5,000 insurgents vigorously attacked the town and its 1,300 GNA defenders. Konitsa was soon surrounded. The Athens government had to drop supplies into it by aircraft. As a sign of how much importance the government placed on this battle, Queen Frederika herself flew into the besieged town to hearten the defenders. On January 4 the attack was broken off, with Konitsa still in National hands. Soon thereafter parliament outlawed the Communist Party.[125]

The principal commander of the Democratic Army was Markos Vafiades, usually called simply Markos. He had come to Greece from his birthplace in Anatolia in 1923 as a teenager and shortly thereafter joined the KKE. It was owing in very large part to his leadership that the insurgents had been able to take control of so much Greek territory and avoid dangerous confrontations with major elements of the National Army. Markos had opposed the assault on Konitsa. After the insurgents' defeat there in January 1948 he wanted to return to guerrilla tactics.

Communist Party boss Nikos Zachariades, however, was opposed to such a return. He instead pressed more and more insistently for a permanent switch to conventional war in order to break the GNA and open the road to Athens. A schoolteacher, born like Markos in Anatolia, Zachariades had gone to Moscow for training in the arts of Communist subversion. He installed himself, on Kremlin orders, as secretary general of the Greek Communist Party in 1931. He spent most of World War II in the infamous German concentration camp at Dachau. Both inside and outside the Greek Communist Party questions arose as to exactly how he managed to emerge alive from that hellhole.[126]

After the ferocious government assault on Mount Grammos in June 1948, Markos had been able to extricate his followers from their precarious position and lead them into Albania. But Zachariades continued to press for the adoption of conventional tactics. That is, he wanted the Democratic Army to attempt to seize and hold territory even in the face of GNA counterattacks.

In November 1948, Zachariades finally succeeded in ousting Markos from command of the Democratic Army and from his seat on the Central Committee. (Zachariades told Markos: "You will become a worm and crawl before me.")[127] Retaining his direction of the KKE, he now exercised control over the Democratic Army himself. Zachariades used his dictatorial power to turn the Democratic Army away from guerrilla warfare, which had brought it control of most of the territory of the country, to conventional warfare, in which it would confront directly the numerically superior and better equipped Greek National Army.

Most critics say that the Democratic Army turned to conventional warfare too early. In fact, however, it is arguable that the switch was made much too late. Whatever one's opinion on that score, by the second half of 1948 defeat for the insurgency was already looming. But when the insurgents, who lacked an air force among other things, engaged in positional warfare with a Greek Army that was improving every month in training, tactics, numbers, equipment, and morale, their defeat became inevitable.

It is not entirely clear why Zachariades made this fateful decision. He was unfamiliar with the nature of guerrilla warfare, having been in prison during the ELAS period. Neither was he well informed about the improvement in training and morale that had been taking place in the GNA during 1948. Other possible explanations include his evaluation of the general strategic situation faced by the Democratic Army in 1948. The main object of the guerrillas had been to disrupt the Greek economy to the breaking point. The inflow of economic aid from the United States, which was reaching serious proportions by mid-1948, meant the failure of this strategic aim. The increasingly bitter dispute between Tito and Stalin (the Cominform expelled Tito on June 28, 1948) and the decision by Zachariades that the Greek Communists would support Stalin meant that the loss of the Yugoslavian sanctuary was only a matter of time. The sands of the insurgency were running out.

Perhaps jealousy of the heroic and popular figure of Markos also motivated Zachariades. He saw to it that no one who joined the Communist Party from the ranks of ELAS was ever again allowed to attain an important post within the party. Later on, he would personally engineer the expulsion from the party of all the most successful guerrilla leaders.[128]

Whatever the reasons that led Zachariades to fire his best military commander and impose conventional warfare tactics on the Democratic Army, they led to fatal error. It ranks with the terrorism against the rural population and the choosing of Stalin over Tito in explaining the ultimate defeat of the Communist insurgency.

In December 1948 and January 1949, under the new policy of Zachariades, the Democratic Army mounted several major conventional attacks on sizable villages and towns, seizing a lot of food and taking many young men and women as hostages. Such assaults made it necessary for the guerrillas to assemble in large columns, a procedure that of course rendered them vulnerable to attacks by the ever improving Royal Greek Air Force and to encircling movements by the GNA. In February 1949, Zachariades directed a renewed attack against Florina. In this battle the Democratic Army employed heavy artillery on a large scale. Nevertheless the attack failed, and the insurgents suffered many casualties.

During 1949 morale within the Democratic Army began to sink. One reason for this, of course, was the very high rate of casualties resulting from the change from guerrilla tactics to conventional warfare. Another was that in the late winter of 1949 the Cominform, under Stalin's orders, proclaimed its support for an independent Macedonia. This announcement caused consternation within Greece and within the Greek Communist Party as well. The negative reaction was only increased, if possible, when Zachariades forced the politburo of the KKE to endorse the Moscow line.

This Cominform ploy was really intended to hurt Yugoslavia's Tito, but it undermined what little prestige remained to the Democratic Army and accelerated desertions from it. Every month the guerrillas were recruiting 1,000 new members and losing 4,000, so that the Democratic Army was more and more composed of forced recruits.[129] Macedonians were the other major component, partly because an increasingly better-trained GNA, employing steadily improving tactics, was destroying or otherwise eliminating guerrilla units in southern Greece.[130] The Democratic Army still had about 25,000 men and women at the end of 1948; by mid-1949, that number was down to around 20,000, of whom seven in ten were Macedonians. Most of the time only about half the insurgents were inside Greece.[131]

In contrast, the National armed forces were growing ever stronger. They included 150,000 regular troops, 50,000 members of the National Defense Corps (whose main function was to take over positions of static defense to release GNA troops for active combat), and 25,000 in the paramilitary gendarmerie. The unified command under Papagos, the gradual weeding out of incompetent officers, the growing impact of American aid and, not least, the increasing conviction that its members were fighting not only about forms of government but for the very territorial integrity of the nation (to keep Macedonia Greek)—all these factors helped to solidify the Greek armed forces into a power that the physically and morally diminishing Democratic Army had no hope of withstanding.

THE YUGOSLAVIAN FRONTIER

But perhaps nothing else did more to raise the morale of the government side and wither that of the insurgents than the disappearance of the Yugoslavian sanctuary. For months, the Yugoslavian dictator Tito had been imposing more and more restrictions on the movement of insurgents. Finally, in July 1949, he closed the Yugoslavian border to the guerrillas.

Tito's move against the Democratic Army and the KKE behind it, as well as his break with Stalin, was made possible in part by British and American assistance to the Greek National government. If the Democratic Army had won in Greece, Tito would then have been nearly surrounded by pro-Moscow Communist satellites, an untenable position from which to defy Stalin.

The border closing damaged the insurgents in several ways. First, it meant that guerrillas in most of northern Greece were no longer free to seek shelter from pursuing GNA troops. From now on, guerrillas who found themselves pressed against the Yugoslavian frontier would face either capture or death. The operations of the GNA, so frustrated for years by the open border, would now almost always bear fruit.

Second, by ending the free passage of armed units from Yugoslavia to Greece and back again, Tito in effect sealed several thousand Greek guerrillas inside Yugoslavia, where they could render no assistance at all to the Democratic Army in Greece.

Third, the GNA was in fairly firm control of that Greek territory lying between the Yugoslavian border and the Aegean Sea. Therefore guerrilla forces in Thrace (the part of Greece closest to Bulgaria) were now cut off from the rest of Greece, to be destroyed or driven into Bulgaria by the GNA at leisure. The isolation of the guerrillas inside Yugoslavia and in Thrace reduced for all practical purposes the number of the Democratic Army's fighting personnel by almost a third.[132]

Last, the closing of the Yugoslavian border stopped most supplies to the Democratic Army from Albania. Albanian territory was still available as a sanctuary, but most of the supplies that used to flow across the Greek-Albanian border had their origin in Yugoslavia, or at least had passed through that country. This compounded the disaster for the Democratic Army, because at least three quarters of its weapons, and all of its heavy equipment (mortars, antitanks guns and so on) came from across the borders. With the defection of Tito, the sealing of the Albanian frontier became the primary strategic objective of the Greek National army.

It was all over but the last act.

Zachariades, ever insistent that the Democratic Army abandon guerrilla for conventional war, had once again erected an "impregnable" bastion in the Grammos mountain area. There he conveniently assembled 12,000 insurgents for the GNA to attack, which it did in August 1949. The Democratic Army lost over 2,000 killed, captured, or surrendered. On August 31, for the last time, sizable guerrilla units scuttled across the Albanian frontier.

And in those same days, Zachariades denounced many high-ranking leaders of the KKE as lifelong traitors and agents of the British government. Zachariades knew that Marxism-Leninism could never be wrong; nor could those who opposed Greek Communism possibly have been popular and strong. He therefore looked elsewhere for the explanation of Communist defeat. He believed he found it in a colossal and evil conspiracy on the part of false Communists to stab the revolution in the back.[133]

On October 16, the voice of the insurgents, Radio Free Greece, announced that military operations were being suspended. And on November 28, President Truman informed Congress that the Greek government had emerged victorious in the civil war.

Greek armed forces, including the gendarmerie, suffered 17,000 dead and 40,000 wounded or unaccounted for. The guerrillas executed more than 4,000 civilians, and burned 12,000 homes and 98 railroad stations.[134] Greek government forces killed 37,000 guerrillas and captured another 20,000.

LESSONS FROM THE GREEK CONFLICT

In 1946, years of war and occupation had ravaged the economy of Greece, underdeveloped to begin with. Defeat and exile had disintegrated the old army. The new national army, badly equipped and poorly trained, seethed with political intrigue and personal rivalries. Disputes between monarchists and republicans bitterly divided the political leadership. On the other hand, with its rugged topography, primitive transportation system, and guerrilla tradition, Greece was a country eminently suited to insurgency. The guerrillas had benefited from several years of struggle against the Germans and EDES during which they had developed and perfected their organization and tactics. And they possessed sanctuaries across the border. These were not only places of safety and sources of supplies. They were as well the outward sign of their alliance with international Communism, a political force that in those days many believed to be the wave of the future.

Why then, with all these advantages, did the Communist insurgency fail? The civil war in Greece is "a textbook case of everything that can go wrong in an insurgency," although this was not so clear in 1947 or even 1948.[135] Looking back, we can see that some of the problems of the insurgents arose uncontrollably from their environment, others were of their own making, and certain weaknesses had at first sight been mistaken for blessings. While students of the war will dispute their relative weight, probably all would agree that the major causes of the final defeat of the insurgency included two external factors, namely, outside foreign assistance to the Greek government and the closing of the Yugoslav border; and two disastrous policies of the KKE, namely, the premature adoption of conventional warfare by the insurgents and Communist alienation of the population.

Foreign Assistance to the Athens Government

Outside intervention spoiled the Communist takeover of Greece not once but twice: by the British in 1944–1945 and the Americans after 1947. In spite of the vaunted power of nationalism in our time, the Greek government's dependence on foreign advice and support apparently did its cause no harm. This seems to have been the case for two sets of reasons. First, Britain had long been the patron and protector of Greek independence and territorial aspirations, and the United States was a land to which many Greeks had emigrated and from which they kept in close contact with relatives and friends left behind in the mother country. Second, in the minds of many ordinary Greeks the insurgents, and especially their leadership, were identified with the country's national enemies, notably Yugoslavia and Bulgaria. However convenient the foreign sanctuaries were to the insurgents, open dependence on Greece's northern neighbors must be accounted a net loss for them. This especially became the case as the Soviet Union trumpeted the idea of detaching Macedonia from Greece and as Macedonians increasingly predominated in the ranks of the insurgent forces. That the KKE endorsed (with much reluctance) the Soviet policy of a "free" Macedonia only underlined the connection between the insurgents and foreign powers who wished Greece little good.

American aid, both economic and military, allowed the Greeks to increase the size of their army and improve its equipment without causing great dislocations in the nation's economy. It provided the wherewithal, as well as the pressure, for the GNA to improve its operations. As the conflict developed, American aid increased while Communist assistance to the guerrillas declined. (In this crucial aspect, the Greek experience was the exact opposite of the South Vietnamese a quarter-century later.)

Losing the Yugoslavian Sanctuary

It is arguable that in the aircraft age, Greece was too small for classical guerrilla warfare. Sanctuary in the Communist states to the north, therefore, provided the insurgents with that space without which they probably would not have been able to function for long. Certainly, the ability of the insurgents, when pressed by the GNA, to retreat across friendly borders and receive shelter, training, and medical attention was a major factor in beginning and sustaining the insurgency.

To appreciate better the importance of the Yugoslavian border closing, one ought to try to imagine the consequences for South Viet Nam if the borders of Laos had been closed to the movement of troops and supplies from North Viet Nam.

The history of guerrilla conflict seems strongly to indicate that guerrillas need to operate astride international borders. Nevertheless, the Greek case suggests that the possession of sanctuaries is not always an unmixed blessing. Dependence on Greece's Communist neighbors identified the guerrillas in the minds of many as an antinational element, and nowhere have Communist insurgents come to power without having first succeeded in wrapping themselves, however incongruously and uncomfortably, in the banners of nationalism.[136] In addition, the availability of escape across friendly borders caused the guerrillas to develop a particular mode of fighting; even when it had become apparent that the Yugoslavian frontier would soon be closed to them, they proved unable to adapt. Finally, secure in their possession of crossborder sanctuaries, many guerrillas also no doubt felt freer than otherwise to express their profound hostility toward their unenlightened countrymen. Thus sanctuaries—ideally so much to be desired—probably worked against the insurgents in the long run.

Abandoning Guerrilla Tactics

Guerrilla warfare—sudden attacks with numerical superiority on isolated targets, rapid dispersal, hiding among the civilian population—is the strategy of the weak, who cannot yet stand up to the superior numbers, training, and equipment of the government's regular armed forces. Conventional armies, moving in large formations and weighed down with equipment, are road bound and easy to observe. These qualities make them vulnerable to guerrilla tactics.

In the classical Maoist strategy, the destiny of guerrillas is to grow in strength until they are able to wage conventional war—that is, to gather and remain together in large numbers to occupy and hold specific territory against attack by the government forces. When guerrillas adopt conventional war, they throw away their great advantage of mobility and give the regular army time to bring its numbers and equipment to bear. Clearly, then, this switch from guerrilla to conventional war ought to occur when the insurgents are gaining in physical and moral strength, and the government forces are losing. The Democratic Army had experimented with conventional tactics in the assaults on Florina and Konitsa in 1947. Even though the Greek National Army was then perhaps in its worst condition, the results had been bad for the insurgents. To directly confront the GNA in the winter of 1948–1949, at a time when American assistance was making itself felt and the insurgency was declining, was an egregious error.

Alienating the People

Could not the Democratic Army have recommitted itself to guerrilla tactics, learned to live without the Yugoslavian sanctuary, and hung on until the Americans lost interest in Greece? The answer to all these questions is: Quite possibly, IF—if it had the support of large elements of the population.

But the insurgents did not have this support, certainly not in 1948 and 1949. Elections in 1949 and 1950, after the fighting had abated, showed that the Communists were able to gather about 10 percent of the electorate, a sufficiently sizable pool from which to have drawn guerrillas, but not nearly enough to have overthrown even the wobbly Greek state. That is why the repeated calls by the leadership of the Communist Party for an uprising of the urban masses never materialized. This uncanny, un–Marxist indifference to the cause of revolution shown by the citizens of Athens resulted in the firing of the whole leadership of the party there. (Similarly, the Vietnamese Communists kept calling for and planning for the Great Uprising in Saigon, which never materialized either—not even after it had become clear that the North Vietnamese army would enter the city.)

Why did the great majority of the population ignore the repeated call to revolution? In the first place, while from a military point of view Greece was close to an ideal choice as a locus for launching a guerrilla-based revolutionary effort, from a political standpoint it was much less than that. Some observers believe that, at least in the short term, a democracy is not very efficient at coping with an insurgency.[137] This may be true. But it is certainly true that to overthrow by internal rebellion a government based on popular consent, or with the trappings of such consent, is very difficult. This is because many who might long for profound changes in the life of the society cannot be mobilized for armed struggle and the fratricidal destruction that comes with it if there exists, or seems to exist, a nonviolent path, such as parliamentary elections, to the desired changes.[138] And however threadbare, Greece was a parliamentary democracy.

But clearly, in a country like postwar Greece, with so much poverty and so many tensions, this need not have been an insuperable handicap. The Communists should have been able to expand outward from their hard core and to gather substantial support behind a program of radical redistribution. They could have at least built up a large popular following among the peasants in those mountainous districts which the insurgents controlled most of the time.

But in fact, this did not happen. The key to the defeat of the insurgents is that they did not have the support of the people: "the rebels failed because the mass of the people was against them."[139] As the conflict went on, support for the Democratic Army and the KKE behind it withered, especially in the villages. Why did this occur? After the end of the civil war, a member of the Greek Communist Politburo provided an explanation for this hostility from the population: the defeat of the Communists, he wrote, stemmed from "the policy of devastation of the countryside."[140]

The guerrillas had safe supply sources over the frontiers and thus were relatively independent of the peasantry, true enough. But clearly not all guerrilla movements that enjoy sanctuaries (such as the Afghan mujahideen) have antagonized the civilians among whom they operated. We must consider the driving force behind the insurgency in Greece, the Communist Party. The hard core of the party was more than merely unrepresentative of the majority of Greeks; it was profoundly hostile to them. Many Communist activists felt contempt and even shame for the mass of the peasantry, whom they considered hopelessly ignorant, superstitious, and petit bourgeois. This is the root of the conscious and unconscious policy of terror in the villages to elicit cooperation or passivity.[141]

This epiphany of hostility was foreshadowed during the German occupation, when ELAS guerrillas would deliberately bring down the Nazi wrath upon helpless villages. The violent propensities of the ELAS were revealed during the Athens fighting in 1944, during which "the Communists, whose many atrocities were perpetrated mostly upon innocent and defenseless hostages, came to be hated with a passion rare in the nation's history."[142] It reached its fruition during the civil war in the policy of gaining power by destroying the economic life of the nation at whatever cost to the peasants. In a Brave New Stalinist Greece the fate of the peasants was to be not liberation, but liquidation. By spreading terror among the peasants, the Communists poisoned the very waters in which they had to swim.

American assistance helped the Greek Army hold together until victory, which was vital, and the closing of the Yugoslav frontier lowered the cost of that victory, which was very helpful. But by violating the two most fundamental rules of guerrilla warfare—never fight the enemy unless you are certain to win, and make friends with the civil population among whom you must exist—the Greek insurgents defeated themselves.

NOTES

1. R. V. Burks, "Statistical Profile of the Greek Communist," *Journal of Modern History*, vol. 27 (1955).

2. C. M. Woodhouse, *The Struggle for Greece, 1941–1949* (London: Hart-Davis, MacGibbon, 1976), p. 226.

3. Greece would be "the first showcase of the American will." Howard Jones, *"A New Kind of War": America's Global Strategy and the Truman Doctrine in Greece* (New York: Oxford University Press, 1989).

4. Douglas Dakin, *The Greek Struggle for Independence, 1821–1833* (Berkeley: University of California Press, 1973).

5. D. George Kousoulas, *Revolution and Defeat: The Story of the Greek Communist Party* (London: Oxford University Press, 1965), Chapter 4 and passim.

6. Kousoulas, *Revolution*, p. 41.

7. Kousoulas, *Revolution*, Chapter 10.

8. D. M. Condit, *Case Study in Guerrilla War: Greece during World War II* (Washington, DC: Department of the Army, 1961), p. 213.

9. John O. Iatrides, *Revolt in Athens* (Princeton, NJ: Princeton University Press, 1972), p. 277.

10. Woodhouse, *Struggle for Greece*, p. 25.

11. Edgar O'Ballance, *The Greek Civil War, 1944–1949* (New York: Praeger, 1966), p. 88.

12. Edward R. Wainhouse, "Guerrilla War in Greece, 1946–1949," in *Modern Guerrilla Warfare*, ed. Franklin Mark Osanka (New York: Free Press, 1962), p. 18.

13. Woodhouse, *Struggle for Greece*, p. 77.

14. O'Ballance, *Greek Civil War*, pp. 81–82.

15. Field Marshal Alexander Papagos, "Guerrilla Warfare," in *Modern Guerrilla Warfare*, ed. Franklin Mark Osanka p. 230; Woodhouse, *Struggle*, p. 106.

16. Condit, *Case Study in Guerrilla War*, pp. 244ff.

17. Papagos, "Guerrilla Warfare," p. 230.

18. Condit, *Case Study in Guerrilla War*, p. 8.

19. Kousoulas, *Revolution and Defeat*, p. 15 and passim; O'Ballance, *Greek Civil War*, pp. 80–81.

20. Condit, *Case Study in Guerrilla War*, Chapter 19.

21. Woodhouse, *Struggle for Greece*.

22. Kousoulas, *Revolution and Defeat*, pp. 175ff; Iatrides, *Revolt in Athens*, pp. 26–27.

23. O'Ballance, *Greek Civil War*, p. 73.

24. Condit, *Case Study in Guerrilla War*, pp. 235ff.

25. Woodhouse, *Struggle for Greece*, p. 101; O'Ballance, *Greek Civil War*, pp. 92, 93.

26. Kousoulas, *Revolution and Defeat*, p. 187.

27. Woodhouse, *Struggle for Greece*, p. 112.

28. Ibid., p. 114.

29. O'Ballance, *Greek Civil War*, p. 97.

30. O'Ballance, *Greek Civil War*, p. 96; Iatrides, *Revolt in Athens*, pp. 160–61.

31. Iatrides, *Revolt in Athens*, p. 226.

32. Winston Churchill, *Triumph and Tragedy* (Boston: Houghton Mifflin, 1953), Chapter 19.

33. O'Ballance, *Greek Civil War*, pp. 98, 105.

34. Woodhouse, *Struggle for Greece*, p. 133; Condit, *Case Study in Guerrilla War*, pp. 85ff.

35. Woodhouse, *Struggle for Greece*, p. 266.

36. Kousoulas, *Revolution and Defeat*, p. 215; O'Ballance, *Greek Civil War*, pp. 111–12; but see also Iatrides, *Revolt in Athens*.

37. O'Ballance, *Greek Civil War*, p. 78.

38. See Churchill's notorious account of his agreement with Stalin over division of the Balkans in *Triumph and Tragedy*, pp. 226–27.

39. See, for example, Kousoulas, *Revolution and Defeat*, pp. 232–33.

40. Woodhouse, *Struggle for Greece*, p. 186.

41. Ibid., pp. 205–6.

42. Ibid., p. 145.

43. See Robert L. Wolff, *The Balkans in Our Times* (Cambridge, MA: Harvard University Press, 1956). There is a good discussion of Macedonian separatist terrorism in Hugh Seton-Watson, *Eastern Europe between the Wars, 1918–1941* (New York: Harper, 1967). A small classic is Elisabeth Barker, *Macedonia: Its Place in Balkan Power Politics* (London: Royal Institute of International Affairs, 1950).

44. William H. McNeill, *Greece: American Aid in Action* (New York: Twentieth Century Fund, 1957), Chapter 1.

45. Woodhouse, *Struggle for Greece*, pp. 212, 254; Kousoulas, *Revolution and Defeat*, p. 252.

46. Condit, *Case Study in Guerrilla War*, p. 18.

47. J. C. Murray, "The Anti-Bandit War," reprinted in *The Guerrilla—and How to Fight Him* (New York: Praeger, 1962), p. 87.

48. McNeill, *Greece*, Chapter 1.

49. Ibid., p. 27.

50. Papagos, "Guerrilla Warfare," p. 234.

51. Woodhouse, *Struggle for Greece*, p. 185. But see the views of Peter Stavrakis in *Moscow and Greek Communism, 1944–1949* (Ithaca, NY: Cornell University Press, 1989).

52. Papagos, "Guerrilla Warfare," p. 237.

53. O'Ballance, *Greek Civil War*, p. 143.

54. Ibid., p. 173.

55. *Foreign Relations of the United States, 1948*, vol. 4, *Eastern Europe and the Soviet Union* (Washington, DC: Government Printing Office) (hereinafter referred to as FRUS 1948), p. 113.

56. The quotation is from U.S. Ambassador Lincoln MacVeagh and appears in *Foreign Relations of the United States, 1947*, vol. 5, *The Near East and Africa* (Washington, DC: Government Printing Office, 1971) (hereinafter referred to as FRUS 1947), p. 252.

57. Woodhouse, *Struggle for Greece*, pp. 205 and 187; Murray, "The Anti-Bandit War," p. 94.

58. Woodhouse, *Struggle for Greece*, p. 183.

59. Murray, "The Anti-Bandit War," pp. 95–96.

60. Woodhouse, *Struggle for Greece*, p. 246.

61. Woodhouse, *Struggle for Greece*, p. 187.

62. Kousoulas, *Revolution and Defeat*, p. 241.

63. Woodhouse, *Struggle for Greece*, p. 213.

64. Kousoulas, *Revolution and Defeat*, p. 229.

65. FRUS 1947, p. 268; Lawrence S. Wittner, *American Intervention in Greece, 1943–1949* (New York: Columbia University Press, 1982), p. 228.

66. John Lewis Gaddis, *The United States and the Origins of the Cold War* (New York: Columbia University Press, 1975); John Spanier, *American Foreign Policy since World War II*, 4th ed. (New York: Praeger, 1971); James F. Byrnes, *Speaking Frankly* (New York: Harper, 1947); George F. Kennan, *Memoirs, 1925–1950* (Boston: Little, Brown, 1967), Chapters 8–12; Dean Acheson, *Present at the Creation* (New York: Norton, 1969), Chapter 22.

67. Iatrides, *Revolt in Athens*, pp. 282–87.

68. FRUS 1947, p. 61.

69. FRUS 1947, p. 30.

70. Kennan, *Memoirs*, vol. 1, p. 318.

71. Howard Jones, in *"A New Kind of War: America's Global Strategy and the Truman Doctrine in Greece"* (New York: Oxford University Press), puts it this way:

Without Soviet and East European documents, who can today determine the extent of Soviet involvement in Greece? In truth, the question is academic: the Truman administration *believed* that the Soviets were at least indirectly involved in that nation's affairs. American documents reveal considerable insight into Soviet behavior during the period, some of which was substantiated years after the civil war." (pp. ix–x, italics in original)

72. Spanier, *American Foreign Policy*, pp. 39–40.

73. Jones, *New Kind of War*, p. 42.

74. George F. Kennan, "The Sources of Soviet Conduct," *Foreign Affairs*, July 1947, pp. 861, 868.

75. FRUS 1947, pp. 220, 222.

76. Gaddis, *The United States and the Origins of the Cold War*, p. 352.

77. Adam B. Ulam, *The Rivals: America and Russia since World War II* (New York: Viking, 1971), p. 125; see Howard Jones, *A New Kind of War*, p. 36.

78. FRUS 1948, p. 3.

79. FRUS 1948, p. 5.

80. FRUS 1948, p. 13; on the concept of the Soviets seeking to outlast the United States in Greece, see the draft report of the Department of State to the National Security Council of November 30, 1948, FRUS 1948, p. 207.

81. FRUS 1948, p. 135.

82. O'Ballance, *Greek Civil War*.

83. Wittner, *American Intervention in Greece*, p. 234.

84. Woodhouse, *Struggle for Greece*, p. 248.

85. FRUS 1947, p. 221.

86. FRUS 1947, p. 20.

87. Wittner, *American Intervention in Greece*, Chapter 4.

88. FRUS 1948, p. 203.

89. FRUS 1947, p. 442.

90. Kousoulas, *Revolution and Defeat*, p. 254.

91. Wittner, *American Intervention in Greece*, p. 223.

92. FRUS 1948, p. 57.

93. FRUS 1947, p. 469.

94. FRUS 1947, p. 460.

95. FRUS 1947, pp. 466–69.

96. FRUS 1948, p. 163.

97. Wittner, *American Intervention in Greece*, p. 236.

98. Acheson, *Present at the Creation*, p. 199.

99. FRUS 1947, p. 273.

100. FRUS 1947, pp. 361, 363.

101. FRUS 1948, p. 208.

102. Wittner, *American Intervention in Greece*, p. 247.

103. FRUS 1947, p. 335.

104. FRUS 1947, p. 383.

105. Wittner, *American Intervention in Greece*, p. 239.

106. FRUS 1948, p. 65.

107. John Lewis Gaddis, *Strategies of Containment* (New York: Oxford University Press, 1982), pp. 22, 62.

108. FRUS 1948, p. 95.

109. Wittner, *American Intervention in Greece*, p. 242; see brief discussion in Jones, *A New Kind of War*, pp. 90–94.

110. Papagos, "Guerrilla Warfare," p. 238. See also Woodhouse, *Struggle for Greece*, p. 237.

111. FRUS 1948, pp. 198–99, 201.

112. Wittner, *American Intervention in Greece*, p. 246.

113. FRUS 1948, pp. 189–91, 211–12.

114. O'Ballance, *Greek Civil War*, p. 216.

115. Kousoulas, *Revolution and Defeat*, pp. 258–59.

116. Ibid.

117. O'Ballance, *Greek Civil War*, p. 214.

118. Kousoulas, *Revolution and Defeat*, p. 257.

119. Woodhouse, *Struggle for Greece*, pp. 238, 246, and 258.

120. Murray, "The Anti-Bandit War," p. 98.

121. R. V. Burks, "Statistical Profile of the Greek Communist," *Journal of Modern History*, vol. 27 (1955).

122. Wainhouse, "Guerrilla War in Greece," passim; O'Ballance, *Greek Civil War*, p. 134.

123. Woodhouse, *Struggle for Greece*, pp. 209, 274.

124. Wainhouse, "Guerrilla War in Greece," pp. 25 and passim. U.S. assistance to Greece during the conflict amounted to $353 million.

125. Woodhouse, *Struggle for Greece*, pp. 220–21.

126. Kousoulas, *Revolution and Defeat*, passim.

127. Jones, *"A New Kind of War"*, p. 190.

128. Woodhouse, *Struggle for Greece*, p. 45.

129. Ibid., p. 263.

130. Ibid., p. 267.

131. Ibid., pp. 257, 262.

132. Murray, "The Anti-Bandit War," p. 74.

133. Kousoulas, *Revolution and Defeat*.

134. Kousoulas, *Revolution and Defeat*, p. 270.

135. David Galula, *Counterinsurgency Warfare: Theory and Practice* (New York: Praeger, 1964), p. 18.

136. See Chalmers Johnson, *Autopsy on People's War* (Berkeley: University of California Press, 1973).

137. See the report of the Policy Planning Staff, November, 1948, FRUS 1948, pp. 199–200.

138. Ernesto ["Che"] Guevara, *Guerrilla Warfare* (New York: Vintage, 1961).

139. Woodhouse, *Struggle for Greece*, p. 233. See also O'Ballance, *Greek Civil War*, p. 210.

140. Woodhouse, *Struggle for Greece*, p. 267.

141. Murray, "The Anti-Bandit War," p. 70.

142. Iatrides, *Revolt in Athens*, p. 288.

Chapter 3

Insurrections in the Philippines

The Filipinos and the Americans are trading partners, military allies, and old friends. They are intimately linked by memories of a gratifyingly victorious struggle against a common foe. The Philippine constitution is modeled on that of the United States, and most Filipinos speak the language their ancestors learned from the Americans. And for students of insurgency, twentieth-century Philippine history provides two instructive examples of defeats of guerrilla movements, one directly and one indirectly at the hands of the Americans.

Aguinaldo and the Americans, 1898–1902

A SKETCH OF THE COUNTRY

The Philippine archipelago consists of over 7,000 islands, only 3,000 of which have names. They stretch north to south for almost a thousand miles, the distance from Seattle to Los Angeles or from Stockholm to Belgrade. The 116,000-square-mile area of the country equals that of Arizona or Italy. Luzon, largest of these islands, is about the size of Kentucky or the former East Germany. With a warm and damp climate, the islands produce rice, hemp, coconuts, and sugarcane.

In modern times the archipelago has been conquered in turn by the Spanish, the Americans, the Japanese, and the Americans again. Magellan the Circumnavigator arrived in the islands, where he was killed, in 1521. Although the Philippines received their name in 1542, in honor of the prince

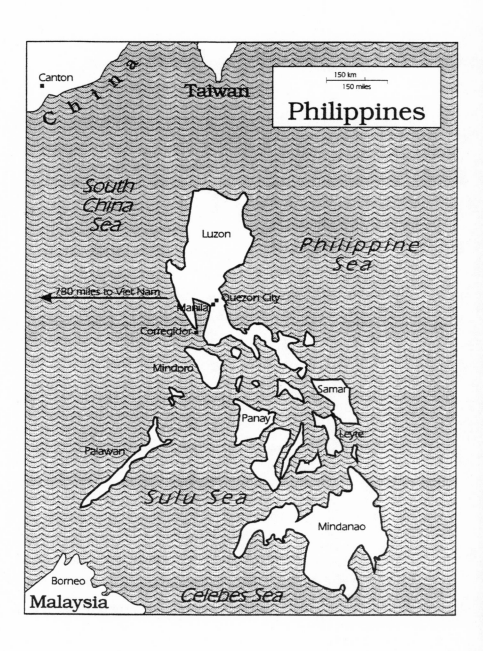

Canton

China

Taiwan

150 km
150 miles

Philippines

South
China
Sea

Luzon

Philippine
Sea

780 miles to Viet Nam

Manila
Quezon City

Corregidor

Mindoro

Samar

Panay

Leyte

Palawan

Sulu Sea

Mindanao

Borneo

Celebes Sea

Malaysia

who as Philip II would one day rule an immense empire, the Spanish did not begin their subjugation of the islands until the 1560s. They founded Manila in 1571.

The Spanish imposed unity on the islands for the first time in their history, and today's Filipino nation grew directly from yesterday's Spanish colony.[1] The Spanish also imposed their economic system, including large landholdings by religious orders. But it was the introduction of Catholic Christianity in its Iberian Reconquista version that most profoundly and permanently shaped the culture of the Filipinos: "The Spaniards put a heavy emphasis on Christianization as the most effective means of incorporating the Filipinos into Spanish culture."[2] Christianity brought the Philippines into the orbit of Western civilization, where they have remained ever since. Indeed "the Filipinos are unique for being the only Oriental people profoundly and consistently influenced by Occidental culture for the last four centuries."[3]

Spanish rule, however, promoted neither economic development nor self-government. By the dawn of the nineteenth century, Filipinos of education and prominence, called *ilustrados*, were chafing under Spanish discrimination against them with regard to appointments in church and state. The Spanish were pursuing similar policies in their Latin American domains, setting Creoles against *peninsulares*. Resentment was also high against the enormous financial and political power of the monastic orders.

Late in the nineteenth century some *ilustrados* founded the Katipunan, a secret society whose purpose was to work toward the overthrow of Spanish power. Emilio Aguinaldo, born in 1869, became head of the Katipunan in Cavite and eventually in all of the islands.

THE SPANISH-AMERICAN WAR

The Katipunan launched a major rebellion in the summer of 1896. About a year later, the revolt came to a halt through an agreement according to which Aguinaldo and several other prominent leaders would go into exile (to Hong Kong) in return for the promise of a substantial payment from the Madrid government. But underlying discontents went unaddressed, and so rebellion broke out again in March 1898. Less than a month later, Spain and the United States went to war. The causes of the conflict had little to do with the Philippines, but its effects on them would be profound. The United States Asiatic Squadron, under Commodore George Dewey on his flagship the *Olympia*, sailed from Nagasaki to Manila Bay. There, on May 1, Dewey won his overwhelming victory against the Spanish fleet under Admiral Patricio Montojo. Dewey then had Aguinaldo brought back to the islands (to Cavite) on May 19.[4]

A few days later, Aguinaldo proclaimed himself dictator of a provisional government of an independent Philippine Republic. By the end of June most of the key island of Luzon was in the hands of his adherents. Aguinaldo was apparently under the impression that Washington would recognize his government.[5]

Meanwhile, the war against the Spanish continued. The first units of the U.S. Army began arriving in the islands on June 30, 1898. Manila fell to the Americans on August 13. These American troops were 10,000 miles from Washington, D.C. The archipelago in which they were deploying consisted of thousands of islands with 7 million inhabitants who displayed a vast cultural diversity, from Hispanicized Manilans at one extreme to the pagan tribes of the Luzon mountains at the other. No one in the Philippines knew what President William McKinley's policy toward the islands was or would be; the U.S. Army leaders on the spot consequently refused to allow Aguinaldo's forces to enter Manila in strength. Nevertheless, the army stood by while many small Spanish garrisons and outposts outside Manila, cut off from supplies and instructions from Madrid, surrendered to Aguinaldo's men. Had they been able to look into the near future, the Americans would have wanted to capture these posts themselves.

The United States had gone to war with Spain over events in Cuba, but Dewey's unexpected and lopsided triumph in Manila Bay meant that the American government now had to decide the fate of the Philippines. At the beginning of the war President McKinley had nothing remotely approximating a policy for the islands. Having conquered the Philippines, for the Americans to return control of them to the Spanish seemed dishonorable, as well as cruel to the Filipinos. But many in Washington (and elsewhere) believed that the islands were not ready to govern themselves. If granted independence in 1898, they would most likely dissolve into civil war and anarchy, tempting other powers with imperial holdings in the Western Pacific (such as Germany or Japan) to occupy them. These considerations began to move some of McKinley's advisers toward the idea of taking temporary American possession of the whole archipelago.

The Spanish-American War came to its predictable end with the signing of the Treaty of Paris on December 10, 1898. The American government had by then adopted the position that the Filipinos could not protect their independence. It believed that the promise of benevolent and efficient administration at the hands of Americans, plus the definite prospect of independence at some future date, would calm and satisfy the inhabitants of the archipelago.[6]

THE INSURGENCY IGNITES

By February 1899, General E. S. Otis was inside Manila in command of about 20,000 American troops. Most of these men were volunteers who a few months previously had been civilians. Around the city were about 30,000 soldiers loyal to Aguinaldo. Relations between the two forces were rapidly deteriorating. Actual combat between the U.S. Army in Manila and Aguinaldo's troops began with a clash on February 4, 1899.

The following month civilian commissioners appointed by President McKinley arrived in the islands. The head of the commission was Jacob Gould Schurman, president of Cornell University; another member was Dean C. Worcester of the University of Michigan, who had made several scientific expeditions to the islands. The commissioners published a proclamation to the Filipinos setting forth the benevolent intentions of the U.S. government. The document promised to protect the Filipinos "in their just privileges and immunities," to "accustom them to free self-government in an ever-increasing measure," and to "encourage them in . . . democratic aspirations, sentiments, and ideals." Elements within the Aguinaldo government wished to accept the terms of the April proclamation; they were stopped only by the vigorous intervention of his armed forces.[7] Nevertheless, numerous respected Filipinos who had been members of the insurgent congress went over to the American side. American forces found that even by the end of the year, many Filipinos had not even heard of the April proclamation. Nonetheless, Filipinos had begun to act as scouts and interpreters for the U.S. Army and to join police units on Luzon and Negros islands.

Aguinaldo commanded the only organized armed force that operated throughout the length of the islands. He also had in the Katipunan an infrastructure that could provide his troops with information and money, distribute propaganda among the civilian population, and punish defectors. Aguinaldo's movement received vital support as well from native clergy. But it would be anachronistic to assume that Aguinaldo was the leader of a movement of full-fledged Filipino nationalism in 1899. In the first place, he had achieved supreme leadership over the insurgency only after his followers had executed Andres Bonifacio, founder of the Katipunan. This act disillusioned many who might otherwise have rallied around a nationalist banner even to the point of armed revolt. Moreover, many in the social elite of the islands were reluctant to assist the rebellion. Even more important in circumscribing support for the insurgents were the ethnic divisions within Philippine society. The center of the revolt was in the Tagalog-speaking regions around Manila. Aguinaldo and a disproportionately large number of the other principal leaders of the insurgency were Tagalog. General Antonio Luna, perhaps the best officer in the nationalist army, was an Ilocano. His murder, under very suspicious circumstances at Aguinaldo's headquarters in 1900, exacerbated ethnic tensions within the islands. The insurgent troops did a lot of indiscriminate pillaging, but probably no group suffered more from this sort of activity that the numerous Chinese minority. The Americans soon learned to take advantage of these conditions by employing non-Tagalog Filipinos in their paramilitary forces.

THE AMERICANS WOO THE FILIPINOS

General Otis, in command of American ground forces, "for all his faults as a troop commander, recognized that the problem facing the Americans in the Philippines was in reality a political one."[8] Otis, that is, understood that he had not only to defeat the rebels but also to set the stage for pacification and reconciliation.

Quite aside from waging war, the U.S. Army in Manila faced a daunting task. The city, which with its immediate environs contained 400,000 persons, was woefully overcrowded. Schools were closed, the port was not operating, rubbish and garbage went uncollected in the streets, the Aguinaldo forces had cut off the water supply. The city was on the edge of epidemic and anarchy.

Many American officers in the Philippines soon demonstrated that they grasped the connection between the present conduct of the army and the future reconciliation between Americans and Filipinos. These officers were of the same Progressive persuasion as many of the folks back home in the states: they believed in honest government, fair taxes, free education and public health measures. In brief, they believed in the power and duty of enlightened government to uplift those in its care. In the words of one American general, "we have got to live among these people, we have got to govern them. Government by force alone cannot be satisfactory to Americans."[9]

The Americans began to clean up the filth in the Manila streets. They appointed municipal health officials and offered free health care to the many indigent inhabitants of the capital. The army vaccinated thousands, first in Manila and then in the countryside, launching the campaign that would soon reduce smallpox from a scourge to a nuisance. As the army moved out from the capital, it distributed food, set up municipal governments, and attacked the deplorable sanitary conditions. The Americans gave the same care to wounded Filipino prisoners as to their own wounded. They reformed the prison system, releasing many who had been held in jail, untried, for years. They built or rebuilt schools, often with soldiers as instructors, and taught many children; this was one of the most popular American programs among a population hungry for education. The insurgent leaders were soon deeply disconcerted by the growing success of what they saw as this American "policy of attraction."

GUERRILLA WARFARE

Along with these popular social policies, General Otis decided to launch a military offensive against Aguinaldo's forces in October. American horses could not live well on the native grasses, and as many as half of the men in some American units were sick. Nevertheless, in the face of aggressive

American tactics Aguinaldo retreated. His troops often broke up into small units, buried their arms, and went home. As a coherent, organized force Aguinaldo's army was finished. As the year 1899 was ending, many Americans hoped that the fighting was ending as well.[10]

Instead, Aguinaldo proclaimed guerrilla war. Some of Aguinaldo's advisers had from the start wanted him to pursue a conventional war against the Americans, to prove that they were a real government and thus gain sympathy and support both inside the United States and from third world countries. But Aguinaldo had leaned toward the strategy of guerrilla warfare from the start and now adopted it for lack of an alternative. Such a move was not without promise of eventual success. U.S. forces in the islands were few in number, far from home, with scant knowledge of the country or its people and with little direction from their own government. Topographically, the country was well suited for guerrilla warfare, and some of Aguinaldo's followers had experience in that type of fighting.

Aguinaldo's guerrillas employed classical tactics with which Americans have become all too familiar. They dug pits and placed sharpened stakes in the bottom, or set up bow-and-arrow booby traps. As a rule, they fought only when they had overwhelming numerical preponderance. After an attack or other armed action, the rebels resumed civilian garb and concealed themselves among the villagers. Thus, American soldiers could never be sure who was a guerrilla and who was a simple peasant—classic conditions for illegal acts or atrocities. Insufficient numbers hindered American action against the guerrillas. Usually they could do no more than hold the principal cities and larger towns. Often an American unit would occupy a town for a period and then move on, so that the rebels came back into possession of it and punished all who had shown themselves friendly to the Americans. Beyond the fighting, many American soldiers found the tropical climate and topography of the islands strange and demoralizing.

The announced object of the guerrilla war was to tire the Americans by making their occupation of the islands as costly as possible, meanwhile awaiting the hoped-for victory of William Jennings Bryan in the approaching presidential election.

THE BRYAN MIRAGE

William Jennings Bryan, former "Boy Orator of the River Platte," evangelist, prohibitionist, future crusader against Darwinism in the famous Scopes "Monkey" trial, was indeed the 1900 Democratic presidential standard-bearer, running on an "anti-imperialist" platform. The specter of a Bryan victory hobbled American efforts in the Philippines: fearing that a Bryan presidency would mean an immediate pullout of U.S. forces from the islands, many Filipinos shied away from cooperating with the Americans. Self-styled anti-imperialist groups in the United States sent propaganda to American soldiers, urging them to abandon this brutal, imperialistic war.

Even though Aguinaldo had very much needed a Bryan victory, the Philippine insurgent later described the American politician as "nearsighted, selfish and unstatesmanlike."[11] Aguinaldo accused Bryan of wanting the United States to annex the Philippines so that there would be a war that he could blame on McKinley. Bryan in fact did go to Washington, where he ordered Democratic senators to vote for McKinley's annexation treaty, which he later denounced during the campaign.[12]

Bryan suffered a rebuff from the American electorate even more decisive than that of 1896. Many Filipinos had wished to make peace with the Americans but had hung back from fear of insurgent reprisal if the Americans abandoned the islands; Bryan's defeat showed that this would not occur, and it certainly hurt morale among the Aguinaldo supporters. Nevertheless, the massive postelection surrenders that American forces had been hoping for did not materialize.[13]

Meanwhile, changes were affecting the American presence at the highest levels. General Otis, a conscientious and hardworking officer, was not cut out to fight guerrillas in the jungle. He relied on sweeps and other time-wasting tactics. Time and again his forces would occupy a village, only to withdraw and have the place reoccupied by the guerrillas. Otis himself was not unaware that he was making little progress, and he asked to be relieved. In May 1900, General Arthur MacArthur took over as commander of the U.S. Army in the Philippines. Within a month MacArthur issued a proclamation of amnesty for guerrillas. He meanwhile made plans for an offensive against remaining insurgent forces. McKinley's decisive defeat of Bryan was the signal to go ahead, and the offensive was launched in December, involving most of the 70,000 troops under MacArthur's command. The Americans initiated numerous small-scale tactical actions. The number of towns with permanent garrisons increased, and in many areas where guerrillas were active the population outside the towns were temporarily gathered inside.

WAR CRIMES

Before 1900, the Americans had the practice of releasing any prisoners once they had been disarmed. As a rule they did not punish villagers even when there was evidence that they had cooperated with the insurgents. The Americans offered the Filipinos many inducements for supporting the United States but exacted few real penalties for opposing. All this was in line with the principle of eventual reconciliation. After the middle of 1900, however, ideas began to change. Many Americans had come to believe that the policy of benevolence toward the guerrillas and their sympathizers had produced a situation in which the rebels were feared more than the Americans.[14] The opinion was widespread that even those Filipinos well-disposed to the Americans viewed the policy of restraint as proof of an essential lack of seriousness. Reprisals, by showing the prohibitive costs of further resistance, would therefore shorten the war and save lives. Hence a new attitude began to appear: benevolence to those who were peaceable, but punishment to those who persisted in obviously useless violence.

General MacArthur resisted pressures from below for a harsher policy, believing that time was clearly on the side of the Americans. There had previously been instances of misbehavior by American soldiers in certain areas, and even the looting of some churches; General Otis and his subcommanders sought to punish those who committed such acts. Nevertheless, by the summer of 1900, some American units were burning down any barrio within whose precincts an ambush or an act of terror or sabotage had occurred.[15] There is no doubt that cruelties and abuses by American forces increased during 1900, and rebel propaganda efforts were unsparing in their depiction of the Americans as steeped in atrocities.

There were also crimes committed in the name of the insurgency. During 1899 many peasants leveled accusations of robbery, rape, and murder against the Aguinaldo forces. Sometimes these incidents reflected the ethnic divisions of the islands, with Aguinaldo and most other leaders of the rebellion being Tagalogs from central Luzon. As 1900 wore on, the tide was obviously turning mightily against the insurgents; the Americans were on the move, and many guerrillas, including officers, were defecting. In their desperation to reinstall discipline into their supporters, the guerrillas resorted more frequently to terrorist acts; killings of officials of American-established municipal governments increased, and guerrilla units even threatened that any town that cooperated with the Americans would be burned down and all its male inhabitants put to the sword.[16] American forces thereafter greatly increased their efforts to protect villages from guerrilla reprisals.

WINDING DOWN THE WAR

In December 1900, MacArthur responded to growing demands for a more vigorously punitive policy toward guerrilla sympathizers. He announced that even men who were only part-time insurgents would receive harsh treatment if captured. The army would no longer accept compulsion or intimidation as an excuse for acts in support of the rebels. The Americans stopped releasing prisoners and began instead to send captured guerrillas to detention on Guam.

Nonetheless, if a Filipino turned in a weapon at a U.S. Army base, he or she could secure the release of a prisoner of war. MacArthur called this one of his "most important policies."[17] The army also began paying bounties for turned-in weapons, no questions asked.

In the spring of 1901, Secretary of War Elihu Root became convinced that the fighting was nearly finished. Wishing to establish closer civilian control over the U.S. Army in the Philippines, and believing he would have an easier time of it with a commander who had not exercised the vast powers of MacArthur, Root replaced him with Brigadier General A. R. Chafee.

The insurgents' desperation intensified; during 1901 their practice of putting whole barrios to the torch became much more common. Filipinos responded to such acts in several quite predictable ways. An increasing number of them joined in active cooperation with the Americans. By June 1901 there were over 5,400 serving as Army scouts or police; almost all of these were non-Tagalog.

Another Filipino response to insurgent terrorism was the appearance of the Filipino Federal Party. Founded at the end of 1900, the Federal Party presented a program of conciliation with the Americans and eventual independence. The insurgents immediately recognized that the Federal Party's peaceful road toward independence was a major threat to them; hence they vowed to execute any party member without trial.

Meanwhile, the Americans had not been neglecting the improvement of their intelligence activities against the insurgents. Between late 1900 and early 1901 they made a serious and fairly successful effort to break up the revolutionary organization in Manila. But the greatest intelligence coup of the war occurred on March 23, 1901, when an American army officer named Frederick Funston captured Aguinaldo himself.[18]

It was clear that the insurgency could not last much longer. American "propaganda of the deed," such as the schools program, the increasing number of permanently garrisoned towns, the aggressive actions by army units that gave the rebels no respite, the growing involvement of Filipinos in peacekeeping activities (such as the Philippine Constabulary, a mobile force of 3,000, mainly under American officers), the efforts of the Federal Party, the capture of Aguinaldo, all resulted in larger and larger numbers of surrenders of guerrillas. In March and April 1901 alone, surrenders totalled 13,000. At the same time, U.S. casualty rates went steadily downward. And on the Fourth of July, William Howard Taft, future president and future chief justice of the United States, was sworn in as civil governor of the Philippines.

As the year 1901 drew to a close, everything was going in the Americans' favor. But toward the end of September, an event occurred that seemed likely to undo much that had been accomplished toward winning over the Filipinos. Through treachery, insurgents massacred a company of the 9th Infantry in the town of Balangiga on Samar, a jungle-covered island with a population of only 250,000. Because the insurgents had carried out the grisly butchery at a stage in the conflict in which it was obvious that their cause could not possibly be victorious, it provoked a furious reaction among American troops on Samar. Brigadier General Jacob Smith, in charge of pacification of the island, vowed to turn the interior of Samar into "a howling wilderness."[19] Smith's punitive campaign on the island involved many violations of the general U.S. policy of benevolence that had seemed to be working so well after three years.

While Smith carried out his drastic campaign against the guerrillas on Samar, General Franklin Bell captured the last insurgent stronghold on southern Luzon, in Batangas. Bell then ordered his subordinate commanders to establish security perimeters around the numerous towns and bring all the inhabitants of the area to come and live inside these perimeters. Soldiers confiscated any food found outside the lines. Eventually over 300,000 people were gathered together inside the lines. To further isolate the guerrillas, Bell instituted a pass system for civilians. By the spring of 1902 Batangas was calm.

On July 4, 1902, the Americans proclaimed another amnesty for all remaining guerrillas, except for a few accused of specific felonies. As the year ended, the number of U.S. Army troops in the islands was down to 15,000. The great majority of politically concerned Filipinos, if not happy about the American occupation, seemed willing to submit to U.S. administration and work within it for independence.

Three decades later, Emilio Aguinaldo ran for the presidency of the Philippine Commonwealth against Manuel Quezon. He was badly beaten.

AN AMERICAN VICTORY AGAINST GUERRILLAS

Defeating the insurrection cost the United States nearly as many lives (4,200 killed, 2,800 wounded) as the conflict with Spain, and several times the original price paid to Spain for the islands.[20] The Americans were a truly foreign force, far from home and few in numbers, with no colonial experience to guide them and little knowledge of the peoples and places among which they were fighting. And of course, they were totally lacking that airpower which Americans later came to regard as the key to victory in any circumstances. They confronted a guerrilla force fighting in its own territory, on terrain favorable to irregular tactics, under the banner of national independence. The situation overflowed with possibilities for disaster; nevertheless, the Americans won a clear-cut and relatively easy victory that laid the foundation for a close future friendship between two peoples at the opposite ends of the broad Pacific. The American victory derived from the combination of increasingly sound counterguerrilla tactics with an intelligent program of social amelioration and political accommodation against a conservative foe lacking a sanctuary.

MILITARY FACTORS IN THE AMERICAN VICTORY

During their struggle against the Filipino insurgents the Americans came to many of the same conclusions about how to fight guerrillas as the great

French colonial commander Louis Lyautey. These included the importance of limiting damage to the civilian economy and winning over the local population through minimal force and good administration. The winning strategy was to hold territory rather than to kill guerrillas.[21] "After 1900 the American stress on the isolation of the guerrilla and the protection of townspeople from terrorism and intimidation was an important element in the success of pacification operations."[22]

One very distinguishing feature of the Philippine insurgency was that the guerrillas had no transfrontier sanctuary from which to receive aid. Hence they started out poorly armed and stayed that way. Elements in the Japanese army wanted to assist Aguinaldo ("Asia for the Asians!"); some Japanese officers did manage to get to Luzon to offer their assistance, and there was at least one unsuccessful attempt to send the insurgents a shipload of weapons and ammunition from Japan.[23] But the Tokyo Foreign Ministry was opposed to such potentially explosive actions and had its way. Not a single foreign state granted recognition to Aguinaldo's government. At one point Aguinaldo said he hoped for help from "perhaps Germany." Maybe he thought that the Germans would help him for nothing or that the Philippines would be better off under Wilhelm II.

One authority on the conflict notes that contemporary U.S. forces have become reluctant to mount operations against guerrillas during the rainy season, when air power is less available. But the evidence from the Philippine insurgency strongly suggests that rainy seasons are at least as hard on poorly equipped and supplied guerrillas as on regular troops. The Americans built all-weather roads in the Philippines; these increased their mobility while not appreciably helping the guerrillas.[24]

THE POLITICAL BASIS OF THE
AMERICAN SUCCESS

The defeat of the Philippine insurgency illuminates with perfect clarity the essential position of political factors in the outcome of this type of struggle. For example, as a guerrilla leader resisting a foreign occupation, Aguinaldo had potentially in his favor the weapon of nationalism, but this he was never able to wield effectively. Why not?

In the first place, a true, countrywide Philippine national consciousness did not exist. Most of the inhabitants of the many islands were peasants who cared for family, village, and church, not for political abstractions. Besides, many ethnic tensions and rivalries existed within Filipino society, and the insurgency aggravated rather than suppressed them, a phenomenon the Americans were quick to exploit.

Aguinaldo might possibly have aroused the peasantry with a program of social revolution, but he was much too conservative to unsheath such an appeal. Instead, he offered political aims that were cloudy to say the best of it. At one point he declared that he wanted the Philippines to be a U.S. protectorate while developing into a free republic—but that was exactly what the U.S. government had promised.[25] He wrote that he and his followers "neither hoped for victory over the Americans nor hated them. But we wanted to gain their respect," and "it was our hope that, if we should perish . . . we would at least earn the respect . . . of the Americans." Reviewing these pronouncements, Aguinaldo later wrote: "I must admit that there was some ambiguity and perhaps even inconsistency in our position."[26]

Nevertheless, his social conservatism did not win him the support of the traditional elites. They recognized right away that Aguinaldo could not defeat the Americans. Consequently, they feared that if they openly supported Aguinaldo, the Americans might confiscate their property or hand the running of the country over to some other group.

Last, but very important, the Americans, although foreign conquerors, were hard to hate. Aguinaldo told his countrymen that the Americans would enslave the Filipinos and abolish Catholicism. This kind of propaganda backfired badly. It soon became clear that the Americans had not come to uproot religion. At the minimum, the Americans, with their schools and sanitation programs and free inoculations, were undeniably a big improvement over the Spanish. Revolutionaries usually promise, and sometimes deliver, literacy and health care to the lower classes; in the Philippines, the Americans provided both. In a real sense *they* were the revolutionaries, not Aguinaldo. And even on the issue of Philippine independence, what the Americans and the insurgents disputed was not the right to independence but merely the timing of it. In retrospect, Aguinaldo wrote that he was glad the United States established its rule over the Philippines, because otherwise the islands probably would have been partitioned among several powers and thus certainly would never have become both free and united.[27]

One final observation: those Japanese military circles that wished in 1899 to go to the Philippines and fight the Americans saw their desires frustrated, but only temporarily. The occupation of the Philippines placed the United States across the Japanese highroad to their Imperial Vision. In less than four decades this awkward juxtaposition would lead to Pearl Harbor and the eventual reconquest of the country by another General MacArthur. And between those two events, the experience of three years of Japanese occupation would deepen the insights of many Filipinos into the essential nature of American administration.

The Huk War, 1945–1953

As in Greece, so in the Philippines, the trauma of defeat and occupation in World War II provided the opportunity for a Communist-organized attempt to take over political power by force of arms. In part because of

American actions, both attempts suffered defeat. The Philippines became the first independent democracy in Asia to overcome a Communist insurgency.

THE JAPANESE AND THE HUKS

July 4, 1946, was the first Independence Day of the Republic of the Philippines. On that day, Manuel Roxas was sworn in as the new country's first president. The republic over which he presided had a population of about 20 million. World War II had ended less than a year previously, and the Philippine Republic was celebrating its birthday amidst great devastation.

In the eyes of many Japanese, World War II, the Pacific War, had been the latest and greatest episode in the epic confrontation between the European and the Oriental races. In the Russo-Japanese War of 1904–1905, for the first time in modern history an Oriental nation dealt a decisive defeat to a major Occidental power. These events had provided compelling evidence to Japanese expansionists that it was their nation's destiny to put an end one day to white domination over Asia. From Shanghai to Sumatra, Imperial Japan must destroy Caucasian colonialism and gather all the teeming lands of the East into the Greater East Asia Co-Prosperity Sphere. Nevertheless, in their three-and-a-half-year occupation of the Philippines, the Japanese committed the most appalling atrocities against its Asian inhabitants. Carlos P. Romulo, who after the war became foreign minister of the Philippines, wrote that the savage behavior of the Japanese arose from the frustration and outrage they felt when so many Filipinos openly sided with the Americans, the white enemy.[28]

In addition to an exceedingly cruel occupation, the Philippines experienced some of the hardest fighting of all of World War II, including the largest naval engagement in the history of the world, the Battle of Leyte Gulf. At war's end, widespread social disorganization and serious economic hardship confronted the fledgling republic; over 70 percent of the city of Manila lay devastated.

During the war many Filipinos had organized to resist the Japanese occupation. In March 1942, a mainly Communist group founded the People's Army against Japan; its Tagalog acronym was Hukbalahap, from which came the nickname "the Huks." By late 1943 there were perhaps 10,000 in the ranks of these Huks. At war's end, they were well armed with weapons acquired from the Japanese or shipped in by the Americans. As in occupied Greece, the Communist-directed guerrilla bands in the Philippines looked to the postwar period; they fought not only against the Japanese but also against guerrillas loyal to the United States government.

The end of the war came and the Japanese departed, but the Huks did not lay down their arms. Instead, tensions increased between the Huks and the authorities of the new Philippine Republic. The United States Army was unwilling to recognize any legal status of the Huks or to pay them for their alleged wartime services. And whereas the Huks wanted severe punishment for all Filipinos who had collaborated with the Japanese occupation, the American policy was to allow these to remain unmolested, and even permit their gradual reentry into positions of influence. Thus Manuel Roxas, born in 1892, had served in the pro-Japanese Laurel government during World War II but had been saved from prosecution by the intervention of Douglas MacArthur. He then achieved election as first president of the republic with the support of the venerable and dominant Nacionalista Party's liberal wing, which set itself up as the Liberal Party. When President Roxas ordered a crackdown on "disorders," the Huks resorted to open armed conflict.

The stronghold of the Huks was on Luzon, the main island, about 40,000 square miles in area. Central Luzon had long been an area of widespread absentee landlordism, one of the greatest curses that can befall an agricultural community. Violent agrarian unrest had been a main theme of the history of this part of the Philippines from time immemorial. Serious social ills went unheeded by a government (if that is the word to characterize Philippine administration in these areas) out of touch and rife with corruption. Officials high and low exploited the peasantry in every conceivable way. During the occupation, the widespread and sometimes quite open collaboration with the Japanese on the part of Luzon landlords stimulated the exasperation of a growing number of peasants with the difficulties of their lives. Luis Taruc, the principal military leader of the Huks, wrote: "when we dealt with [the landlords] harshly, it was because they were betraying our country to the Japanese and oppressing the common people. This knowledge of the period is essential to an understanding of Huk activities."[29] The Huk conflict with the Japanese had been in part a response to the oppressive nature of the occupation, but also an expression of the deep anxieties produced by overpopulation and the breakdown of traditional patron-client relationships in the countryside. Carlos P. Romulo noted that "the majority of Huk complaints came out of injustices concerning the land."[30] General Douglas MacArthur, a man whose name is inextricably linked with the history of the Philippines, once tartly observed: "If I worked in those sugar fields, I'd probably be a Huk myself."[31] And years after the rebellion was over, Luis Taruc wrote that "it must be fully understood that one cannot separate the problem of rebellion from that of the peasantry. It is most important to recognize that this is an urgent problem—perhaps the most urgent of our day—in every one of the newly developed [*sic*] countries."[32]

THE FIRST YEARS OF THE STRUGGLE

When the Huks took up arms against the Philippine Republic, they employed the classic methods of guerrilla warfare so familiar to the islands.

They were especially efficient at robbing payroll offices, trains, and cargo trucks in central Luzon.[33] Their success in such operations no doubt owed a great deal to the fact that they had recruited or absorbed some bands of what can only be called common criminals.

The government's main instrument for dealing with this challenge, the paramilitary Philippine Constabulary, was not well equipped for this or any other sort of warfare. The United States had handed over to the new Philippine Republic surplus war equipment worth billions of dollars in the money of the 1990s. Very little found its way into the hands of the armed forces; much of it was simply stolen. The Constabulary's tactical response to the Huks was unimaginative and largely useless. Edward Lansdale, who would one day be a security adviser to the presidents of both the Philippines and South Viet Nam, wrote critically of the usually futile and often destructive encirclement tactics used by government forces.[34]

But the problems of the Constabulary extended beyond inadequate equipment and poor tactics. The treatment of the peasants of Luzon at the hands of the Constabulary and civil officials fueled the Huk revolt. The propensity of soldiers to help themselves to the possessions of the peasants and to commit even worse offenses against these humble citizens of the republic whom they were supposed to be serving and protecting, created many recruits and supporters for the Huks, especially between 1948 and 1950.[35] Soldiers led by good officers do not systematically abuse civilians, especially those of their own nationality. The oppressive behavior of Filipino troops reflected in large part the influence of political interference within the officer corps that corrupted the soul of the armed forces and reduced their anti-guerrilla efforts to worse than nothing. Years later, Luis Taruc consistently maintained that the true generative source of the Huk rebellion was government provocation and terrorism against the hapless civilians.[36] Without abuses of this kind the Huk rebellion might never have assumed the serious proportions it eventually attained.

The presidential elections of 1949 directly benefited the guerrillas. On the death of Manuel Roxas in 1948, Vice President Elpidio Quirino (born 1890) succeeded to the presidency. The Huks believed that Quirino's continuation in the Malacanan Palace would prolong and aggravate the corruption and inefficiency of the national government and thus smooth their path to power. They therefore cynically supported his reelection efforts as much as they could.[37]

But Quirino did not need the help of the Huks. He held onto office by the aid of vote buying, vote stealing, and voter intimidation on a massive scale. The "dirty election of 1949" was a boon to the Huks: by undermining the faith of both intellectuals and common citizens in the processes of democracy, it seemed to close off the path to peaceful change.[38] If there was no hope of removing a corrupt and incompetent government through the ballot box, then all disaffected elements in the population would eventually have to turn to armed rebellion under the leadership of the Huks. Taruc maintains that several members of the wartime Huk movement who had been elected to Congress in 1947 were illegally deprived of their seats, thus convincing them that armed revolt was the only valid option. The perversion of the electoral process in the Philippines was thus worth thousands of fighters to the Huk cause.

As the decade of the 1940s drew to a close, civil war raged in Greece, the long struggle in China neared its fateful climax, and the Communist-led rebellion in the Philippines increased in strength. The Huks had between 11,000 and 15,000 fighters.[39] Opposing them were perhaps 25,000 members of the Constabulary. At the end of 1949, Mao proclaimed the end of the Chinese civil war and the triumph of Communism; in imitation of their victorious ideological brothers in China, the Philippine Communists changed the name of their armed forces to the "People's Liberation Army."

By mid-1950, when the North Koreans invaded the South, the Huks were able to deploy around 20,000 guerrillas.[40] Although the guerrilla leader Luis Taruc wrote afterward that there was never any real danger that Manila would fall to the Huks, during 1950 the rebellion was nevertheless obviously reaching a new and dangerous level.[41] In March and again in August 1950, the Huks carried out some spectacular raids in the Manila area. The size and boldness of these operations jolted the Quirino administration into a realization that the war was going very badly and that it was necessary to do something drastically different.[42] President Quirino called in the army to assist the outclassed Constabulary. And shortly thereafter (September 1950) he appointed as secretary of defense, and therefore as the man most directly in charge of anti-Huk operations, Ramón Magsaysay.

THE COMING OF RAMON MAGSAYSAY

Magsaysay was born in 1907, of Malay stock (unlike most of the Philippine elite). His father had been a carpentry teacher in a secondary school. Before World War II, he himself had managed a bus company. He had served as a Liberal Party congressman from 1946 to 1950 and had become chairman of the House National Defense Committee. But in the view of the Quirino Administration, Magsaysay's primary credentials were that he had fought as a guerrilla against the Japanese occupation and therefore presumably would know how to fight the Huks. This expectation proved to be exceedingly well founded.

It is a sound principle that when "competing with a vigorous rebellion, a precarious authority should be concerned with respect for the people's dignity at least as much as with the level of their income."[43] Clearly, the first order of business for Magsaysay was to improve relations between his troops and the peasantry. Ex-guerrilla Magsaysay knew from experience that big sweeps by government military units were hardly ever effective.

Even if the rebels have not previously been tipped off by informants, guerrillas can hear the movement of large numbers of troops from very far away. But worse than that, sweeps provide too many occasions for the abuse of civilians: tired soldiers, unable to catch their ever elusive enemies, may vent their frustrations on the civilians at hand. Magsaysay therefore instructed his commanders that troops should never enter a village in an attitude of hostility unless they were sure it contained active guerrillas. On the contrary, soldiers should approach peasants as if they were, or were soon to become, allies. Remembering the American GIs of World War II, Magsaysay supplied candy for his soldiers to hand out to village children.[44] He also saw to it that the army provided medical help to peasants who needed it. Within a matter of months Magsaysay's reforms began to improve the image of the armed forces and undermine the hopes of the Huks.[45]

Ranking second as a cause of Huk success only to the armed forces' poor relations with villagers was their poor campaigning tactics. (These two deficiencies seem almost always to go together.) Demanding more aggressiveness from his soldiers, Magsaysay organized new Battalion Combat Teams to enter areas where the armed forces had not gone before. Feeling safe in these unvisited areas, the Huks had been using them to improve their living standards by growing food in fields they had laboriously cleared. The discovery of these food-growing areas by government forces meant serious hardships for many Huks.[46] Interference with their food supplies can have an even more disruptive effect on guerrillas than interference with their weapons supplies. Eventually, the troops learned not to move in until just before the crops were ready for harvesting. Toward the end of 1951, aggressive tactics on the part of Magsaysay's troops forced the remaining Huks to retreat into swamps and other undesirable areas; there they were cut off from contacts with civilians, unable to obtain sufficient food, and exposed to numerous illnesses.[47]

Magsaysay knew the fate of reforms whose author simply issues instructions and then sits in his office, expecting them to be carried out. To make sure that commanders were indeed observing his policies concerning correct treatment of civilians and aggressive tactics against guerrillas, Magsaysay made numerous and unexpected visits, usually by plane, to military forces, even in remote areas. Edward Lansdale, a close adviser to Magsaysay, has recorded how the defense secretary's unscheduled descents from on high to bestow medals and praise or to remove on the spot lazy and incompetent commanders electrified the military into conformity with his wishes.[48] Magsaysay introduced a special telegraph service to his headquarters; for a nominal fee, any citizen in the country could send the secretary of defense a message about abuses or problems in his or her own area.

Magsaysay also placed the Constabulary under military (that is to say, under his) control. He fired all the incompetents and criminals he could find (unfortunately, there were a lot) and also those who had established comfortable or lucrative relationships with the Huks.

There is no weapon more effective against guerrillas than a good intelligence organization. Under Magsaysay the intelligence available to the armed forces greatly improved, partly because the image of the soldiers benefited from their new respect for civilian dignity, partly because Magsaysay offered big rewards for information leading to the capture of guerrillas or the discovery of arms caches, and partly because of the universal rule that intelligence flows more freely to what is perceived to be the winning side.[49] Intercepted couriers often provided invaluable information. As in other insurgencies, captured guerrillas, when treated well, often changed sides and offered all kinds of interesting information.[50] Through such methods Magsaysay was able to bag most of the members of the Politburo of the Philippine Communist Party, along with truckloads of documents that provided much fascinating reading for him and his military commanders.[51]

Magsaysay also had some weapons for use specifically against the leaders of the insurgency. He offered what to an ordinary Filipino would be fabulous rewards for the arrest of individual Huk leaders, identified by name—not as rebels but as felons, wanted for a particular criminal act, such as murder, rape, or arson, at a particular time and place. Magsaysay widely publicized the names of Huk leaders captured in this way. These procedures helped reduce the image of the Huks from Robin Hoods to common criminals. They also sowed dissension between Huk leaders and their followers: no insurgent commander could be sure whether or for how long all of his comrades would be able to resist the allure of sudden wealth. Another special weapon against the Huks consisted of small ranger units whose unique function was to track down and kill notorious Huk leaders.[52] In these circumstances, leadership posts among the Huks rapidly began to lose their former attractions.

But the easiest and cheapest solution to guerrilla war is to overcome the guerrilla's will to fight and induce him to surrender. The increased pressure on the Huks was having that effect, but Magsaysay went farther. He knew that many who fought with the Huks were neither convinced Communists nor hardened criminals; he could win them over with the right approach. Thus Magsaysay developed his amnesty policy. The announcements of amnesty carefully avoided the word "surrender," using in its place euphemisms like "coming in." It also excluded real criminals, thus further sowing discord within rebel ranks.[53] (Government forces should take great care to rigidly segregate guerrillas who have surrendered from those who have been captured.)

But Magsaysay understood that many Huks could not just "come in." Some Filipinos had joined the Huks when they were mere boys; for them and for others the movement had been home and family for a decade. Once they left the guerrilla organization, they had no place to go. It was therefore necessary to provide these unfortunates with a new life. Magsaysay's solution to this problem was to open up virgin lands on southern islands to provide a homestead to any surrendered guerrillas who desired one. The former Huk would normally receive 20 acres; he also got help from the army to build a little house, a small loan to tide him over until the first crop, and maybe a work animal or two. Those who accepted this amnesty-with-a-farm changed overnight from threats to the constitutional order into productive and eventually tax-paying citizens. And, the final payoff, once the land-to-surrendered-Huks policy was seen to be working, popular opinion began to turn against those Huks who continued fighting: since the war was obviously lost, was it perhaps that these holdout guerrillas did not want to give up because they did not wish to do hard work on the land like the peasants?

Beat the guerrillas with a house, some cash, and a little land: so simple a concept, so inexpensive a program, so effective a weapon. Naturally, these methods did not work with the ideologically motivated intellectuals who composed the hard core of the insurgency, but Magsaysay's progressive isolation of these from their peasant base reduced them to the status of fish out of water.

As the 1951 congressional elections approached, some members of the Commission on Elections wished to avoid a repetition of the travesties of 1949. They requested the assistance of the secretary of defense. With the help of a civic action group called the National Movement for Free Elections (NAMFREL), which is still in existence today, Magsaysay deployed the army to ensure relatively peaceful balloting and an honest count. Compared to the 1949 presidential contest, the 1951 elections were models of orderliness and probity; in fact, the opposition Nacionalista Party won every single senate seat up for election that year. By demonstrating that there was indeed a realistic alternative to violence for the adjustment of grievances, the elections dealt a major blow to the insurgency. "To all intents and purposes, the 1951 elections sounded the death knell of the Hukbalahap movement."[54]

MAGSAYSAY TO THE PRESIDENCY

As secretary of defense, Magsaysay improved military tactics against the Huks, cut down military abuse of the civil population, and ensured clean congressional elections in 1951. He employed the same combination of tactics against the Huks that the Americans had used a half-century before against Aguinaldo's followers: unrelenting military pressure plus the mitigation of serious social irritants. As a result of all this, thousands of Huks were captured or killed, gave themselves up, or just melted away from the movement.

Yet, in the office he held, subordinate to President Quirino, Magsaysay lacked the full power to uproot the political and economic abuses that fed the Huk movement. "Good troops employing proper tactics cannot make up for an unsound government and political base."[55] Hence in March 1953, Magsaysay resigned his defense post to campaign for the presidency. Another Quirino cabinet member was also seeking election to the highest office: this was Carlos P. Romulo. Born in 1899 under the U.S. flag, he had been Philippine ambassador to the United States and to the United Nations, president of the U.S. General Assembly, and secretary of foreign affairs under President Quirino. Like Magsaysay, Romulo had concluded that the Huks would never be thoroughly defeated while Quirino and men like him ruled the country.

In the 1953 campaign of Ramón Magsaysay, Filipinos saw for the first time a major presidential candidate leave the comfortable and predictable route of the large cities to seek votes and speak to the people in the villages and the remote islands.[56] A great deal was riding on this election. Luis Taruc urged his followers to support Quirino (as he had in 1949).[57] In Washington, Secretary of State John Foster Dulles agreed with Edward Lansdale that the presidential contest had to be free and honest if the Huks were to be finally overcome.[58] Besides verbal warnings, the United States took several measures to prevent Quirino from using the tactics of 1949 against Magsaysay in 1953. The State Department saw to it that numerous American reporters went to the Philippines to cover the elections; U.S. government funds discreetly bolstered the Magsaysay presidential campaign. President Quirino, aware that he was in trouble, tried to stir up anti-Americanism over U.S. interference in the campaign, but without success (having experienced the Japanese occupation, Filipinos found anti-Americanism to be very weak tea.) Magsaysay received the vital support of NAMFREL (whose establishment in 1951 had been facilitated by CIA funds), and the Filipino press was much more vigilant than in 1949. Impressed with the clear evidence of Magsaysay's popularity, and fearful of splitting the anti-Quirino vote, Romulo withdrew from the race and asked his supporters to vote for Magsaysay. Finally, the leaders of the powerful Roman Catholic Church forcefully reminded their adherents of their duty not only to go to the polls but also to vote to prevent the triumph of corrupt men.[59]

Magsaysay won a tremendous victory: 2.4 million votes for him, 1.15 million votes for Quirino. (In 1949, the announced results gave 1.6 million votes to Quirino, and 1.5 million to his opponents, principally José Laurel, who had served the Japanese occupation as "president of the Philippine Republic" from 1943 to 1945 and had been pardoned for this by Quirino in 1948.)

With Magsaysay in the Malacanan Palace, completely in control of the armed forces and fully in position to expand his land-to-surrendered-Huks program, the end of the struggle was clearly in sight. In May 1954, Luis

Taruc himself came out of the jungle to surrender; this event is the conventional date for the end of the Huk insurgency. When Taruc gave himself up (to receive a twelve-year prison sentence), some in the government said that he was merely a Trojan horse, that this move was just some Communist deception.[60] They were wrong. A few Huk units went on fighting, but these were composed mainly of hard-core Communists or real criminals (or both), and they never posed a threat to Manila or any other sizable town. Perhaps 10,000 Huks lost their lives between 1946 and 1954; 4,000 were captured and another 16,000 surrendered.[61]

In March 1957, while campaigning for reelection, President Magsaysay died in a plane crash not far from the spot where Magellan had been killed in 1521.

THE LEADERSHIP OF THE COMMUNISTS

Luis Taruc writes, perhaps accurately, that in the early days of World War II, Communist leaders of the Huk guerrillas had no serious plans beyond resistance to the Japanese occupation.[62] It was inevitable, however, that the Communists would soon turn their thoughts to postwar conditions and would consider the probabilities of a "proletarian" revolution led by its "vanguard" party. (It may be hard for us to keep in mind that in those days—1943–1946—the Maoist model of revolution that would so dominate global political thought during the 1960s was not yet available.)

The leaders of the Philippine Communist Party were mostly urban, often of good education. Their chief was Vicente Lava, who had obtained a Ph.D. from Columbia University and was professor of chemistry at the University of the Philippines. Luis Taruc, who would become the major hero of the Huk movement, was born not far from Manila in Pampanga province; he had studied medicine for years at the University of Manila but had had to withdraw in 1934 for lack of funds.[63] Elected to Congress in 1947, he was not permitted to take his seat because of accusations that he and others like him had used terrorism to gain election.[64]

Many Communists were sympathetic to the peasants but did not share their goals nor really understand them. Of those peasants who bore arms as Huks, the majority apparently wanted merely a return of the system of stable tenant farming with its traditional patron–client relationships as it had existed before the 1930s. The Communists, in contrast, wanted a real social and political revolution, based on the urban masses, pursuing a Stalinist policy of forced industrialization and efforts to uproot the traditional family structure and local relationships.[65]

While the tactics of the government forces under Magsaysay greatly improved, the tactics of the Huks and their Communist leadership deteriorated. The Communists needed to expand their base from central Luzon, but they were reluctant to reach out to other opposition groups to form the classic Leninist broad front.[66] Instead the Huks tried to spread their rebellion into adjacent areas by sending small detachments of guerrillas into them. Usually such efforts were not successful. Many Huk leaders wore better clothes and smoked better cigarettes than the peasants whose acceptance they sought as their liberators.[67] Often the men sent into a new district to start up a rebel movement were criminals, or men who acted like criminals.[68]

By 1951, the Huk rebellion was clearly sinking into an irreversible decline.[69] Confronted with the mounting evidence of inevitable defeat, the Communists began to turn their frustration and anger against the members of the Huk movement. They executed young fighters and sympathizers for such infractions as sleeping while on duty or asking leave to go home, behaviors the Communists viewed as a prelude to surrender. If a Huk's relatives asked him to give up, the Communists told him that the only way he could prove his continuing loyalty to the movement was to kill those relatives.[70] Senseless acts of destruction and cruelty, such as the murder of the widow of President Manuel Luis Quezon, hurt the Huk cause both inside and outside the movement.[71] Taruc is bitterly critical of the Communist Party leadership for insisting on prolonging the fighting after 1950, when it was clear that the military effort was lost.

THE QUESTION OF U.S. COMBAT INVOLVEMENT

The United States had an enormous emotional and ideological stake in the Philippines. In 1950, the Philippines had been independent for less than a half-decade. For fifty years before that, Americans in large numbers, civilian as well as military, were present in the islands and involved with Philippine affairs in the most intimate ways. In 1907, only a few years after the Aguinaldo insurgency had come to an end, the Americans set up the first popularly elected legislature in the history of Southeast Asia. By 1916, all literate Filipino males had the right of suffrage. The Americans fostered labor unions, pressed for the limitation of absentee landlordism, and constructed a well-paid civil service staffed more and more by Filipinos. American English was in wide use, and many Filipinos felt admiration, or at least amused affection, for Americans. All this elicited one day an exasperated sigh from Nationalist Party leader Manuel Quezon: "Damn the Americans, why don't they tyrannize us more?"[72] As the world entered the post–World War II period, Washington wanted the Philippines to become the showcase of democracy in East Asia.

The introduction, therefore, of U.S. ground combat forces into the struggle against the Huks was not so unthinkable as a later generation of Americans (or Filipinos) might imagine. President Quirino himself was anxious to have American troops, in some capacity at least, in the Philippines.[73]

The Truman Administration did in fact send some U.S. military personnel to help train the Philippine armed forces. But until 1950, no one in

Washington seems to have given serious consideration to a possible large-scale commitment of U.S. troops, mainly because a Huk victory did not appear likely to American political or military leaders. Besides, Washington was preoccupied with the conflicts in China and Greece and the construction of the North Atlantic Treaty Organization.

In April 1950, the chargé at the U.S. Embassy in Manila, Vinton Chapin, cabled to his superiors in Washington his belief that the Huk rebellion had grown out of the need for agrarian reform. The Huks were able to point to Quirino's fraudulent election and also liked to brand him a tool of "American imperialists." Chapin noted that the Philippine armed forces were not doing very well because of their passive tactics and their alienation of the peasantry. This latter failure was aggravated by the tendency of the Philippine troops to rely too much on artillery, a tool that obliterates the distinction between guerrillas and civilians. At the same time, the U.S. military mission to the Philippines consisted of officers who were unskilled in counterguerrilla operations. While the sending of American ground forces would shift the balance of power against the Huks, nevertheless "the employment of United States troops against Filipinos outside our bases should probably be considered only as a last resort. Such action would provide our enemies all over Asia with valuable propaganda and might be expected to cause many Filipinos to regard us as invaders and to join forces with the Huks." The Americans would probably be better off doing in the Philippines what they had done in Greece: sending better-prepared U.S. advisers in larger numbers.[74]

The deterioration of the Philippine government's position in early 1950 alarmed the Truman Administration. The president wrote to his secretary of state that "failure of the Philippines experiment which all Asia watches as evidence of American intentions and abilities could only have the most unfortunate repercussions for the United States both abroad and at home."[75]

Shortly after this presidential pronouncement, North Korean troops crashed across the 38th parallel. Soon United States forces were in Korea literally fighting for their lives around Pusan. Later that year the Chinese Communists intervened massively in the conflict. At the same time, Washington was assuming a greater and greater responsibility for the supply of French and Vietnamese forces fighting the Viet Minh in Indochina.

Yet even in those desperate circumstances U.S. Ambassador to Manila Cowen stated his belief (September 29, 1950) that the United States should at least consider sending a reinforced division to the Philippines.[76] And a "top secret" draft paper by the deputy director of the Office of Philippine and Southeast Asian Affairs, dated January 19, 1951, reads in part as follows:

It is assumed that the United States is determined, regardless of the cost and despite any eventualities, as part of its Pacific policy to retain the Philippines within the orbit of the democratic powers and to deny it to the Soviet orbit. This is the irreducible minimum of American security and interests in the Pacific and the Far East.[77]

To that end, the author of the secret document approved the idea of sending two American divisions to the Philippines.[78] On the other hand, a National Security Council Staff Study had concluded in November 1950 that the Philippine armed forces, if well trained and adequately equipped, ought to be able to defeat the Huks, provided that the Huks received no important outside aid.[79]

Washington analysts often focused on the dual need for good leadership and land reform. A Department of State paper prepared in June 1950 for the staff of the National Security Council stated in part: "Since the tragic death of President Roxas in 1948, Philippine leadership has been discouragingly weak and short-sighted."[80] A National Security Council Staff Study noted that "leadership of the Philippine Government has been largely in the hands of a small group of individuals representing the wealthy propertied classes who, except in isolated instances, have failed to appreciate the need for reform and the pressures generated among the less prosperous and more numerous groups of the population." Secretary of State Dean Acheson had a particularly unfavorable opinion of the ethics and ability of President Quirino and was annoyed by the latter's "overweening vanity and arrogance."[81] Washington policymakers were also aware that the fraud and violence of the 1949 presidential election seriously undermined public trust in the government and thus increased the attraction of the Huks.[82]

U.S. Ambassador Cowen cabled the State Department on February 15, 1951, that the Communists automatically placed outside the law any peasants to whom they gave land. The United States and the Philippines must therefore defeat the Huks by carrying out effective land reform programs, including resettlement of landless peasants on desirable lands. Cowen also reminded Washington that everyone who was killed by United States–supplied arms had relatives who might thus support the Communists, making necessary new expenditures for arms.[83] The secretary of state reflected this general stance. "We strongly believe," he wrote, "that the only way to beat the Communists is to show our ability to carry out under democratic processes those reforms they advocate which are worthwhile. Land redistribution is one such reform."[84]

The accumulation of such views began moving the Truman Administration toward the position of making assistance to the Manila contingent on internal political, military, and economic reforms.[85] Unfortunately, however, the Philippine leaders felt that they could do whatever they wanted and ignore the need for reform, since they could in the last analysis count on the United States to save them.[86] Acheson wrote to President Truman: "If there is one lesson to be learned from the China debacle it is that if we are confronted with an inadequate vehicle it should be discarded or immobilized in favor of a more propitious one." On the other hand, if the U.S. government encouraged the removal of President Quirino, it would become known and would resound all over Asia, presumably to the detriment of American foreign policy on that continent.[87]

One very important reason that the United States did not send combat units to the Philippines was that among the least anxious to get involved in the fighting were the leaders of the United States armed forces. General George Marshall told Carlos P. Romulo that he "did not wish to have the same experience that he had in China in supplying arms to an Army which was guided by political interests."[88] And on September 6, 1950 (a few days after the appointment of Magsaysay as defense secretary and at a time when the early stages of the Korean War were going very badly for the Americans), a memorandum from the Joint Chiefs of Staff to Secretary of Defense Louis A. Johnson noted that the possibility was definitely developing that a militant minority organized by the Huks would overthrow a corrupt and discredited regime. The United States had guaranteed the security of the Philippines by the agreement of March 14, 1947; but "such intervention would require, in light of the present world situation [the fighting in Korea and the building up of NATO] a considerable increase in the extent of mobilization currently envisaged." Present conditions in the islands, the memorandum went on, did not warrant the sending of U.S. combat forces. Instead the United States should increase shipments of military materiel to the Philippines, augment the number of security personnel on U.S. installations there, and raise the American military mission to Manila, Joint U.S. Military Advisory Group (JUSMAG), to a strength of 32 officers and 26 enlisted.[89] JUSMAG itself opposed the direct assignment of American officers to Philippine combat units.[90]

Above all, it was their evaluation of the political roots of the Philippine rebellion that raised serious doubts among the Joint Chiefs about the advisability of widening American participation in the conflict. In the same memorandum, dated September 6, 1950, the Joint Chiefs stated their belief that "the basic problem [in the Philippines] is primarily political and economic. Military action should not be an alternative for a stable and efficient government based on sound economic and social foundations." It was inequities in land ownership that constituted the roots of the Huk rebellion, as well as the preference for guerrilla life that some men had acquired under the Japanese occupation. Therefore "direct United States military intervention in the Philippines would be justifiable, from a strategic point of view, only if there remained no other means of preventing Communist seizure of the islands."[91]

In any event, by the end of 1951, the prospects of a Huk victory had clearly evaporated, and so had any possibility of deploying U.S. combat units in the Philippines.

CONCLUSIONS

Guerrillas probably have their best chance in a country ruled by a foreign power. But the mere foreignness of the foreigner is no magic formula for insurgents; the foreigners must cooperate by being hateful as well. More than forty years before the Huks, the efforts of the Aguinaldo forces to rally support by an appeal to anti-Yankeeism and national independence had crashed upon that rock. Far from invading a previously independent country, the Americans were only superceding a Spanish colonial regime compared to which they were manifestly a vast improvement. Moreover they provided written promises of eventual independence. The Huks were of course even less able to use national independence as an issue, fighting as they were against a republican government of their own people. Communist efforts to rally the nation against "American imperialism"—especially in the aftermath of the Japanese occupation—were simply not relevant or even credible to the peasantry or, ultimately, to most of those in the guerrilla bands.

Unable to wrap themselves in the mantle of outraged nationalism, the Huks found themselves increasingly deprived of domestic issues as well. This had a profoundly important effect on the insurgents because compared to their Communist leaders, most rank-and-file Huks were fighting for very limited goals. When Magsaysay restored elections as an alternative to the violent path to change and began making obvious efforts to mitigate the worst social irritations fueling the rebellion, the peasant footsoldiers of revolution abandoned the struggle in large numbers.[92]

Simultaneously, Magsaysay increased the military pressure on the Huks. He did this without relying on highly destructive weapons, especially the jet aircraft and long-range artillery that assumed such controversial dimensions in Viet Nam. He put more vigorous commanders in the field who moved into those areas the guerrillas had come to rely on for rest and food. He sowed discord within the Huk ranks by offering rewards for the capture of individual leaders. He provided ordinary guerrillas with a way out through amnesty and resettlement. But the most important of all Magsaysay's military measures, the one that most effectively undercut the insurgency, was his successful insistence that military abuse of civilians came to a halt.

Thus the Huks eventually confronted an indigenous reformist government defended by increasingly effective armed forces and backed by the resources of the United States. In such circumstances, the only hope of the insurgents would have been assistance from outside. Here the geography of the Philippines exerted its decisive influence: for the Huks as for Aguinaldo, there could be no sanctuary, no possibility to obtain any systematic aid from outside. In this vital matter the contrast between the Philippine case on the one hand and those of Viet Nam and Afghanistan on the other is as broad as the South China Sea.

Against both Aguinaldo and the Huks, the government eventually linked good military tactics and effective political programs that doomed the geographically isolated guerrillas to extinction. The similarities of these two insurgencies suggest that there may be something like a law of successful counterinsurgency to the effect that governments enlightened enough to pursue a sound political strategy will also adopt sound military tactics. They further suggest that those who will seek to defeat insurgency tomorrow would do well to study the insurgencies of yesterday. Yet, despite the generous rewards that reflection on these Philippine experiences could yield, it is not at all clear that the United States Army, or civilian policymakers, at the time or after, learned very much from them.[93] And for this negligence many would pay a high price.

NOTES

1. When the Indonesian nationalists demanded independence from the Netherlands, the territories they claimed for the new state of Indonesia consisted of exactly those parts of the archipelago ruled by the Dutch, no more and no less. The territorial consciousness of the Indonesian nation was created by their imperial rulers. Rupert Emerson, *From Empire to Nation* (Cambridge: Harvard University Press, 1960), p. 125.

2. John Leddy Phelan, *The Hispanization of the Philippines* (Madison: University of Wisconsin Press, 1967), p. ix.

3. Ibid., p. 161.

4. It was here that Dewey uttered the remark that became, for some reason, so famous: "You may fire when you are ready, Gridley."

5. John Morgan Gates, *Schoolbooks and Krags: The United States Army in the Philippines, 1898–1902* (Westport, CT: Greenwood Press, 1973), Chapter 1.

6. Gates, *Schoolbooks and Krags*, Chapter 1; Margaret Leech, *In the Days of McKinley* (New York: Harper and Row, 1959).

7. Gates, *Schoolbooks and Krags*, pp. 92–93.

8. Ibid., p. 278.

9. Ibid., p. 215.

10. Ibid., pp. 111–13.

11. Emilio Aguinaldo, *A Second Look at America* (New York: Robert Speller, 1957), p. 87.

12. Leech, *In the Days of McKinley*, p. 350; Louis W. Koenig, *Bryan: A Political Biography of William Jennings Bryan* (New York: Putnam, 1971), p. 292.

13. Gates, *Schoolbooks and Krags*, p. 220.

14. Ibid., p. 168.

15. Ibid., p. 175.

16. Ibid., p. 164.

17. Ibid., p. 218.

18. See interesting details of this and other events in Chapter 7 of Frederick

Funston, *Memories of Two Wars: Cuban and Philippine Experiences* (New York: Scribners, 1911).

19. Gates, *Schoolbooks and Krags*, p. 254.

20. Henry F. Graff, ed., *American Imperialism and the Philippine Insurrection* (Boston: Little, Brown, 1969), p. xiv; Garel A. Grunder and William E. Livezey, *The Philippines and the United States* (Norman: University of Oklahoma Press, 1951), p. 55.

21. See Jean Gottmann, "Bugeaud, Gallieni, Lyautey: The Development of French Colonial Warfare," in *Makers of Modern Strategy*, ed. Edward Mead Earle (Princeton, NJ: Princeton University Press, 1941).

22. Gates, *Schoolbooks and Krags*, p. 271.

23. Ibid., p. 101.

24. Ibid., p. 186.

25. Aguinaldo, *Second Look*, p. 83.

26. Ibid., pp. 116, 83.

27. Ibid., p. 66.

28. Carlos P. Romulo, *Crusade in Asia* (New York: John Day, 1955), p. 63. See also the illuminating study by John W. Dower, *War without Mercy: Race and Power in the Pacific War* (New York: Pantheon, 1986).

29. Luis Taruc, *He Who Rides the Tiger* (New York: Praeger, 1967), pp. 145–46.

30. Romulo, *Crusade in Asia*, p. 148.

31. William Manchester, *American Caesar: Douglas MacArthur, 1880–1964* (Boston: Little, Brown, 1978), p. 420.

32. Taruc, *He Who Rides the Tiger*, p. 188.

33. Benedict J. Kerkvliet, *The Huk Rebellion: A Study of Peasant Revolt in the Philippines* (Berkeley: University of California Press, 1977), p. 215.

34. Edward G. Lansdale, *In the Midst of Wars: America's Mission in Southeast Asia* (New York: Harper and Row, 1972), pp. 20–21.

35. Taruc, *He Who Rides the Tiger*, p. 38.

36. See for example Taruc, *He Who Rides the Tiger*, p. 144.

37. Romulo, *Crusade in Asia*, p. 88.

38. Che Guevara maintained that a democratic government, or one with at least democratic trappings, could not be overthrown by armed force, because there appeared to be an alternative road to change; see his *Guerrilla Warfare* (New York: Vintage, 1961); Lansdale agrees that the corruption of the 1949 elections helped the Huks.

39. Kerkvliet, *Huk Rebellion*, p. 210.

40. Kenneth M. Hammer, "Huks in the Philippines," in *Modern Guerrilla Warfare*, ed. Franklin Mark Osanka (Glencoe, IL: Free Press, 1962), p. 181.

41. Taruc, *He Who Rides the Tiger*, p. 88.

42. Ibid., pp. 89–90.

43. Nathan Leites, *The Viet Cong Style in Politics* (Santa Monica, CA: Rand Corporation, 1969), p. 17.

44. Napoleon D. Valeriano and C.T.R. Bohannan, *Counterguerrilla Operations: The Philippine Experience* (New York: Praeger, 1962), p. 206.

45. Kerkvliet, *The Huk Rebellion*, p. 208.

46. Ibid., p. 208.

47. Ibid., p. 242.

48. Lansdale, *In the Midst of Wars*, pp. 42–44 and passim.

49. Taruc, *He Who Rides the Tiger*, p. 97; Geoffrey Fairbairn, *Revolutionary Guerrilla Warfare* (Harmondsworth, England: Penguin, 1974).

50. Lucian Pye, *Guerrilla Communism in Malaya* (Princeton, NJ: Princeton University Press, 1956).

51. Romulo, *Crusade in Asia*, p. 135.

52. Valeriano and Bohannan, *Counterguerrilla Operations*, pp. 97–98; this controversial practice antedated Magsaysay's secretaryship.

53. Sir Robert Thompson, *Defeating Communist Insurgency: The Lessons of Malaya and Viet Nam* (New York: Praeger, 1966), Chapter 8.

54. Valeriano and Bohannan, *Counter-guerrilla Operations*; Kerkvliet, *The Huk Rebellion*, p. 238; see also Lansdale, *In the Midst of Wars*.

55. Peter Paret and John Shy, *Guerrillas in the 1960s* (New York: Praeger, 1962 revised), p. 45.

56. Romulo, *Crusade in Asia*, p. 200 and passim.

57. Taruc, *He Who Rides the Tiger*, p. 130.

58. Lansdale, *In the Midst of Wars*, p. 106.

59. Cecil B. Currey, *Edward Lansdale: The Unquiet American* (Boston: Houghton Mifflin, 1988), Chapter 6.

60. Taruc, *He Who Rides the Tiger*, p. 138.

61. Boyd T. Bashore, "Dual Strategy for Limited War," in Osanka, *Modern Guerrilla Warfare*, p. 198.

62. Taruc, *He Who Rides the Tiger*, p. 24.

63. Ibid., p. 12.

64. Ibid., p. 26.

65. Kerkvliet, *The Huk Rebellion*, Chapter 7.

66. Taruc, *He Who Rides the Tiger*, p. 161.

67. Kerkvliet, *The Huk Rebellion*, p. 217.

68. Ibid., p. 229.

69. Ibid., p. 233.

70. Taruc, *He Who Rides the Tiger*, p. 149.

71. Kerkvliet, *The Huk Rebellion*, p. 217.

72. James C. Thomson, Jr., Peter W. Stanley, and John Curtis Perry, *Sentimental Imperialists: The American Experience in East Asia* (New York: Harper and Row, 1981), p. 120.

73. *Foreign Relations of the United States, 1951*, vol. 6, *Asia and the Pacific* (Washington, DC: Government Printing Office, 1977), p. 1536. Hereafter abbreviated FRUS 1951.

74. *Foreign Relations of the United States, 1950*, vol. 6, *East Asia and the Pacific* (Washington, DC: Government Printing Office, 1976), pp. 1433, 1435–38. Hereafter abbreviated FRUS 1950.

75. FRUS 1950, p. 1443.

76. FRUS 1950, p. 1495.

77. FRUS 1951, p. 1498.

78. FRUS 1951, pp. 1501–2.

79. FRUS 1950, p. 1517.

80. FRUS 1950, p. 1462.

81. FRUS 1950, pp. 1403, 1442.

82. FRUS 1950, p. 1441.

83. FRUS 1951, p. 1507.

84. FRUS 1951, p. 1537.

85. See National Security Council Statement NSC 84/2, "The Position of the United States with Respect to the Philippines," November 9, 1950.

86. FRUS 1950, p. 1408.

87. FRUS 1950, pp. 1442–43.

88. FRUS 1951, p. 1504.

89. FRUS 1950, pp. 1485–89.

90. FRUS 1951, p. 1549.

91. FRUS 1950, pp. 1485–89.

92. Kerkvliet, *The Huk Rebellion*, pp. 207–8.

93. Larry E. Cable, *Conflict of Myths: The Development of American Counterinsurgency Doctrine and the Viet Nam War* (New York: New York University Press, 1986), Chapter 4.

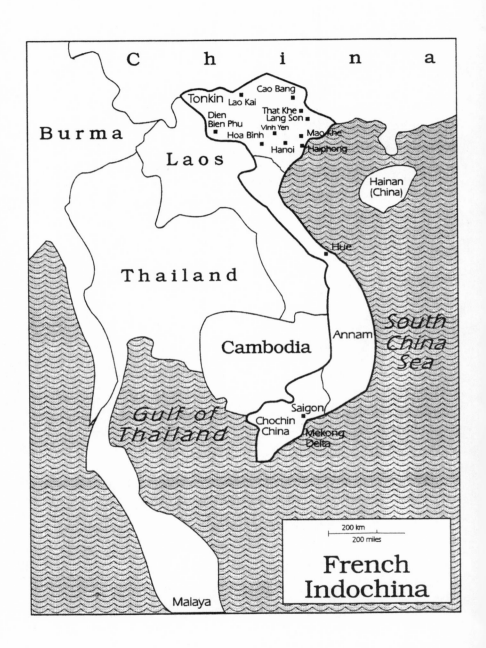

Burma

Tonkin
Lao Kai
Cao Bang
Dien
Bien Phu
That Khe
Lang Son
Vinh Yen
Mao Khe
Hoa Binh
Hanoi
Haiphong

Laos

Hainan
(China)

Thailand

Hue

Annam

South
China
Sea

Cambodia

Saigon
Chochin
China
Mekong
Delta

Gulf of
Thailand

200 km
200 miles

French
Indochina

Malaya

Chapter 4

The Agony of French Indochina

There are no neutrals on Viet Nam.

Peter M. Dunn, *The First Viet Nam War*

It is an invariable axiom of war to secure your own flanks and rear and endeavor to turn those of the enemy.

Frederick the Great

THE THIRTY YEARS' WAR

Lying across the communications links between India and the Pacific, Southeast Asia is a region rich in rice, rubber, and petroleum. The Japanese desire to possess these resources led to the attack on Pearl Harbor. In 1941, in this whole vast area only Thailand was independent; the Americans governed the Philippines, the Dutch controlled sprawling Indonesia, the British held Burma, Malaya, and Singapore, and the French ruled Cambodia, Laos, and Viet Nam, together known as French Indochina. Within a few years of the end of World War II, European rule in this region would come to an end, except for that of the French. They would pursue at great cost their vision of *la mission civilisatrice* from the steaming jungles of Indochina to the blazing sands of North Africa well into the 1960s. The French became the first European colonial power to face a full-fledged Maoist revolution, although it took them several years to realize it. The Cold War would link French efforts to maintain great-power status with American efforts to contain the Sino-Soviet bloc. Thus, as World War II drew to a close, in Indochina another conflict was about to begin. It would be a twentieth-century Thirty

Years' War, an ideological and geopolitical contest that would eventually involve directly or indirectly most of the great powers of the globe.

THE SETTING

Stretching north to south about 1,000 miles, the distance from Rome to Copenhagen, Viet Nam is roughly the size of Illinois and Missouri combined. In essence the country is two great deltas, those of the Red River and the Mekong, linked by a narrow coastal plain that tapers down to 50 miles at the waist. Vietnamese compare their country to a carrying pole with a rice basket suspended on each end.

Difficulties of communication across the great distances between north and south helped produce regional differences, rivalries, and wars. Viet Nam existed under unified government for only about three decades in the five centuries before the battle of Dien Bien Phu. Most of the time there were two warring states, based on the deltas, separated by a boundary somewhere between the 16th and 18th parallels and supported in their conflicts with each other by the Dutch and the Portuguese. After the French established themselves, they pursued different policies in the north (Tonkin), center (Annam), and south (Cochinchina), which perpetuated or increased deep-rooted regional diversities. During their occupation from 1940 to 1945, the Japanese also adopted distinctive policies for the three regions.

Early in the seventeenth century the rulers of Japan closed their country to foreigners. Thus the powerful Catholic missionary effort in Asia shifted to Viet Nam. Jesuit missionaries invented the present-day system of written Vietnamese; by World War II, a tenth of the Vietnamese, and in some provinces fully half, were Catholic.

Bloody clashes between Vietnamese rulers and the growing Catholic community resulted in French military intervention. In 1859 France took Saigon, a small town in those days but with a good harbor. Before the end of the century the whole of Viet Nam was under direct or indirect French control.

The French brought peace and order to Viet Nam. They set up a good public health system and turned thousands of acres of wasteland into farmland. On the other side of the picture, in 1954 the majority of Vietnamese were illiterate, absentee landlordism was widespread, especially in Cochinchina, and conditions for many industrial workers were close to slavery. A century of French tutelage had not prepared Viet Nam for self-government.

In economic terms France profited very little from Viet Nam: on the eve of World War I, Vietnamese trade was worth less than 1 percent of France's gross national product. If the French colonial effort had been all about money, the conflict that erupted after World War II would probably never have occurred; indeed, the French would sink billions of dollars into the fruitless effort to hold onto Viet Nam, more than all of the aid it received through the Marshall Plan.[1] But to many Frenchmen the value of their worldwide empire could never have been expressed in mere accountants' terms: the empire was the embodiment of the validity of French culture and a counterweight to the ever-growing power and population of Germany.

Early anti-French revolutionary movements in Viet Nam were parochial affairs. In a country like Viet Nam a serious attempt at revolution would have to involve the peasantry, but traditional elites were both disdainful of the peasants and also afraid of rousing them to a frenzy that could sweep away not only the French but the native elites themselves. National revolution—as opposed to provincial rebellion—would require a Viet Nam—wide organization of persons who could both wield revolutionary theory and mobilize large numbers of peasants.

Pre–World War II Vietnamese nationalism drew heavily upon foreign models: French, Soviet and Chinese, both Nationalist and Maoist. Early nationalist parties were urban and elitist, without serious appeal to the peasant majority or prospects of developing any. Internal strife and factionalism weakened them further; so did police harassment. The best-known of the non-Communist nationalist parties was the Nationalist Party of Viet Nam (VNQDD), founded in Hanoi in 1927 under the influence of Chiang Kai-shek's Kuomintang. Trying to build support within the peasantry, the VNQDD extorted money from the wealthy and lent it to peasants at low rates, hoping to obligate them.[2] The party staged a premature and poorly coordinated uprising in 1930, which the French authorities easily crushed. The leaders who escaped prison fled to Nationalist China. There they remained until the middle of World War II.

While French law and order bottled up the warlike energies of the Tonkinese, French social policy created a new, Westernized Vietnamese elite. By frustrating that elite's natural desires for influence and status, the French stimulated its desire for national independence. At the same time the French, in contrast to the British in India or the Americans in the Philippines, did not permit organization for or even advocacy of eventual independence. Political opposition was subjected to police punishment.[3] With no possibility of peaceful and lawful expression, any Vietnamese nationalist movement had to become revolutionary. In an example of truly Gallic irony, by breaking up the VNQDD in the 1930s, the French destroyed the very sort of organization with which they would seek to counteract the Communists in the 1950s.

THE JAPANESE INVASION

In the late 1930s, Japan launched her ferocious attempt to conquer China. Once the Japanese had occupied China's coastal cities, the only access route besides Burma for military supplies to Chiang Kai-shek's beleaguered Nationalist armies was Indochina. The Japanese wished to close this backdoor supply route to Chiang. They also wanted Indochina's resources for themselves and viewed the area as a strategic base for further incursions into Asia. Hence the Japanese demanded from the French administration in Viet Nam that they be allowed to occupy bases there. The Blitzkrieg had just struck down Metropolitan France; the isolated French authorities in Viet Nam believed themselves to have no choice except to bow to the Japanese ultimatum. Japanese forces began occupying Viet Nam in September 1940; Saigon became the headquarters of the Japanese armies in Southeast Asia. Soon afterward the Japanese would attack Pearl Harbor, capture mighty Singapore, and sweep aside Dutch resistance in Indonesia.

It would be impossible to overemphasize the effect of these Japanese invasions on the future of East and Southeast Asia. Surrounded by an aura of omnicompetence and invincibility, the Europeans had for many decades been able to hold their vast imperial territories with remarkably small armed forces. The defeat and humiliation of the Europeans—at the hands of Asians—stripped them of their prestige and signaled that they had at last lost the Mandate of Heaven. By breaking the mythic power of the Europeans, the Japanese paved the way for postwar revolution in the East, and thus for Ho and his Communists.

THE COMMUNIST PARTY

In January 1930, under orders from Moscow, three tiny cliques of squabbling Communists united to form the Communist Party of Viet Nam, with a total membership of 211. Different from all other parties in the country, "it was a subversive movement launched from outside Viet Nam by the Soviet government as an instrument for embarrassing France."[4] Belatedly caught up in the ill-planned nationalist uprising of 1930, the new party fell easily into the hands of the French police: "virtually the entire Party Central Committee had been sold out by fellow Communists."[5]

From these disasters the party leadership drew two fundamental conclusions. First, the French could not be defeated from inside Viet Nam; some international upheaval would be necessary to break the power of the state, as in Russia in 1917. Second, when such an upheaval arrived, the party must be ready with a long-tested, tightly disciplined organization.[6]

From the beginning, the leader of the Vietnamese Communists had been Ho Chi Minh. Like almost every modern revolutionary leader, he had been born in comfortable circumstances. Descendant of scholars and bureaucrats, Ho (born Nguyen That Thanh in 1890) attended the best secondary school in Hue. Rejected for a government position in 1911, Ho took a job on a French steamship and did not return to his country for thirty years. During that time he visited London, New York, Thailand, the China of Chiang, and the China of Mao. He helped found the French Communist Party, went to prison in Hong Kong, crossed the Gobi Desert, and took courses on revolutionary theory and practice in Stalin's Moscow. He learned to speak passable French, Russian, English, and Chinese. No major leader of world Communism, and certainly not Stalin or Mao, could remotely match the knowledge and experience of the wide world possessed by Ho.

Having gone to Paris to press for Vietnamese self-government at the Versailles Conference of 1919, Ho came into contact with the teachings of Lenin. The Bolsheviks, seeing the colonial empires as the Achilles' heel of world capitalism, were advocating the emancipation of subject peoples. (Lenin, of course, did not apply these ideas to the subject peoples of the Tsarist and Bolshevik empires.) To Ho, Communism seemed to offer a satisfactory explanation of Vietnamese backwardness, a realistic strategy for revolution, and the promise of support from a major European state all in one. Unmarried, ascetic (except for chain-smoking American cigarettes), Ho the world traveler and Moscow-trained subversive deliberately cultivated the image of a gentle and naive uncle, while he simultaneously determined to impose his political will on his country at whatever cost in blood and tears. By the outbreak of World War II, Ho completely dominated the party because of his long and wide experience and his contacts in Moscow. Besides, having been out of Viet Nam for most of his adult life, he had been spared the embarrassments of having to enforce the ever changing Comintern line.

In the world's underdeveloped areas Communism has historically attracted not the peasant majority, nor the often tiny working class, but rather the urban middle-class intellectuals. Marxism-Leninism was the negation of existing Western society; in the Viet Nam of the 1930s, "to be a Marxist represented a grand gesture of contempt for the corrupt past as well as the humiliating present."[7] There was another attraction: in Communist theory, revolutions require the leadership of the "proletariat," the working class, even in peasant societies. In practice this meant the leadership of the revolution by the Communist Party and thus of the intellectuals who controlled it. Marxism-Leninism offered dissatisfied intellectuals psychic consolation for the present and exciting promises for the future. Yet, with weak roots and few contacts among the population at large, on the eve of World War II, Vietnamese Communism remained a very small operation.

In August 1939, Hitler and Stalin came together in their pact to destroy Poland. Following this infamous agreement and in subservience to orders from Moscow, the French Communist Party assumed a violently neutralist and pro-German stance. One consequence of this shameful behavior was that in Viet Nam the police authorities carried out a major crackdown on the local Communist Party. Police activity was so effective and the Communist organization in Viet Nam was so weak that the party was almost completely dismantled in the cities and forced to make its new home in the remote mountains along the Chinese border, with momentous conse- quences for the future development of the revolution.

FORMATION OF THE VIET MINH

The small, harried, but disciplined Communist Party finally got its chance with the entrance of the Japanese into Viet Nam. In May 1941, the Eighth Plenum of the Indochina Communist Party assembled in the hamlet of Pac Bo, a stone's throw from the Chinese frontier. This miniature convocation laid down the bases of the new program that would help carry the Com- munists to victory. The Eighth Plenum proclaimed two fundamental points. First, national independence took primacy over the class war. The party leaders declared that if Viet Nam did not achieve independence, then no class within it would receive what it wished or needed; the class struggle must therefore give way to the national struggle against the Japanese and the French.[8] Thus the Communists gave up their demands for land redis- tribution in favor of the seizure only of French lands and reduced rents on the rest. By substituting a kind of "racial patriotism" for classic Marxist slogans, the Communist appeal became broader, especially to formerly non- Communist intellectuals.[9] The second fundamental point: the Communists must create a new front organization uniting all anti-imperialist elements in the country, whatever their class or political affiliation. The name of this front organization would be the League for the Independence of Viet Nam, or (in short form) the Viet Minh. The Communists would form the nucleus of the Viet Minh front.

Communists all over the world routinely used this "front" tactic. It helped them establish contact with and gain influence over individuals and groups who would not join or listen to an openly Communist organization. How- ever profoundly un-Marxist an appeal to nationalism may be, it proved an ideal basis on which to establish such a front. Indeed "the primary political tactic of communist revolutionaries since the time of Lenin has been to attempt to forge a 'united front' with genuine nationalist movements, thereby hoping to gain mass support for a communist organization not on the basis of the organization's communist values and goals but on the basis of its tactically adopted nationalist values and goals."[10]

Working to widen its attraction beyond the small circle of urban intel- lectuals who formed its heart, the Vietnamese Communist Party would henceforth pursue not the orthodox urban and class strategy but a heterodox rural and nationalist strategy. If the Communists had not taken this mo- mentous step, it is difficult to see how they would have achieved their future success.[11]

THE VIET MINH AND THE ANTI-JAPANESE WAR

During 1941, in the face of the Japanese occupation, most non-Communist nationalist leaders either retired from politics, cooperated with the French, or fled into Chiang's China. In contrast, the Viet Minh persisted in its efforts and grew in size and prestige. By the end of 1943 the Viet Minh army under General Vo Nguyen Giap counted several hundred soldiers and controlled the provinces of Cao Bang, Lang Son, and Bac Kan on the Chinese border.[12] The fact that the Viet Minh exercised control over Vietnamese territory—no matter how small or remote a piece—helped legitimize the Front's claim to be an alternative government, an identity none of its nationalist competitors could remotely match.

Looking forward to the inevitable defeat of the Japanese, the Viet Minh conducted only minimal operations against them.[13] Nevertheless, the Allies gave the Viet Minh full credit for being the only serious anti-Japanese resistance in the country, and the Americans parachuted arms and supplies to them. This recognition from the Allies further bolstered the growing prestige of the Viet Minh.

The Japanese shipped a lot of rice out of Viet Nam. They also forced many peasants to abandon rice cultivation for jute. Meanwhile, Allied bombings damaged transportation lines from the rice-rich south to Tonkin. As a result, in the winter of 1944–1945 a serious famine struck northern Viet Nam; perhaps as many as 2 million people died. Seizing on a popular issue, Communists led demonstrations demanding the opening of government granaries, activities that were "a key to the development of the movement in rural areas throughout the north."[14]

On March 9, 1945, in the face of looming defeat, Japanese occupation forces ended the fiction of shared control of Viet Nam. They arrested French colonial officials and disarmed and imprisoned those French military units they could lay hands on. Two days later, under Japanese encouragement, Emperor Bao Dai proclaimed the independence of the ancient state of Annam, along with Tonkin (the Japanese insisted on maintaining firm control of Cochinchina, which consists of Saigon and its surrounding area, plus the populous Mekong Delta region).

The Japanese could easily wipe out the vestiges of French power but lacked the troops to occupy the countryside effectively. Hence the Viet Minh was freer now than ever before to fill the expanding power vacuum. By the summer of 1945, Ho Chi Minh and General Giap controlled an armed force of over 5,000 ruling over a million peasants in provinces near the Chinese border. Thus, into the space left by the imprisonment of the French, the disinterest of the Japanese, and the weakness of their competitors, the Viet Minh stepped, with their program of unity behind national independence and their tough little army.

THE AUGUST REVOLUTION

At war's end, no Vietnamese political organization, not the Viet Minh or the VNQDD or anybody else, had anything that could be called a mass following in Tonkin. The events that were to go down in history as the August Revolution were the work of a small elite. At the time, according to Ho himself, the total number of Communist Party members in all of Indochina was a mere 5,000.[15]

But in Leninist strategy, a revolutionary situation exists not when there is wide support for the Communists but when there is only minimal support for the government. In such circumstances the role of the armed forces becomes crucial. In the late summer of 1945, after the stunning announcement of Japan's surrender, the 30,000 Japanese troops in Viet Nam stood by in supreme indifference to local politics, and the police and militia of Bao Dai's fledgling regime wavered in the face of Communist discipline and speed. The August Revolution was not a revolution but a coup d'état.

The primary and decisive circumstance for the August Revolution was the power vacuum in Tonkin. Next in importance were the success of the Viet Minh Front in concealing from many the Communist face under the nationalist mask and its possession of small but disciplined armed units. At first, numerous leading non–Communist elements, including several Catholic bishops, joined or supported the Viet Minh provisional government. American officers of the OSS (forerunner of the CIA) in Hanoi prominently associated themselves with Ho, marched into Hanoi with Giap's little army, and publicly saluted the revolutionary flag on top of the Hanoi Hilton. Believing that such actions signaled the support of the United States government for the Viet Minh, Emperor Bao Dai abdicated and accepted the post of "supreme adviser" to Ho's government.[16] On September 2, 1945, before a huge crowd in downtown Hanoi, Ho Chi Minh proclaimed the independence of the Democratic Republic of Viet Nam.

Without the acquiescence, indeed without the benevolence, of the Japanese army in Viet Nam, the Viet Minh would never have established their predominance over the other nationalist groups in the country. More than this, elements in the Japanese armed forces were determined that the surrender of their own country would not stop resistance to the Western allies: in the confused days after the surrender, the Japanese delivered money, tanks, artillery, and over 31,000 rifles to Giap's forces. Several thousand Japanese soldiers, rather than surrender to the Allies, joined the ranks of the Viet Minh outright.[17]

The Viet Minh revolution of 1945, like the Bolshevik Revolution in 1917, was the result not of Communist popular appeal but of the temporary weakness of their enemies in the chaos of war. Once these unusual conditions disappeared, the Viet Minh would not be able to hold on in Hanoi but would be forced back into the jungle whence they had recently and briefly emerged.

THE DEFEAT OF THE NONCOMMUNIST NATIONALISTS

The emergence of a nationalist movement in Viet Nam was inevitable. Also inevitable, in light of French attitudes toward independence, was the turn of nationalism toward violent revolution. But the domination and manipulation of revolutionary nationalism in Viet Nam by Communists was *not* inevitable. How the Communists defeated their rivals for the predominant rule in Vietnamese nationalism is a revealing chapter.

Of course, the skillful leaders of Vietnamese Communism cleverly cloaked their true program under a call for nationalist unity; that was the essential purpose of the Viet Minh front. But the ties of Ho Chi Minh and the leadership group of the Viet Minh to international Communism were of immense importance. The Comintern provided them with financial assistance, training in Moscow in the arts of subversion, an external source of discipline, and the tremendously morale-building knowledge that they enjoyed the support of a worldwide movement orchestrated by a major European state. The French Communist Party helped too, especially when the Popular Front cabinet came into power in Paris in 1936: jailed Communist leaders in Viet Nam were given an amnesty and permitted to enter the political mainstream.

Leninist tactics—especially the maintenance of armed forces, no matter how small, ready to seize power at the opportune moment—enabled the Viet Minh to take advantage of the temporary chaos in Hanoi in the last weeks of August 1945. The August Revolution, elitist and ephemeral as it was, gave the Viet Minh an enormous advantage over their nationalist rivals: once Ho Chi Minh proclaimed the independence of the Democratic Republic of Viet Nam in Hanoi, many Vietnamese who wished actively to oppose the return of French power felt they had no real alternative but to back the Viet Minh.

In contrast, non-Communist nationalist groups had many weaknesses. They had no powerful protectors in France or in any other country. Their indiscipline exposed them to the ravages of factionalism; their inexperience in subversion exposed them to the ravages of the police. Apparently viewing the VNQDD as more intransigently anti-French than the Viet Minh, the police pursued them remorselessly.[18] The Vietnamese public closely associated the VNQDD with the Chinese Nationalists. When Chinese troops occupied Tonkin after the Japanese surrender, their arrogant attitude and exploitative behavior discredited the VNQDD, and the withdrawal of these forces left it exposed to the wrath of both the Viet Minh and the French.

But the non-Communist nationalists were also the victims of two very special weapons that the Viet Minh employed with great effect against them. One was the tactic of "decapitating the opposition," that is, the murder of the leaders of non-Communist groups, a strategy explained by Truong Chinh, chief theoretician of the Communist Party, in his *Primer for Revolt.*[19] The Communists began killing their opponents well before the August Revolution, but this practice reached a crescendo once Ho proclaimed independence. In Cochinchina the Viet Minh assassinated the spiritual leader of the powerful Hoa Hao religious sect; they tied sect members together in bundles and threw them into the Mekong. They also executed leaders of the Trotskyite Party. In Tonkin, the Viet Minh killed many hundreds of authentic nationalists, leaders and followers, especially of the VNQDD.[20]

Sometimes, instead of murdering their rivals, it was more convenient for the Communists to betray them to the French. Many have accused the Communists of this practice, both before and after the August Revolution. The accused include Ho Chi Minh; his otherwise inexplicable escapes from French and other prisons have given rise to the charge that he bought his release by acting as a police informer.[21] Some results of this betrayal and decapitation of the opposition appeared in the 1946 elections, in which Ho reportedly received 169,000 votes in Hanoi, a city whose total population was supposed to be 119,000.[22]

Numerous commentators have believed that the secret of Communist victory in Viet Nam, both in 1954 and in 1975, is their takeover of the nationalist movement. Certainly, the Viet Minh victory over non-Communist nationalists was an accomplishment of immense importance. But whether that is the fundamental reason for Viet Minh success in the conflict with the French will require more discussion later on.

THE OUTBREAK OF THE FRANCO–VIET MINH WAR

In the waning months of World War II, President Franklin Roosevelt was inclined to oppose the restoration of French rule in Indochina. But General Charles de Gaulle and many other French leaders were determined to re-establish control, an aim which enjoyed the favor of Prime Minister Winston Churchill.

In February 1946, Ho Chi Minh announced the formation of a coalition government at Hanoi, admitting some representatives of groups other than his Viet Minh. He did this because he had decided not to oppose the peaceful reentry of French troops into Viet Nam, and wished to protect himself from any negative consequences by implicating his potential opponents.[23]

In March 1946, Jean Sainteny, the representative of General de Gaulle's Provisional Government, signed accords with Ho Chi Minh in Hanoi. The accords recognized Viet Nam not as an independent state but as a "Free State" within the worldwide French Union. This Free State of Viet Nam was to have its own parliament and administration, its own treasury and armed forces. The French would maintain 15,000 troops north of the 16th parallel for up to five years and were to train and equip the Vietnamese army. A plebiscite would be held in Cochinchina to determine whether that region wanted to become part of Ho's new state. The French invited Ho to come to Paris to negotiate the final settlement, thus granting him enormous legitimacy. The apparent reconciliation between French imperialism and Vietnamese nationalism received a jarring blow when Admiral Thierry D'Argenlieu, high commissioner for Indochina, acting on his own authority in Saigon, recognized Cochinchina as a separate republic in the same terms in which the French government had recognized Ho's regime.[24]

Whatever the events in the diplomatic field, in Tonkin relations between the French and the Viet Minh were deteriorating dangerously. The French troops did not trust the Viet Minh: in December 1944, Giap's forces had attacked two remote French outposts, and on August 3, 1946, near Ban Minh, they attacked and destroyed a French convoy on an authorized mission.[25] On November 9, Ho's government, now with 50,000 troops of its own, approved a constitution with no mention of Viet Nam as part of the French Union.

Two weeks later occurred the infamous Haiphong Incident. In retaliation for some serious attacks on French personnel in Hanoi, the cruiser *Suffren* began to shell the port of Haiphong, a callous and stupid act in which many hundreds of innocent Vietnamese civilians were killed.[26] But the real beginning of the war is commonly taken to be December 19, 1946, when Viet Minh units tried to overwhelm French forces in Hanoi and many other places and perpetrated grisly attacks on French civilians. In Paris, Socialist Premier Léon Blum declared that France's response would be one of firm military containment.

The August 1945 seizure of Hanoi was the Leninist phase of the Viet Minh revolution. After 1946 it would enter the Maoist phase. (There would be no return to a Leninist phase for seizing South Viet Nam in the 1960s because support for the Communists in the southern cities was negligible.) The influence of the Chinese model is apparent: the national independence united front, the party-army, the secure base in remote areas, the guerrilla tactics. Just as the Japanese had been able to control China's cities but were too weak to dominate the countryside, so the French were able to drive the Viet Minh from Hanoi, but not to establish tight control in rural areas. To these places the Viet Minh retreated. It was the adoption of this rural guerrilla strategy that ensured a protracted conflict and thus made the Viet Minh victory possible.[27]

In his *Primer for Revolt* Truong Chinh observed, "Strategy decides tactics. Our strategy is to protract the war; therefore, in tactics, we should avoid unfavorable fights to the death because we must maintain our forces."[28] The Viet Minh from the start employed classic guerrilla tactics with Maoist refinements: cultivate the civilian population, always plan and carry out a military operation for its political impact, surprise the enemy through speed of movement and good intelligence, never fight except with overwhelming superiority, attack enemy morale, disguise Communist control, and maintain at least the appearance of a broad political coalition.

In the terrain and climate of northern Viet Nam "the advantage lies with the well-trained and lightly equipped rifleman accustomed to life in the jungle."[29] The Viet Minh knew the countryside and were used to the climate. Coolie labor was plentiful, able to work in areas unsuited to trucks, and easy to conceal against air attacks. The Viet Minh built shops to produce bullets, mines, and even light machine guns. And not least, Tonkin was a region with an immemorial fighting tradition, for centuries the shield of the Vietnamese against Chinese incursions, the last area of the country to fall under the control of the French.

The Viet Minh maintained conventional forces as well as guerrilla units. At the bottom of the ladder were the so-called popular troops. These were local and part-time, with some political training and instruction in sabotage but few weapons. Those among the popular troops who showed aptitude might be promoted into the conventional forces.

Of necessity, the original Viet Minh conventional forces were few in number. These regular troops fought like guerrilla units in that they were always under orders to break off contact with superior or determined enemy forces. But the conventional units had more training and better weapons. The main object of guerrilla units was to cause damage; that of regular units was to surround and annihilate an enemy force.[30]

The Viet Minh lacked reliable signals communications. They ignored medical facilities up until the early 1950s; this meant leaving wounded men behind on the battlefield, bad for morale. But they spent a lot of time on political indoctrination of their fighters, especially the regular forces, stressing national independence, not Communization. They placed great emphasis on good intelligence, careful planning, and rehearsal for an operation. In the early years, morale was high and desertions few.[31]

The Viet Minh were also counting very heavily on benefiting from the weaknesses of Metropolitan France. The trauma of defeat, occupation, and liberation had left that country deeply divided and spiritually exhausted. The Americans had granted independence to the Philippines, the British were about to do the same in Burma and India, as were the Dutch in Indonesia; the French thus seemed to be trying all alone to hold back a regional and even global tide of independence. The armed forces of France were distributed all over the empire, and Saigon was a very long way from Paris. General Philippe Leclerc, who represented France at the surrender ceremonies in Tokyo Bay, assumed command of the forces in Saigon. In early 1947 he expressed doubt that France could go back to the old relationship in Indochina. "Anti–Communism will be useless as a tool as long as the problem of nationalism remains unresolved."[32] The author of *Primer for Revolt* put great stress on the fact that there was already by 1947 an antiwar movement in France.[33]

GENERAL GIAP

The outstanding military commander of the Viet Minh, destined to become the Vietnamese revolutionary leader second in fame only to Ho himself, was Vo Nguyen Giap. Born in 1912, graduating from the same school in Hue that Ho and Ngo Dinh Diem had attended, Giap went on to take a law degree at the University of Hanoi. He contemplated pursuing a doctorate in political economy but instead married and took a teaching position at a private school in Hanoi. Soon after the Japanese occupied Tonkin, Giap found himself in command of the fledgling armed units of the Viet Minh. He often boasted that the only military academy he ever attended was the jungle. That is not a bad school in which to learn about war, especially the kind the Viet Minh had to fight much of the time. But the jungle has no libraries where one can study books by and about the great commanders of history. Thus Giap's military self-education was strong on tactics but weak on strategy; time would show the importance of this imbalance. In any event, during the exhilirating days of the August Revolution this Communist revolutionary and jungle war-college graduate liked to display himself in Hanoi resplendent in white suits and striped ties.[34]

For about three years after December 1946, there were very few major military operations by either side. The French did not grasp the nature of the challenge they were facing, while Giap's main effort, aside from preserving and increasing his forces, was to get the French to leave Bac Can. By 1949, the fighting had reached a stalemate. The French, assisted by the forces of Bao Dai, were in control of the population centers, but without the necessary numbers to flush the Viet Minh out of their frontier strongholds. The Viet Minh, while free to harass the French, lacked the firepower to inflict a major defeat on them.

All this changed when the Maoists triumphed in China. The Communist victory across the border meant that the Viet Minh would have both a safe refuge and a reliable source of invaluable supplies. Chinese officers equipped and trained Giap's conventional forces into a real army, and large numbers of Chinese military advisers served with the Viet Minh.[35] Although during 1951 China's assistance decreased somewhat owing to her intervention in the Korean War, a steady flow of vehicles and artillery (including American 75mm recoilless rifles, superior to the French 57mm gun) continued to sustain the Viet Minh.

All this aid was not entirely free of charge. The Viet Minh sold opium to raise cash for some of its needs.[36] And Ho paid another price too: in 1950 he proclaimed Viet Minh adherence to the Marxist-Leninist camp in its global struggle against the West. By irrevocably revealing the Stalinist sword under the nationalist silk, Ho and the Viet Minh won for themselves the lasting enmity of the United States. For the next quarter-century the Americans would strive, by aiding first the French and then the South Vietnamese, to prevent the final victory of the Vietnamese Communists. Ho's public embrace of Stalinism would cost his people untold suffering. Thus "the extremists in the Viet Minh movement incurred a grave responsibility to the Vietnamese people."[37]

Until 1950, the French could delude themselves that they were actually winning the war, that they were taking territory and driving the rebels ever backward. But the arrival of Maoist forces on the frontier was the decisive event of the Franco–Viet Minh conflict. And the entry of the Chinese into war against the United States and the United Nations in Korea meant that a Chinese army might rush into Tonkin at any time and annihilate the French, who would have no hope of an evacuation.[38] The best strategy—the only strategy—left for the French and their Vietnamese allies was to fall back onto Saigon and Cochinchina. Instead, they decided to pursue a completely opposite course.

By 1950, Giap's regulars were disciplined, vigorous in assault, and receiving Chinese help. In a radio broadcast in February of that year, Giap announced that the guerrilla phase of the war was over and the "war of movement" had begun. In the autumn campaign season, Giap achieved some spectacular successes over French outposts along the Chinese border (see below). These victories, however, led to overconfidence; Giap decided he was ready for full-scale attacks against the seat of French power in the north, the great Hanoi–Red River Delta area. Giap launched major assaults at Vinh Yen (January), Mao Khe (March), and along the Day River (May–June). In these battles the French were operating on interior lines, close to their supply area, with the advantages of air and even naval support. These encounters cost the Viet Minh 20,000 casualties (and 500 prisoners at Vinh Yen).[39]

Almost anybody can be a successful commander if he doesn't care how many casualties his forces take. Giap showed "a callous disregard for casualties among his own troops" but failed to produce any gains for this bloodshed.[40] Worse, Giap publicly blamed the defeat at Vinh Yen on the "cowardice" of his soldiers.[41] These disasters forced Giap to revert to classical guerrilla warfare, far from the Delta, at the maximum range of French troop movements and air power. Fortunately for Giap, the French lacked the men and material to mount a serious counteroffensive. Equally fortunate for the Viet Minh, the French failed to seize this opportunity—the morrow of a real triumph—to make persuasive concessions to anti-Communist nationalists.

THE FRENCH EFFORT

The French were trying to fight a serious war thousands of miles away from their home base. Their forces consisted of units of diverse nationalities, languages, and dietary requirements (Muslim soldiers, for instance, could not eat the canned pork ration of the French Army). Most Vietnamese units in both the French and Bao Dai armies harbored Viet Minh infiltrators.[42] Such conditions would have severely sapped the strength of any army. But in addition, French forces suffered from inadequate training, inappropriate tactics, and insufficient numbers.

"Our units," states the principal French military study of the war, "organized for warfare in Europe, proved to be ill-suited to . . . a struggle against rebel forces in an Asiatic theater." French infantry was "poorly trained, weighed down by its impedimenta, and excessively burdened with supplies and ammunition." The French did not like to make major troop movements at night; hence when they did move, everybody knew about it. Time after time they would try to encircle guerrilla bands, but "in the jungle one encircles nothing."[43] *Primer for Revolt* advises guerrilla attacks against the enemy when they have just completed a difficult march, when they are eating or sleeping, or when it is nighttime or raining. The French often cooperated in all this, inviting attack by making camp too early or in an exposed area.[44]

Most of all, the French had a grave problem of numbers. All those who would fight against guerrillas face a classic problem: how to divide limited forces between static defense and mobile operations. In the Indochina war French commanders confronted this problem in an extreme form because of the demonstrably insufficient numbers of troops available to them. In May 1953, at the height of the war, there were approximately 190,000 troops in the French Expeditionary Force, including air and naval personnel. Of this number 70,000 were Vietnamese. Only 54,000 were army troops from Metropolitan France, whose population at that time was over 42,000,000. After adding in Bao Dai's national army, and even the immobile militias of the Cochinchina sects, the grand total of all French and allied forces reached only about 550,000 personnel. In the 1950s General Giap had about 300,000 fighters under his command. From the viewpoint of contemporary counterguerrilla doctrine, which required a ratio of ten to one for a government victory, the French position in Viet Nam was utterly hopeless.

The French wore themselves out in a numbers game that was rigged against them. The Viet Minh, like all guerrillas, were free to strike or not as they pleased. Since most of them went into action infrequently, they had plenty of time to rest and train. In contrast, French forces had to be on the alert and on patrol every day and every night.[45] Time and again the French would mount thrusts into enemy territory far from their own bases. To obtain sufficient troops for such operations, they would strip other areas of manpower, making them vulnerable. After a while they would order the attacking unit to return to base because there were no reinforcements or replacements to send them. The returning column would then suffer heavy casualties because the small French air force could not provide sufficient protection from enemy ground harassment. As an example of this scenario, after Giap's costly failures of 1951, the French attacked Hoa Binh, severing the main Viet Minh north-south communications line. But lacking sufficient troops to hold the area, the French soon withdrew with heavy losses.

The Viet Minh usually had good intelligence on how many enemy troops were available for a particular operation. They could also calculate how many of these troops would be necessarily employed in protecting each mile of communications between the attacking unit and its home base. Thus they could figure out with great accuracy where and when a French offensive would run out of steam.[46]

FRENCH AIR POWER

In modern warfare, air superiority is perhaps the most prized possession. The French always controlled the air in Indochina, at least in the sense that the Viet Minh had no air force with which to challenge them. The French derived little benefit from their superiority. The Viet Minh were excellent at camouflage; they usually attacked at night, when French planes were ineffective; they were often able to sabotage even the most carefully guarded French aircraft. (Sabotage, camouflage, parachute—French words.) Rain and fog could interfere with French flying either at the launch point or the planned attack point, and in Tonkin the rainy season usually ran from late April to late September. Aircraft were misused in ground support or for wholly illegitimate purposes, as illustrated by the stupid remark of General Chassin, air commander in Viet Nam, who said that his planes were going to kill water buffalo because they were the "tractors" of the Viet Minh.[47] By 1953, General Giap was receiving good Soviet antiaircraft weapons (so important later at Dien Bien Phu). In view of the enormous reliance American and Soviet forces placed on helicopters in South Viet Nam and Afghanistan, it is sobering to recall that the French forces in Viet Nam had no helicopters until 1950, when they acquired two.[48] As late as April 1954—that is, when their forces inside Dien Bien Phu were fighting for survival—the French never had as many as 10 helicopters operational in all Indochina.[49] Given the French penchant for creating outposts that they could not supply adequately on the ground, this weakness in helicopters explains much about the outcome of the war.

The French used paratroopers with great color, but not with great effect. The mystique of the paratroops played its role in the practice of establishing an outpost by leaping over guerrilla-controlled territory. But then the French were faced with the problem of supplying the outpost, which often proved too costly and thus led to its abandonment and heavy casualties on the retreat.

One of the most spectacular (although unsuccessful) episodes involving paratroops occurred in October 1947; landing near the headquarters of the Viet Minh, French airborne troops almost captured both Ho and Giap, who escaped with only an hour to spare, one of the great what-ifs of history.[50] On July 17, 1953, three parachute battalions descended upon Lang Son, of unhappy memory, destroying tons of Viet Minh equipment and ammunition. It was symptomatic of the way in which the home country supported the effort in Indochina that airborne troops had to spend a lot of time and energy recovering the parachutes they had just used, because they were always in short supply.[51]

FRENCH COUNTERGUERRILLA TACTICS

Like many other students of guerrilla warfare, Trinquier says that victory over guerrillas requires the support of the native population and the destruction of the political infrastructure of the guerrilla movement. These two factors are often closely linked. Only an extended occupation of a given area permits the infrastructure to be destroyed. But such extended occupations, loosely called "clear and hold," never achieve the spectacular results so beloved by glory-seeking military commanders, especially ones brought up in a Napoleonic tradition.[52] The French would occupy a district town or a village and begin to root out the local Communists, often with the help of local inhabitants. Then, for reasons of inadequate manpower or change in plans, they would abandon that place, exposing all the civilians who had helped them to ghastly reprisals. In the worst cases, village searches by French forces were usually quite superficial, so that the rear guard of a unit would be fired upon as it left the village that had just been "searched."[53]

French troops often conducted themselves in ways that alienated the village populations among whom they had to operate. And as the war went on, French units increasingly relied on artillery and air support. This was a sure sign of declining morale and an abandonment of any effort to win over or at least neutralize the Vietnamese civilian population.[54]

Searching villages for the hidden enemy is best left to local troops and/ or police, assisted by local sympathizers. This is not a quick or a glamorous undertaking, but it is vital. But the French army often assigned the collection of intelligence to officers who were strangers to the area of their responsibility and/or could speak no Vietnamese or any local dialect.[55] Such an unenlightened approach to intelligence cost the French forces many lives that would otherwise have been easily saved.

It is especially important for regular troops fighting guerrillas to grasp that every guerrilla movement, and almost every guerrilla unit, contains members who were either coerced into it or have repented of their joining but don't know how to get out. Such individuals will often be taken prisoner. Every captured guerrilla must therefore be viewed as a potential gold mine of information, and even as a possible recruit for the government side. It is of the essence that prisoners be carefully interrogated as soon as possible and potential converts carefully segregated from the hard core.

OUTPOSTS, CONVOYS, AND AMBUSHES

For much of the war, the major military activity of the Viet Minh was the ambush of French motor columns. The French were not very successful at countering these attacks: indeed "the French lived in fear of ambushes to the end of the war."[56]

The Viet Minh emphasis on ambush was a response to the French strategy of establishing outposts far from their base in the Red River Delta. These outposts had to be supplied with food and ammunition. Since French air power was not sufficient for this task, outposts depended for supply on road-bound convoys. In order to combat ambushes, the French began to build strongpoints or other outposts at any place where an ambush had once occurred. These posts in turn had to be supplied by convoys. The whole system was very odd: the supply of outposts required convoys, and the protection of convoys required outposts.[57] The protection of anti-ambush posts necessitated the sweeping of the jungle around them for several hundred yards on either side of the road on which the post had been established. But there were never enough troops to hold the Delta, garrison the outposts, protect the convoys, and sweep the sides of the roads.[58] For every hundred kilometers of road kept open in Viet Nam, French forces suffered three of four casualties per day.[59]

Even when protected by tanks or other armored vehicles, convoys were inviting prey to guerrillas. Between 1952 and 1954 the French lost 398 armored vehicles to enemy action. The great majority of these were destroyed by mines and booby traps, only a few by conventional antitank weapons.[60] In the month of June 1954 alone, they suffered 240 vehicles lost and 1,100 casualties and missing.[61] And all this to little good, because in the chilling words of an official French army evaluation, "each night the roads were left to the enemy."[62] The French eventually decided to overfly convoys with helicopters and light aircraft, but there were never enough of these. The inadequacies of the outposts-and-convoys system meant that from time to time the French would abandon an outpost with the intention of retreating by road to a safer place. Thus the withdrawing garrison of the abandoned outpost became another convoy subject to attack. Some of the worst disasters that befell the French occurred in this way, as the garrison of an abandoned outpost, laboriously carrying inadequate supplies of food and ammunition, lacking good maps and reliable guides, tried to make its way over poor roads through dense jungle filled with the waiting foe.

BORDER DISASTERS

In order to have reliable access to supplies from Communist China, Giap had to clear French forts and outposts lying at key transportation points along the rugged border area of northern Tonkin. In February 1950, under Viet Minh pressure, the French high command ordered the abandonment of the post at Lao Kai, against the will of the commanding officer there. The French forces retreating from Lao Kai brought with them a lot of opium but left behind the non–Vietnamese tribesmen who had long been loyal to them and who had fought the Viet Minh ferociously. After the evacuation of Lao Kai, Viet Minh troops rushed into the town and slaughtered hundreds of civilians.[63]

In October of the same year occurred the affair at Cao Bang. The French had a very nice fort at Cao Bang, with good natural and man-made defenses, a tough garrison, and many friendly civilians. Under orders from Hanoi to give up the place, the French garrison of 1,600, accompanied by 1,500 Indochinese civilians, set out for Lang Son, 85 miles to the south. They made their way down Colonial Route 4, which was "no more than a narrow trail of patched-up, roughly mended, blackened earth, a wretched kind of track that wound through the overwhelming majesty of the forest."[64] Advancing from the south to meet and escort the Cao Bang column to safety were 3,500 Moroccan troops. These two groups linked up but then were overwhelmed in hand-to-hand fighting. After incredible hardships a large number of survivors eventually reached the post at That Khe, only to find that it too had been abandoned. Thus they fell into the hands of the Viet Minh. One author has called the Cao Bang debacle "the greatest defeat in the history of French colonial warfare."[65] Truly, in the eyes of many Frenchmen, "the gods had fallen from their pedestals."[66] And not in the eyes of the French alone.

Cao Bang would not have happened if the French had had the kind of air power, especially helicopters, possessed by the Americans who succeeded them. But in the circumstances of the time, the real key to the Cao Bang disaster was French underestimation of the abilities of General Giap and his forces. The French would repeat this mistake at Dien Bien Phu. The Cao Bang episode was also, on a small scale, a foreshadowing of the disaster that would engulf the Army of South Viet Nam a quarter of a century later.

The most important French strongpoint of the entire border region was Lang Son, a city of 100,000 inhabitants. The events of Cao Bang persuaded the French to abandon Lang Son even before the Viet Minh had appeared near it. In order not to alert the enemy of their plans, the French did not blow up their stores. Hence, when Giap's forces marched into the abandoned city, they found tons of invaluable supplies waiting for them, including 10,000 75mm shells, thousands of automatic weapons, gasoline, clothing, and medicines enough to last for years.[67] Bernard Fall called Lang Son "France's greatest colonial defeat since Montcalm had died at Quebec."[68]

These disasters meant the end of French power north of the Red River Delta. Henceforth the Viet Minh could raid the Delta at will and retreat back into their border redoubt; they also had unrestricted access to China. In these border battles, the Viet Minh had employed mortars, bazookas, and other heavy weapons. Giap's manpower advantage over his enemies ran from three-to-one to eight-to-one.

The experience of the French and their outposts suggests at least two principles: (1) outposts are worthless unless they can be surely and safely supplied, and (2) it is safer for troops inside strongpoints to stay and try to fight off the enemy than to expose themselves to attack on inadequate roads.

These events of the fall of 1950 should have convinced the French that they could not hold onto Tonkin, that they should turn Hanoi-Haiphong into an enclave, regroup the rest of their forces into Cochinchina (Saigon and the Mekong Delta), and await better days, which might include more troops from France and more supplies from the United States. Instead, they continued with the same strategy and the same tactics until the end. In November 1951, French paratroopers descended upon Hoa Binh. The operation quickly outgrew French ability to reinforce and supply the place. Also, Giap was attacking with good weapons that he had obtained from the Chinese, including first-class American weapons captured in Korea. In February 1952 the French abandoned Hoa Binh in a two-day fighting retreat that eventually involved close to 20,000 French troops. In October 1952, Giap attacked French positions on the Nglia Lo Ridge: the French evacuated and managed to reach the safety of the Black River, with very heavy losses. In April 1953, French forces abandoned the fortifications at Sam Neua; they were cut to pieces, with only about 230 survivors from the original three battalions. The last of the great French outpost battles would, of course, occur at Dien Bien Phu.

THE FRENCH TRY TO REGROUP

The disasters of Cao Bang and Lang Son provoked Paris into recalling from Viet Nam both the high commissioner and the commanding general. The government named General Jean De Lattre de Tassigny to fill both positions. Brave and charismatic, De Lattre infused new vigor and heart into the French forces, whose morale had been badly damaged by the recent catastrophes along the Chinese border. He put a stop to plans to evacuate women and children from Tonkin, believing that French soldiers would fight better if the civilians stayed. De Lattre also concluded that French control of the rice crops of the Delta was having seriously negative effects on the enemy.[69] To restrict even further the flow of Delta rice to the insurgents, De Lattre began the construction of a line of fortifications around French-controlled territory. Eventually known as the De Lattre Line, by the end of 1951 it consisted of over 1,200 strongpoints constructed in groups of five or six, each group about a mile from another. He augmented the number of troops available for raids on enemy territory and laid plans for a major increase in the size of the loyal Vietnamese army. It was De Lattre who administered the severe defeats to Giap when the Viet Minh launched their ill-fated attacks on the Delta in spring 1951.

A sound strategist, popular with French soldiers and civilians, De Lattre in fact managed to change very little of the reality of the war in Tonkin. The De Lattre Line did not halt Viet Minh infiltration into the Delta; by 1952 they had at least 30,000 fighting men there. Although defense of the Delta tied down 100,000 French and allied forces, the Viet Minh actually controlled as many as 5,000 of the Delta's 7,000 villages.[70] The expanded Vietnamese army remained largely on paper. De Lattre had not retaken any territory held by the enemy and was responsible for the failed operation against Hoa Binh. Most of all, De Lattre did not even try to regain control over land communications with China: this was a clear sign of his conviction that the French could not win the war.[71] His death from cancer in Paris in January 1952 was undoubtedly a blow to French morale but probably a blessing for his reputation.

De Lattre's successor, Raoul Salan, decided to attack the Viet Minh supply and communications line along the Red River; this would draw Giap away from any operations in Laos, capture much valuable booty, and perhaps cut Giap off permanently from his main base. Operation Lorraine began in late October 1952, involving over 30,000 troops, the largest French force ever deployed in Indochina up to that time.[72] Operation Lorraine started out well, but it depended for supplies on only a single road and ran out of thrust at Phu Yen, about 60 miles northwest of Hanoi. On November 14, Salan ordered the units in the operation to return to the cover of the De Lattre Line. Viet Minh ambushes inflicted much damage; in exchange for destroying some Viet Minh supplies, the French suffered 500 casualties.

The next French commander in Indochina was Henri Navarre, who took over in May 1953. Navarre stunned his officers in his first formal address to them when he said, "I am counting on the contacts I shall have with you . . . to speedily remedy my inexperience."[73] When Navarre took command, the Viet Minh had about nine divisions operating in Tonkin; the French, because of their broad defensive strategy, had only the equivalent of three mobile divisions to meet them.[74] Navarre informed Paris that he could hold the Red River Delta and Cochinchina but could not do anything else unless he received substantial reinforcements. The government replied that Navarre must make no new plans that would require such reinforcements, but rather should tailor his plans to his means (in the circumstances, good advice).

THE BAO DAI SOLUTION

Like the British in Malaya, the French in Indochina treated minority tribesmen much better than the native majorities ever had. Consequently, Navarre was able to compensate somewhat for his lack of manpower by employing minority tribesmen behind Giap's lines. Some of these tribal units were very effective and tied up many Viet Minh battalions away from the main scene of action.[75] But the project was not very large, and the French High Command did not believe in the whole concept enough to expand it to its potential. Besides, the creation and maintenance of these irregular forces was hampered by a shortage of officers familiar with their ethnic and geographical background. The French Colonial Army rotated its units to posts all over the globe; hence there were never many true specialists in a particular area.[76] Some of these tribal units were still fighting the Communists as late as 1959, years after the French had departed Tonkin.

Clearly, the solution to French manpower problems was to build a real Vietnamese army. General Juin had called for the construction of such an army after the catastrophe of Lang Son, back in 1950. A substantial Vietnamese army could only be the instrument of an independent, anti-Communist Vietnamese state: hence the French decision to employ the "Bao Dai solution" against the Viet Minh.

Before the Japanese invasion, Bao Dai had been nominal emperor under French protection. When Japan surrendered, he wrote to General De Gaulle, President Truman, and Chiang Kai-shek appealing for the recognition of Vietnamese independence. But the August Revolution swiftly took control of Hanoi. Convinced that the Americans supported the Viet Minh, Bao Dai abdicated. Ho thereupon named him "supreme political adviser," seeking to attach Bao Dai's prestige to his new regime. Bao Dai soon realized that he was the tool of Communists and fled Viet Nam. Nevertheless, in June 1948, after two years of negotiations, he exploded a political bombshell by signing with the French a treaty beginning with the arresting sentence: "France solemnly recognizes the independence of Viet Nam."[77] This treaty, by capitalizing on the contrast between Ho Chi Minh's Marxist revolutionism and Bao Dai's traditional legitimacy, could have provided the framework on which to build a national Vietnamese army and defeat the Viet Minh.

The next year a Vietnamese military academy opened its doors, but the school attracted a disappointingly low number of qualified applicants, partly because the Vietnamese middle classes were disappointed by French reluctance to follow up on the promise of an independent state under Bao Dai.

Besides, the Vietnamese army received only secondhand French equipment.[78] The French never gave the Vietnamese troops enough training to familiarize them with their weapons and tactics. Instead, employing the excuse that Vietnamese units would learn fighting by fighting, the French threw them into combat against veteran Viet Minh forces much too early, with predictable results.[79] General De Lattre had intended to maintain the De Lattre Line with Vietnamese troops, freeing his French forces for aggressive assaults. But even though Bao Dai's government introduced conscription in the summer of 1951, enough Vietnamese soldiers were never forthcoming. General Salan planned to use the Vietnamese army mainly in Cochinchina, where the Viet Minh were unpopular and the French had the upper hand, but again lack of numbers, especially of Vietnamese officers, thwarted this project.

Nevertheless, in the 1950s fully half of the casualties on the anti–Viet Minh side were Vietnamese; in 1954, 300,000 Vietnamese were serving either under the French colors or those of Bao Dai, as compared to 120,000 French, Colonial, and Foreign Legion forces, and 300,000 in the Viet Minh. According to the standard formulas of counterguerrilla war, French and allied forces would have been enough to deal effectively with perhaps 50,000 guerrillas, but the Viet Minh had more than six times that number.[80]

COCHINCHINA

By 1953 the situation in Viet Nam seemed to be this: a substantial minority of Vietnamese supported the Viet Minh; a substantial minority opposed them; and a very large group, perhaps the largest of the three, stood with neither side.

But the picture varied greatly from one section of Viet Nam to another. All the serious fighting between the Viet Minh and the French and their Vietnamese allies took place in Tonkin. The Viet Minh weakness in the south had many causes. The famine of 1944–1945, which had brought the Communists so much favorable attention, had not struck in the south. The Chinese had occupied Tonkin until 1946, giving the Viet Minh time to get consolidated, whereas Cochinchina was back under French control by October 1945. The south was far away from the Chinese Communist border and its military supplies; the cohesive Catholic minority was aloof or hostile to the Viet Minh. Finally, the politically sophisticated population of Saigon was not attracted to the peasant-based Viet Minh.

But most important in explaining the weakness of the Viet Minh in the south were the religious sects, the Hoa Hao and the Cao Dai. Most southern Vietnamese outside Saigon belonged to one or the other. The well-armed sect militias and the Viet Minh had fought each other ferociously in the winter and spring of 1946. The sects were not exactly pro-French but were totally and irrevocably alienated from the Communists.

Immediately after the surrender of Japan, Paris appointed Admiral Thierry d'Argenlieu as high commissioner of Indochina. In June 1946, in an effort to save what he could from what appeared to be a French surrender to the Viet Minh, d'Argenlieu, "the most brilliant mind of the twelfth century,"[81] and his French and Vietnamese cohorts in the south proclaimed the "autonomous republic of Cochinchina."[82] But Paris abandoned the Cochinchina gambit (which may actually have been the best way to prevent a totally Communist Viet Nam) in favor of the Bao Dai solution, a plan to unite the urban areas with the sects and other anti–Viet Minh and moderate nationalist elements under French protection.

In 1950, an ill-advised Viet Minh rising in Cochinchina was cut to ribbons (a foreshadowing of Tet 1968). After that there would be very little fighting in the south until the French surrender. In the countryside the armed sects lived in uneasy peace with the French administration; in Saigon effective police work, the indifference of the population, and the terrible impression made by a Viet Minh bomb-throwing campaign in 1949 left the city without any sort of effective Viet Minh organization (the Viet Minh were weak in Hanoi as well).[83] From late 1952 until the collapse, not one major terroristic incident occurred in all of Saigon.[84]

With the French firmly in control of Saigon, supported by the Catholics and the prewar nationalist parties, with the sects and pro-French "warlords" dominating the rural areas, there was no space in Cochinchina for the growth or even the survival of a Viet Minh threat.[85] General Navarre at one time had wished to fall back to Cochinchina while holding the De Lattre Line and the rich and populous Delta area inside it and wait for U.S. supplies and the buildup of the Vietnamese army to turn the tide. But the French moved away from this eminently sensible strategy back to their outpost illusions, and to their final calamity: Dien Bien Phu.[86]

By 1954 the struggle had clearly become stalemated. Aside from lack of sufficient manpower, the French saw their principal problem in the fact that Giap had learned not to face them in pitched battles. As long as the war remained essentially guerrilla, the French would continue at a grave disadvantage. They must therefore entice Giap into offering a major battle, along the lines of his disastrous attacks at Vinh Yen and the Day River in 1951. Thus the French High Command came to the decision to build a fortress at Dien Bien Phu. This would serve several purposes. Minimally, by preventing the easy passage of Viet Minh troops from Viet Nam to Laos, it would shore up the pro-French regime there (enemy troops making this passage would probably wind up in southern Viet Nam anyway). More importantly, a French stronghold so far from its Red River Delta base would surely provide Giap with an irresistible temptation; he would send in his best regular units, which superior French firepower and training would then chop into pieces. The French believed that the Viet Minh possessed little heavy artillery. In any case, it would be impossible to transport sufficient artillery from the Chinese border through jungles and mountains to the Laotian border and keep it supplied with sufficient ammunition. And just for the sake of argument, even if the Viet Minh did bring artillery to bear on Dien Bien Phu, French gunners inside the fortress would destroy it. If the siege should go on longer than anticipated, headquarters at Hanoi would keep the defenders of Dien Bien Phu supplied—by air. So the French parachuted men and material into the valley of Dien Bien Phu.

Giap decided to take up the French challenge. Viet Minh casualty rates had been very high, and the great powers were preparing to gather at Geneva to deal with the Viet Nam situation. At Dien Bien Phu, Giap would have an overwhelming advantage in numbers, and the Viet Minh would be close to their base, while the French would be isolated from theirs. If all went well, Dien Bien Phu would be the chance to strike a powerful and perhaps decisive blow not at a fortress in Indochina but at opinion in metropolitan France and at the Geneva Conference. That is what Dien Bien Phu came to be about.

At Dien Bien Phu, about 13,000 French, colonial, and Vietnamese soldiers fought 100,000 Viet Minh. The battle began on March 13, 1954—with a Viet Minh artillery bombardment! The defenders of Dien Bien Phu knew immediately that they were lost.

The Communist artillery destroyed the landing strip in the first hours of the contest. Since no planes could land, food and ammunition had to be dropped into the shrinking perimeter of the fortress. The defenders needed approximately 200 tons of supplies a day, but French aircraft from Hanoi were able to deliver no more than 100 tons.[87] Much of this material fell into the hands of the enemy. The French had planned to evacuate the wounded at Dien Bien Phu by aircraft, but this was now impossible. Without adequate medical supplies and care, without even clean drinking water, the rapidly increasing numbers of seriously wounded at Dien Bien Phu endured truly terrible suffering.

The French had committed about one-twentieth of their forces to Dien Bien Phu, but Giap had committed one-half.[88] All this was foreseeable. What doomed the fortress was that the defenders soon faced a four-to-one Communist superiority in artillery. That the Viet Minh possessed such power, that they could haul heavy pieces to Dien Bien Phu, that they could transport enough ammunition for them—all this simply astounded the French. Knocking out the French artillery at Dien Bien Phu opened the way for the Viet Minh to bring their overwhelming numerical superiority to bear. "The failure at Dien Bien Phu was due to the fact that this isolated base was attacked by an enemy with artillery and antiaircraft."[89] Yes. And where, *where* were the French intelligence services?

The French had been underestimating their enemy for years; Dien Bien Phu was the payoff. Methodically surrounding the fortress, applying overwhelming power, the Communists captured its strongpoints one at a time until toward the end the defenders were holding an area no bigger than a football field.

The French might have tried to save Dien Bien Phu by mounting a rescue effort on the ground. This would have meant stripping every strategic place in the country of troops and sending a relief expedition across trackless wastes into the teeth of Viet Minh harassment, an expedition that might not arrive (or return) in time. Dien Bien Phu is more than 180 air miles from Hanoi.

Massive air attacks would have saved the garrison of Dien Bien Phu, but the French at the best of times had no more than 100 fighting aircraft operational, not nearly enough. In addition, the antiaircraft fire over Dien Bien Phu was thicker than that over Germany in World War II.[90] Many Viet Minh antiaircraft batteries had Chinese advisers.[91] What air power the French had sometimes worked against the defenders of the fortress: on April 15, a French pilot accidentally dropped out of his cockpit a packet of photographs of the whole battle area, and this invaluable intelligence was soon in the hands of General Giap.

Everyone knew from the first days of the battle that Dien Bien Phu was doomed; yet right up to the end hundreds of French and Vietnamese volunteers parachuted into the caldron. The whole world stopped to watch the last days of the drama. Exactly nine years after the surrender of Nazi Germany, the fortress fell. For years the French had wished to entice the Viet Minh into a major battle out in the open. When at Dien Bien Phu they got what they wanted, they lost. The 56-day battle was a metaphor for the entire French effort in Viet Nam: abundant heroism, questionable strategy, inadequate means.

While the French had suffered an utter defeat tactically, strategically Dien Bien Phu was in no way decisive, because the French still had 95 percent of their forces intact. Nevertheless, as the leaders of the Viet Minh had hoped, the fall of Dien Bien Phu broke the will of the French government to continue the war.

A conference of the great powers, along with delegations representing various forces in Indochina, opened in Geneva as Dien Bien Phu fell.[92] Elements of the Viet Minh leadership always believed that if the Geneva Conference had not met until later, the Communists would have been able to take over all of Viet Nam. But even though Pierre Mendès-France had become prime minister on a pledge to end the war quickly or resign, the French, backed by the Americans, were insisting on partition, that is, saving southern Viet Nam. Even in the bitter aftermath of Dien Bien Phu, the West was not without cards to play: the Viet Minh were tired, there was a great deal of hostility to the Viet Minh in the south, the Americans were increasing their aid to the French, and when the Viet Minh showed themselves opposed to partition Mendès-France ordered tropical inoculations for French troops in Germany.[93] The Soviets and Chinese wanted to make some settlement with Mendès-France, because if he failed he might be replaced with a conservative cabinet that would renew the fighting.

Thus under pressure from its Communist big brothers, the Viet Minh had to settle for partition. Bao Dai and his new prime minister, Ngo Dinh Diem, who claimed quite correctly to be the only legal government of all of Viet Nam, also opposed partition. But if partition there had to be, then the Viet Minh demanded that it be along the 13th parallel; this line, by giving South Viet Nam more compact borders, would in the long term have served it better than the 17th parallel on which the Geneva Conference finally settled.

THE VISIBLE COSTS OF THE WAR

A young French officer once remarked, "We French had come back to Indochina to fight a war of colonial reconquest, but very soon, almost in spite of ourselves . . . we have become the only force which keeps the Vietnamese from falling into the Kafkaesque world of Asiatic Communism."[94] What did this failed effort cost?

It cost the French ten times the value of their investments in Viet Nam, more than all the aid that France would receive under the Marshall Plan.[95] That money would easily be replaced. The cost in blood was of another order.

Approximately 74,000 soldiers from Metropolitan France were casualties; of these 21,000 died. This would be roughly equivalent to 110,000 American dead in 1993. There were perhaps 78,000 casualties among Foreign Legion and African units, of whom probably 22,000 died.[96]

The battlefield and the prison camp destroyed the cream of the French officer corps: 1,300 lieutenants alone, 4 generals, at least 21 sons of French marshals and generals.[97] By the 1950s, more French officers were being killed annually in Viet Nam than were graduating from the national military academy at St. Cyr.

Two thousand women served with the French ground forces, another 150 in the air force and navy. Almost 100 of these were killed in action.[98]

Vietnamese casualty figures are more imprecise. The best estimates may be that close to 80,000 Vietnamese lost their lives fighting the Viet Minh, in the ranks of the French or the Vietnamese National armies; this figure includes about 23,000 Vietnamese soldiers taken prisoner and never accounted for.[99]

Nobody knows how many Viet Minh died, but estimates run to 400,000. Civilian deaths almost certainly exceeded 500,000.

The moral right of the French to rule over the Vietnamese was, to say the least, highly debatable. But in 1948, France recognized, however halfheartedly, the independence of the state of Viet Nam under Bao Dai, and as time passed the de jure independence of that state would certainly have evolved into de facto independence. But Ho Chi Minh and his cohorts did not want an independent Viet Nam; they wanted an independent Viet Nam under their control, something quite different. And to achieve this, they were willing to see the blood of their countrymen spilled in frightful quantities. In the end, they obtained only half their goal and spent the next twenty years causing more Vietnamese blood to be spilled in order to have all things their own way.

THE VIEW FROM WASHINGTON

The famous Domino Principle or Domino Theory helped to shape the attitude and policies of the Truman Administration (1945–1953) toward the Viet Nam conflict. Major pronouncements of the National Security Council set forth the grim results for American foreign policy if Viet Nam fell to the Communists. "In the absence of effective and timely counteraction, the loss of any single country would probably lead to relatively swift submission to or an alignment with communism by the remaining countries of this group."[100] Above all, "the neighboring countries of Thailand and Burma could be expected to fall under Communist domination if Indochina were controlled by a Communist-dominated government. The balance of Southeast Asia would then be in grave danger."[101]

In the time of the Korean conflict, "the danger of overt military attack against Southeast Asia [was] inherent in the existence of a hostile and aggressive Communist China, but such an attack [was] less probable than continued communist efforts to achieve domination through subversion."[102]

And so what of it? Even assuming the validity of the Domino Principle, why was it necessary for Washington, already preoccupied with the economic reconstruction and military defense of Western Europe, to concern itself with subversion in Southeast Asia? Because the ascendancy of Communism in that region through armed subversion would have grave implications in other areas of the globe. If parts or all of Southeast Asia became Communist, it would "strengthen the claim that the advance of Communism is inexorable."[103] Indeed, the future of Japan–United States relations might be at stake: "the loss of Southeast Asia, especially of Malaya and Indonesia, could result in such economic pressures in Japan as to make it extremely difficult to prevent Japan's eventual accommodation to communism."[104] Obviously, therefore "it [was] important to United States security that all practicable measures be taken to prevent further Communist expansion in Southeast Asia."[105]

The Truman Administration had from the beginning of the war pressed France to grant real autonomy to Viet Nam, believing this to be the best way to undercut the appeal of the Viet Minh. When the French formally ratified Vietnamese independence in February 1950, President Truman recognized Bao Dai's government the next day. Washington nevertheless always felt that it had inadequate leverage with which to force Paris to see the war its way: after all, if pushed too hard, the French might pull out of Viet Nam completely. Besides, Washington's highest priority after 1948 was getting NATO started and Europe rearmed. The French weapon against Washington's pressure was European defense: without American aid in Viet Nam, the French hinted strongly that they would be forced to reconsider their participation in the Western military alliance.

Aware of France's manpower problems in Viet Nam and extremely reluctant to commit U.S. ground forces, especially after the outbreak of the Korean War, the Truman Administration constantly suggested that the French train and equip a large Vietnamese national army.[106] The Americans knew that the French were reluctant to do this, and that many Vietnamese, especially the middle class, were less than enthusiastic about fighting for nothing better than the perpetuation of French rule, however thickly disguised.

In effect, Washington wanted the French to fight and beat the Communists in Viet Nam and then leave. But as French Ambassador Georges Bonnet said to Secretary of State Acheson, it would be difficult to get the French army to fight and die for Vietnamese independence.[107] Besides, what would be the effect on France's position in North Africa if the French withdrew from Indochina?

The United States began making serious financial contributions to the French effort in 1950, which by 1954 totalled $1 billion (the equivalent of many billions in 1993 dollars).[108] When Dwight Eisenhower became president in January 1953, the Americans were paying approximately 75 percent of the costs of the French military effort in Indochina.[109] Even though Washington might have expected to exert great influence in these circumstances, its desires to see the French implement true Vietnamese independence and build a powerful Vietnamese army were fruitless. The French even opposed the idea of any American assistance going directly to Bao Dai's government; they insisted that all aid be channeled through them. When the American military mission arrived in Viet Nam in August 1950, the French forbade its members to have any contact with the Vietnamese government. Nevertheless, Washington apparently expected a French victory until 1953 and still had some hopes after that date.[110]

The new Eisenhower Administration took Viet Nam very seriously. As Richard Nixon wrote: "We were all convinced [in 1953] that unless the Communists knew that their so-called wars of national liberation would be resisted by military means if necessary, they would not stop until they had taken over Southeast Asia just as they had taken over Eastern Europe."[111] Viewing nationalism and Communism as ultimately and radically incompatible, Secretary of State John Foster Dulles longed to see doomed European colonialism in Asia replaced with independent nationalist regimes.[112] But anachronistic French ideas of empire were delaying the appearance of such governments. Thus on one hand Washington wished to help the French defeat the Viet Minh, but on the other it saw continued French rule as an obstacle to a stable settlement in the long-term interests of the West.

The progressive deterioration of the French position in Viet Nam deeply disturbed Eisenhower. Why were the French, with their technical superiority and massive American assistance, unable to bring the conflict to a successful conclusion?[113] "The French could win in six months if the people were with them," he told Dulles on April 3, 1954.[114] For Eisenhower, sending U.S. ground forces to Viet Nam was out of the question: "there seemed to me no dearth of defensive ground strength in Indochina."[115] The main French problem was that they would not effectively employ the strength they had; Eisenhower was therefore skeptical that the French would be able to win, even with U.S. troops assisting them.

THE AMERICANS AND DIEN BIEN PHU

In his *No More Viet Nams*, Richard Nixon identifies the refusal of President Eisenhower to intervene at Dien Bien Phu as the first critical mistake that the United States made in Viet Nam.[116] On April 5, 1954, and later that same month, the French government requested United States air strikes to prevent the collapse of the fortress.[117] The CIA was in fact flying relief missions to Dien Bien Phu through their Civil Air Transport company. But this was not nearly enough.

The previous January, General Walter Bedell Smith and Admiral Arthur Radford advised President Eisenhower that he should consider the employment of naval and air units in Viet Nam only as a last resort and certainly not with ground forces.[118] Many high-ranking officers questioned the possibility of limiting intervention against the Viet Minh to air and naval forces alone. For one thing, any U.S. air base located in Indochina would need ground forces to protect it. As Vice Admiral A. C. Davis observed, "there is no cheap way to fight a war, once committed."[119]

The Chiefs of Staff, under Admiral Radford, prepared a study called Operation Vulture, which looked at the feasibility of using tactical nuclear weapons to save Dien Bien Phu; army strategists concluded that "the use of atomic weapons in Indochina would not reduce the number of ground forces required to achieve a military victory [there]."[120] Actually, the thinking of the Joint Chiefs of Staff was rapidly crystallizing against any American intervention in Viet Nam at all. After the fall of Dien Bien Phu they would send a memorandum to the secretary of defense stating in part,

The Joint Chiefs of Staff desire to point out that, from the point of view of the United States, with reference to the Far East as a whole, Indochina is devoid of decisive military objectives and the allocation of more than token U.S. armed forces in Indochina would be a serious diversion of limited U.S. capabilities.[121]

On April 28, 1954, President Eisenhower received a National Intelligence Estimate stating that the fall of Dien Bien Phu need not mean the collapse of French resistance in Viet Nam; the political consequences would be greater than the military consequences.[122]

President Eisenhower was extremely skeptical of the possibility that air strikes alone would have any serious effects on the war. He had warned the French against their Dien Bien Phu venture in the beginning; now he had "no intention of using United States forces in any limited action when the force employed would probably not be decisively effective."[123] What kind of force, then, would be effective? Army Chief of Staff Matthew B. Ridgeway told the president that the United States would have to go into Viet Nam with from 7 to 12 divisions, perhaps a quarter of a million men.[124] Supported by Walter Bedell Smith, director of Central Intelligence from 1950 to 1953, Eisenhower utterly rejected the idea of sending large ground forces.[125] He believed that the American people would not accept such a massive unilateral commitment, that a huge American presence in Viet Nam would completely undercut U.S. responsibilities elsewhere, especially in Europe, and that it would destroy the principle of collective defense against Communist expansion that Truman and Eisenhower had labored so hard to establish.[126] An army position paper of April 1954 opposed the use of U.S. ground combat units in Indochina.[127] Besides, the French did not want allied ground forces in Viet Nam, which they viewed as completely an internal French affair; they wanted American air strikes alone, an option most American military leaders opposed.[128]

President Eisenhower thus faced an extremely difficult problem. He believed that the complete loss of Indochina to Communist military conquest would have adverse long-range effects on the security of the United States. He also believed that to a large degree the French had got themselves into this predicament by not granting more self-rule to the Vietnamese.[129] Then there were the domestic political considerations that no president can ignore. Eisenhower was keenly aware that the most popular act of his presidency so far had been the ending of the Korean Conflict; and he strongly suspected that the American people would reject large-scale intervention in Viet Nam. On the other hand, an outright turning down of French pleas for help with Dien Bien Phu could have serious consequences for NATO. Thus, Eisenhower informed Paris that the United States would intervene in Viet Nam under certain conditions. One of Eisenhower's principal biographers has offered the judgment that he knowingly set down conditions impossible to fulfill.[130] The Eisenhower Administration would enter the combat in Viet Nam if (1) France and the Associated States of Indochina requested it, (2) Britain, Australia, and New Zealand agreed to participate, and (3) both houses of Congress consented.[131] The second condition was the most crucial, because without allied collaboration there was no chance at all of congressional approval.

The British government was unconvinced of the Domino Theory's validity outside Indochina. It also did not believe that the fall of Dien Bien
Phu need bring the French effort to an end. Prime Minister Churchill made
it clear that Britain would not send any troops to Viet Nam, observing that
"if his people had not been willing to fight to save India for themselves,
he did not think they would be willing to fight to save Indochina for the
French."[132] Besides, Churchill was worried that Western intervention in
Viet Nam might be countered by Chinese intervention, as in Korea.

On April 2, a delegation of congressional leaders of both parties told
Secretary of State Dulles that they could not authorize President Eisenhower
to intervene at Dien Bien Phu without British participation. Leading Republican senators were especially determined to prevent any U.S. involvement in Vietnamese combat: the GOP had successfully branded the
Democrats as the war party in the 1952 campaign and prided itself on the
end of the Korean stalemate. Thus, the United States did not intervene to
save Dien Bien Phu, and the Geneva Conference partitioned Viet Nam.

President Eisenhower and Secretary Dulles were not completely sorry to
see French rule in Indochina come to an end. They believed that the French
failure there was rooted in the attempt to hold onto an anachronistic colonial
position. Unburdened by this selfish legacy, the United States would now
assist the new state of South Viet Nam and succeed where the French had
failed.[133]

REFLECTION: WHY THE FRENCH LOST

Americans find it very tempting to blame the French for everything that
went wrong in Viet Nam, not only for their inability to defeat the Viet
Minh but also for setting the stage on which the American tragedy would
soon commence. The standard American evaluation of the Franco-
Vietnamese situation goes something like this: If the French, it is said, had
only realized that World War II had finished classical colonialism in Asia,
they could have avoided war, or at least avoided defeat, by making some
prudent concessions to the rising tide of Vietnamese nationalism. The
French should have heeded American advice, granted the Vietnamese real
self-government, and helped them to raise a powerful Vietnamese army to
defeat the Communists. But the French rejected these American aims. Their
military reentry into Vietnam in 1945–1946 had been not anti-Communist
but imperialist. Humiliated by their experiences in World War II, blind to
the fact that Europe's brief if impressive dominion was finished, the French
dealt arrogantly, even brutally, with the Vietnamese, thus forcing nearly
all Vietnamese nationalists into the arms of Ho Chi Minh. In fighting against
the Viet Minh, the French were fighting against the tide of history. In the
succinct summary of one eminent authority, "to have underrated the force

of nationalist feeling and to have disregarded all opportunities for genuine compromise may be called the basic French mistakes in Indochina."[134]

WAS NATIONALISM THE KEY?

This version of events is certainly not without value. Nationalist sentiment would probably have forced the French out of Viet Nam eventually—but not necessarily in 1954, and not necessarily under the leadership of the Viet Minh. However satisfying to Americans it may have been (and still is) to say "the French lost in Viet Nam because they were engulfed by the irresistible tide of nationalism," such impressive metaphors obscure certain empirical aspects of the conflict.[135]

In the first place, it is too simple to view the Viet Minh as the mere and sole embodiment of a righteous and spontaneous nationalist upsurge against French oppression. Until 1940 the Vietnamese Communists were a minuscule group with no realistic prospects for coming to power. It was World War II that established them as a serious force through the anti-Japanese Viet Minh front. Because the Japanese occupation army had been unconcerned with maintaining order outside the urban areas, the Viet Minh had been able to establish their control over extensive areas of the Tonkinese countryside. In these districts they would later use not only political slogans and programs but also coercion and even terror against the families of recalcitrant peasants.[136] It was the mantle not of anti-French independence but of anti-Japanese resistance that procured help for the Viet Minh from the Allied powers. It was the war-created famine of 1944–1945 that allowed the Viet Minh to attract the favorable attention of the Tonkinese peasantry.[137] While the effects of famine still ravaged the northern provinces, Japan's unexpected surrender extended the power vacuum from the countryside into Hanoi itself.

The Japanese had not only ended French control but also shattered the myth of French invincibility. This unexpected cataclysm opened up vast new possibilities. Then, as the Japanese had broken the power of the French, so the Americans broke the power of the Japanese. It was the collapse of the Japanese, not the strength of the Viet Minh, that enabled Ho Chi Minh to seize Hanoi, however briefly, and set himself up as a legitimate and plausible alternative to the French.

Yet, even under these classical revolutionary circumstances, the August Revolution was a small, elite affair, unfolding mainly in the environs of Hanoi. If in 1945 the French had "recognized the changed times," that is, if they had decided to grant independence to Viet Nam right away, it would have meant in practical terms handing power over to the Viet Minh, a group which, however disciplined and determined, was small, urban, Marxist (that is, culturally alien) and thus in no honest way representative of the majority of the population.

Another problem with viewing the war as a straightforward contest between French imperialism and Vietnamese nationalism is this: Ho Chi Minh and the other Communist leaders of the Viet Minh waged bloody combat against authentic nationalist groups from the beginning. Great numbers of Vietnamese fought, in the armies and militias of the sects, of the Catholics, of the French, of Bao Dai, against the Viet Minh. After the French had gone, even greater numbers would fight to preserve the South Vietnamese Republic, and many of these would eventually flee their native land rather than live under Ho's conquering successors.[138] If the main weapon of the Viet Minh was nationalism, from the 1940s through the 1970s impressive numbers of Vietnamese were strangely invulnerable to it.

Then there is this inconvenient fact: during the very years that the French were losing in Viet Nam, the British were dealing quite efficiently with a Communist-racial revolution in Malaya. The British in Malaya were just as foreign, just as racially alien, as the French in Viet Nam. Why did not "the inexorable tide of history" inundate British Malaya? Of the many differences between the two cases, was the most significant difference perhaps the fact that in Malaya the insurgents had no sanctuary?

Clearly, the formula "Viet Minh = nationalism = irresistible force" needs some more exploration.

THE REVOLUTIONARY ALLIANCE

European imperialism in Asia eventually created a native elite of teachers, lawyers, journalists, writers. Educated in European schools, either at home or in the imperial country, these elements came into contact with such concepts as the juridical equality of all persons, government by consent, and the nation-state as the preferred form of political organization: in short, the Principles of 1789. The educated middle class was also that segment of society most likely to have frequent contact with Europeans; often the latter were occupants of positions in government and business that the native educated elites would have liked to fill themselves. For the urban middle class, national independence and personal advancement coincided. Hence the middle class became the vehicle of nationalism (and vice versa).

So it was in French Viet Nam. In the early decades of the twentieth century, a growing number of Vietnamese received an education in French-run schools. Many of these graduates quite naturally aspired to positions of leadership in the country's administration, professions, and businesses. But educated Vietnamese found themselves second-class citizens in their own country. Many positions, and almost all the top ones in every field, were reserved for Frenchmen. Where they did obtain employment, they typically found themselves working under Frenchmen with less education than they had. A Frenchman doing the same job as a Vietnamese would receive from two to five times the salary. In 1937, there were three times as many Frenchmen working for the government in Indochina, with a population of 30 million, as there were Britons working for the government in India, with 300 million. In Hanoi, Frenchmen were even serving as traffic policemen as late as 1953. In dramatic contrast, before World War II government services in the Philippines, including police, customs, and health, were staffed almost exclusively by Filipinos.[139]

The twentieth-century obsession with economics and the so-called class struggle has obscured just how much the desire of middle-class intellectuals to get into power has shaped the history of our era.[140] Yet both the lack of suitable employment and the artificial roadblocks to positions of authority for educated Vietnamese are the very roots of modern revolution in Viet Nam: "for most of those who became revolutionaries, it was clear that their own opportunities for advancement were inseparably bound up with eliminating French rule in Viet Nam."[141] The leaders of the Vietnamese revolution, like those of the Bolshevik and National-Socialist revolutions, were upwardly mobile elements who had experienced frustration of their ambitions.

The French unquestionably undermined themselves by first producing an educated Vietnamese middle class and then blocking the predictable and legitimate ambitions of that class. But this mistaken policy would not have produced a revolutionary movement capable of defeating the French. By itself, the Vietnamese middle class lacked the strength even to offer the French a serious challenge.

The attractions of nationalism to the middle classes of a colonialized country are clear. On the other hand, nationalism has not normally had great effect on the peasantry. Words like "nation," "independence," and "revolution"—these form the vocabulary of city men with soft hands and agile tongues. Uncomfortable with political abstractions, preoccupied with the mundane but essential aspects of everyday life, peasants tend to identify the motherland with the village. If they adopt a broader identification, it is most often in religious rather than political-national terms. Peasants had relatively little contact with the Europeans, did not perceive them as competitors for jobs, and often found them not much more objectionable than the previous native overlords or their ethnically different neighbors.

Thus, the middle class (and especially the "intelligentsia") embraces the idea of national independence but lacks the numbers to challenge the imperial power effectively. On the other hand, while the peasants have the requisite numbers, they find nationalistic concepts and slogans irrelevant. The revolution requires an alliance between intellectuals and peasants—between ideas and numbers. The central problem—aside from military inferiority—facing those who would make a nationalist revolution in a predominantly peasant society is for the revolutionary elite, educated city people psychologically cut off from the mass of their countrymen, to discover some way to arouse and organize great numbers of peasants to fight for independence.[142] This is a very difficult task, and it is one of the most important reasons that true revolutions have been so rare. Ho Chi Minh's Leninist and Comintern training undoubtedly made him especially sensitive to the necessity and complexity of constructing an alliance with the peasantry.[143]

If the foreign rulers are brutal, like the Japanese in China and the Soviets in Afghanistan, they will themselves force peasants into the arms of the revolutionaries. But however grave its shortcomings or surprising its insensitivities, French rule in Viet Nam, at least in the twentieth century, was not brutal. Before the Japanese invasion, keeping the peace among 30,000,000 Vietnamese required the presence of only 11,000 French regular troops.[144]

The Communists therefore erected their revolutionary alliance of intellectuals and peasants on the platform of distributing the wealth of the French and their rich Vietnamese collaborators. Since the execution of this program required the expulsion of the French, the social revolution had to become a nationalist revolution. Ho, Giap, Pham Van Dong—every one a European–educated son of privilege—sought to mobilize the peasantry by portraying the French not only as colonialists (not per se very offensive to the peasantry) but as the guarantors of a social order that worked to the detriment of the peasant majority. During the anti-Japanese struggle the Viet Minh sought to downplay class antagonisms in the interest of uniting all Vietnamese in the patriotic struggle and attracting help from the Anglo-Saxon powers. This deemphasis on social revolution was unpopular; poorer peasants saw little reason to risk life and limb against the Japanese merely in the interest of obtaining some reduction in their rent.

It is by no means obvious, therefore, that the French faced the choice of either granting complete and immediate independence to the elite group around Bao Dai or the other one around Ho Chi Minh or suffering inevitable expulsion at the hands of an aroused Vietnamese nationalism. On the contrary, by carrying out land reform or by reducing those taxes and curbing those landlord practices that the peasantry perceived as unjust, the French might well have loosened or even severed the connection between the irreconcilable revolutionaries and the potentially very reconcilable peasantry.

But the French did not seriously address the socioeconomic aspirations of the peasantry. Instead, they sought to maintain their control through military force. Later, they tried to split the nationalist middle class and isolate the Viet Minh by setting up a self-governing Vietnamese state under Bao Dai. This was potentially a successful gambit. Certainly Bao Dai, the representative of Annamese legitimacy who needed help from the French, was no less Vietnamese than Ho Chi Minh, the Moscow-trained Leninist who needed help from the Chinese. And Bao Dai's state, which had diplomatic recognition by the Americans, the British, and others, would almost certainly have evolved toward total independence while allowing the French to retain an important role in Vietnamese society. But even here the French missed their opportunity; they were grudging and graceless in their dealings with Bao Dai and his government, undermining its legitimacy in the eyes of the very Vietnamese it was supposed to attract. Thus the more intransigent nationalists like Ngo Dinh Diem refused to join the Bao Dai government. And then the battle of Dien Bien Phu cut the ground from under French interest in the royalist experiment.

OTHER IMPORTANT REASONS FOR FRENCH FAILURE

Vietnamese nationalism played an important role in the French debacle, principally by providing a legitimizing ideology for frustrated Vietnamese intellectuals. But other powerful factors were operating as well. Prominent among these were political divisions in France, military mistakes in Viet Nam, and the actions of third countries, most of all the Chinese.

Deep political cleavages and uncertainties afflicted the French political class. From the bombardment of Haiphong to the fall of Dien Bien Phu, France had no less than sixteen prime ministers, as well as eight commanders in Viet Nam. In the 1951 national elections anticonstitutional parties received over 47 percent of the vote. These domestic difficulties were not caused solely by the war in Indochina, but they certainly made a single-minded prosecution of it impossible.

Early in 1947, the Viet Minh theoretician Truong Chinh wrote that the longer the war went on, the more the Viet Minh would find allies inside France. He was right.[145] France's free press happily published all kinds of information about the war, which the Viet Minh happily received.[146] Many Frenchmen had lost faith in the right of Europeans to rule over distant peoples, and their number was growing. When French cabinets tried to switch the moral basis of the war from preservation of colonial grandeur to resistance to Communist expansion, many of the French were unwilling to fight Communism at so high a price in an arena so far away. Besides, there were plenty of Communists at home: in the early 1950s the French Communist Party was the largest in the nation. After Ho Chi Minh openly proclaimed his unity with the international Marxist-Leninist cause, the French Communists mobilized against the war: they attacked the moral basis of the conflict, they urged desertion and sabotage in the army, they actually stoned hospital trains unloading wounded soldiers in their home towns.[147] It would be an understatement to say that such actions, along with defeatist and "war criminal" propaganda emanating from other sections of French society, damaged army morale.[148] The army of France began to act like one "that does not have the nation solidly behind it, whose heart is not wholly engaged and whose approach is merely professional."[149]

Far away in Viet Nam, allies or would-be allies of the French were not unaware of these currents within France, and one can only imagine the effect on anti-Communist Vietnamese of speeches like the one in which Pierre Mendès-France warned in December 1951 that France could not go on stripping her European and North African forces to find men for Viet Nam.

The Japanese conquest had gravely undermined the prestige of France. The only real hope for reestablishing it was to make a display of military power that would overawe the Vietnamese. But the French were both unwilling to send many of their own young men to Viet Nam and unable to come up with a formula that would have provided enough Vietnamese troops. Thus the Viet Minh fought a total war on their home ground for the highest stakes; the French fought a limited war in a faraway land for hotly debated aims. That was the essence of the strategic situation in Viet Nam from 1946 to 1954. Hence General Navarre, reflecting on the conflict, identified the first cause of the French defeat as "inadequacy of means."[150]

This assessment by Navarre, however, does not fill in the entire picture. Halfhearted support for the war in France explains why the French command in Hanoi had numbers of troops and aircraft inadequate to the kind of war they were pursuing. It does not explain why the French command did not eventually adapt their method of fighting to their means. French air power was weak in Viet Nam, yes; but what kind of airpower did the Americans have against Aguinaldo? American air strikes might have saved Dien Bien Phu, yes; but did not the French put themselves into Dien Bien Phu in the first place?

By 1950 at the latest, the most sensible French option would have been to play for time by employing a very conservative strategy: holding the Red River Delta with armed force and Cochinchina with political support while slowly building up an adequate Vietnamese army. Instead, the French forces constantly violated "the first great rule of war in Indochina, the rule which states that every undertaking which is not a total success is fated to become a total disaster."[151] The combination of grandiose schemes with inadequate resources meant that most French military operations were "both parsimonious and at the same time exceedingly costly."[152]

The key to the French failure to adapt their strategy to their means was that they consistently underestimated Giap and the Viet Minh: their numbers, their equipment, and their capabilities.[153] Dien Bien Phu was only the most spectacular result of this flawed evaluation of the enemy.

Then there was China. If France was psychologically exhausted, politically divided and geographically remote, Maoist China was none of these things. The role of the Viet Minh's sanctuary-cornucopia across the Chinese border after 1949 cannot be exaggerated; without it the Viet Minh would have had to wage war in a much lower key.[154] France's allies did not like so many French troops fighting in Indochina instead of bolstering NATO, doubted her ability to win, and consequently skimped on aid to her. In contrast, General Giap's Chinese allies believed he could win, wanted him to, and gave him a great deal of assistance.[155] Chinese artillery and oil reached Giap's forces in crucial quantities, and after the Korean truce of 1953 such aid greatly increased. By the time of Dien Bien Phu, perhaps 40,000 Viet Minh soldiers had received training inside China.[156] And over the heads of the generals in Hanoi, over the heads of the politicians in Paris, there constantly floated the black cloud of potential Chinese invasion of Tonkin, against which French resistance could have availed nothing. The dreaded specter of a Chinese inundation helps explain in part the reluctance of French cabinets to send sufficient forces to Viet Nam.

The nature of the French defeat appears most clearly if one considers those conditions that would have produced the continuation of French power. They include:

1. either a much larger commitment of troops and resources from Metropolitan France or an adjustment of French strategy to French resources;
2. a socioeconomic program that effectively addressed some fundamental peasant grievances;
3. the creation of a large and well-equipped Vietnamese army; and
4. the diplomatic or military closing of the Chinese border.

If any two of these conditions had been present, a French defeat would have been very unlikely; but of course all four were absent.

Vietnamese nationalism, Japanese imperialism, Chinese proximity, American doubts, and French hubris all contributed significantly to the outcome of the conflict. One might expect that efforts to assess the relative importance of these factors would have preoccupied the Americans as they took up the burden of anti-Communist resistance in Viet Nam. In fact, however, "the French experience in Indochina was almost totally written off and disregarded."[157]

NOTES

1. Bernard Fall, *Street without Joy* (Harrisburg, PA: Stackpole, 1964), p. 314n.
2. Dennis J. Duncanson, *Government and Revolution in Viet Nam* (New York: Oxford University Press, 1968), p. 128.
3. Ellen Hammer, *The Struggle for Indochina, 1940–1955* (Stanford, CA: Stanford University Press, 1966), p. 79.
4. Duncanson, *Government and Revolution*, p. 140; see also *Thirty Years of Struggle of the Party* (Hanoi, 1960); William J. Duiker, *The Communist Road to Power in Viet Nam* (Boulder, CO: Westview, 1981), p. 45.
5. Douglas Pike, *History of Vietnamese Communism, 1925–1976* (Stanford, CA: Hoover Institution, 1978), p. 20.
6. Duncanson, *Government and Revolution*, p. 146.
7. Duiker, *Communist Road to Power*, p. 26.
8. The similarities in this program to that of the former Socialist revolutionary–

turned-fascist Benito Mussolini is striking. See Anthony James Joes, *Mussolini* (New York: Watts, 1982), Chapter 5; A. James Gregor, *The Fascist Persuasion in Radical Politics* (Princeton, NJ: Princeton University Press, 1974).

9. Samuel L. Popkin, *The Rational Peasant* (Berkeley: University of California Press, 1979), p. 218; Paul Ely, *Lessons of the War in Indochina*, trans. (Santa Monica, CA: Rand Corporation, 1967), vol. 2, p. 32.

10. Chalmers Johnson, *Autopsy on People's War* (Berkeley: University of California Press, 1973), p. 12.

11. Hoang Van Chi, *From Colonialism to Communism: A Case History of North Viet Nam* (New York: Praeger, 1964), p. 30.

12. Robert J. O'Neill, *General Giap* (New York: Praeger, 1969), p. 29.

13. Peter M. Dunn, *The First Viet Nam War* (New York: St. Martin's, 1985).

14. Duiker, *Communist Road to Power*, p. 103.

15. John T. McAlister, *Viet Nam: The Origins of Revolution* (Garden City, NY: Doubleday-Anchor, 1971), p. 217; Dunn, *First Viet Nam War*, p. 23.

16. Duiker, *Communist Road to Power*, p. 107; Philippe Devillers, *Histoire du Viet-Nam de 1940 à 1952*, 3d ed. (Paris: Editions du Seuil, 1952), p. 186; Dunn, *First Viet Nam War*, p. 43ff.

17. "It was the acquiescence of the Japanese rather than Viet Minh strength which ensured Communist predominance over the disoriented Vietnamese caretaker government." McAlister, *Viet Nam: Origins*, p. 149; also Duiker, *Communist Road to Power*, p. 107; Hammer, *Struggle for Indochina*, p. 101; Bernard Fall, *The Two Viet Nams: A Political and Military Analysis*, 2d ed., rev. (New York: Praeger, 1967), p. 65; Huynh Kim Khanh, *Vietnamese Communism, 1925–1945* (Ithaca, NY: Cornell University Press, 1982), p. 335; Truong Chinh, *Primer for Revolt*, (New York: Praeger, 1963), p. 37n. Bernard Fall says some Nazis stranded in Hanoi when the Japanese surrendered also decided to stay and fight on Ho's side, *Street without Joy*, p. 29.

18. Joseph Buttinger, *A Dragon Defiant: A Short History of Viet Nam* (New York: Praeger, 1972), p. 86.

19. Truong Chinh, *Primer for Revolt*, p. 24.

20. Fall, *Two Viet Nams*, p. 101; McAlister, *Viet Nam: Origins*, pp. 190–92; Lucien Bodard, *The Quicksand War: Prelude to Viet Nam* (Boston: Little, Brown, 1967), pp. 208–9; Hammer, *Struggle for Indochina*, pp. 158, 176.

21. Hoang Van Chi, *From Colonialism to Communism*, p. 44; Robert F. Turner, *Vietnamese Communism: Its Origins and Development* (Stanford, CA: Hoover Institution, 1975), pp. 8, 9, 11; Pike, *History of Vietnamese Communism*, p. 29; "Mendacity was a cornerstone of Ho's career and that of his party" (Robert M. Blum, *Drawing the Line: The Origin of the American Containment Policy in East Asia* [New York: Norton, 1982], p. 218).

22. McAlister, *Viet Nam: Origins*, p. 221; Turner, *Vietnamese Communism*, p. 48; Devillers, *Histoire du Viet-Nam*, p. 201.

23. Buttinger, *Dragon Defiant*, p. 85.

24. Fall, *Two Viet Nams*, pp. 73–74.

25. O'Neill, *General Giap*, p. 31.

26. For an account of this episode sympathetic to the French see Fall, *Two Viet Nams*, pp. 75–76.

27. Alexander Woodside, *Community and Revolution in Modern Viet Nam* (Boston: Houghton Mifflin, 1976).

28. Truong Chinh, *Primer for Revolt*, p. 180.

29. Ely, *Lessons of the War in Indochina*, p. 162.

30. George K. Tanham, *Communist Revolutionary Warfare: From the Viet Minh to the Viet Cong*, rev. ed. (New York: Praeger, 1967), p. 84; and Truong Chinh, *Primer for Revolt*, passim.

31. Tanham, *Communist Revolutionary Warfare*, p. 64.

32. The Pentagon Papers: The Defense Department History of United States Decisionmaking on Viet Nam, vol. 1 (Boston: Beacon Press, 1971), p. 24 (hereinafter abbreviated PP).

33. Truong Chinh, *Primer for Revolt*, p. 158.

34. O'Neill, *General Giap*, p. 45.

35. Tanham, *Communist Revolutionary Warfare*, p. 39ff.

36. Le Monde, quoted in Bernard Fall, *Hell in a Very Small Place* (Philadelphia: Lippincott, 1967), pp. 20–21.

37. Hammer, *Struggle for Indochina*, p. 248.

38. Roger Trinquier, *Modern Warfare: A French View of Counterinsurgency*, trans. Daniel Lee (New York: Praeger, 1964), p. 98.

39. Fall, *Street without Joy*, p. 39; O'Neill, *General Giap*, p. 99.

40. Phillip B. Davidson, *Viet Nam at War: The History, 1946–1975* (Novato, CA: Presidio, 1988), p. 13.

41. O'Neill, *General Giap*, p. 90.

42. Ely, *Lessons of the War in Indochina*, p. 59.

43. Ibid., pp. 193, 217, 161.

44. Ibid., p. 152.

45. Ibid., pp. 93, 216.

46. The French had faced similar problems, and made similar errors, in their campaign of conquest in Tonkin in the 1890s. See, for example, J. Kim Munholland, " 'Collaboration Strategy' and the French Pacification of Tonkin, 1885–1897," *Historical Journal*, vol. 24, no. 3 (1981).

47. Tanham, *Communist Revolutionary Warfare*, pp. 107–10; Denis Warner, *Certain Victory: How Hanoi Won the War* (Kansas City: Sneed, Andrews and McMeel, 1978), p. 89.

48. Ely, *Lessons of the War in Indochina*, p. 299.

49. Fall, *Street without Joy*, p. 242.

50. Davidson, *Viet Nam at War*, p. 49; Tanham, *Communist Revolutionary Warfare*, p. 9; Bodard, *Quicksand War*, p. 13.

51. Ely, *Lessons of the War in Indochina*, p. 249.

52. Trinquier, *Modern Warfare*, pp. 8–9, 58, and 65.

53. Ely, *Lessons of the War in Indochina*, pp. 110, 91, and passim.

54. Ibid., p. 200.

55. Ibid., p. 34.

56. Tanham, *Communist Revolutionary Warfare*, p. 90.

57. Bodard, *Quicksand War*, p. 239.

58. Ibid., p. 53.

59. Fall, *Street without Joy*, p. 252.

60. Ibid., p. 354.

61. Ely, *Lessons of the War in Indochina*, p. 166.

62. Ibid., p. 76.

63. Bodard, *Quicksand War*, pp. 330–335.

64. Ibid., p. 54.

65. Donald Lancaster, *The Emancipation of French Indochina* (London: Oxford University Press, 1961), p. 218.

66. Bodard, *Quicksand War*, p. 283.

67. Ibid., p. 323; Fall, *Street without Joy*, p. 33.

68. Ibid., p. 30.

69. Davidson, *Viet Nam: Origins*, p. 71.

70. Lancaster, *Emancipation of French Indochina*, p. 265; Tanham, *Communist Revolutionary Warfare*, p. 102; Fall, *Street without Joy*, p. 180.

71. Lancaster, *Emancipation of French Indochina*, p. 242. The French had made little headway in their campaign of conquest in Tonkin in the 1890s until they had by various expedients secured the Chinese border; see Munholland, "Collaboration Strategy."

72. Fall, *Street without Joy*, p. 78.

73. Lancaster, *Emancipation of French Indochina*, p. 264.

74. Ibid., p. 265.

75. Ely, *Lessons of the War in Indochina*, p. 156.

76. Ibid., p. 158.

77. Devillers, *Histoire du Viet-Nam*, p. 431.

78. Fall, *Two Viet Nams*, p. 200.

79. Ely, *Lessons of the War In Indochina*, p. 250 and passim.

80. Henri Navarre, *Agonie de l'Indochine*, rev. ed. (Paris: Plon, 1956), p. 46; Edgar O'Ballance gives different figures for Spring 1953 in *The Indo-China War, 1945–1954* (London: Faber and Faber, 1964), pp. 195–96.

81. Fall, *Two Viet Nams*, p. 72.

82. Devillers, *Histoire du Viet-Nam*, pp. 248–70.

83. Duiker, *Communist Road to Power*, p. 152.

84. Fall, *Street without Joy*, p. 61.

85. Duncanson, *Government and Revolution*, p. 189.

86. The best books on this epic encounter include Fall, *Hell in a Very Small Place*; and Jules Roy, *The Battle of Dien Bien Phu*, trans. Robert Baldick (New York: Harper and Row, 1965); but see also Navarre, *Agonie de L'Indochine*.

87. Davidson, *Viet Nam at War*, p. 219.

88. Fall, *Hell in a Very Small Place*, p. 225.

89. Ely, *Lessons of the War in Indochina*, p. 154.

90. Fall, *Hell in a Very Small Place*, p. 337.

91. Ibid., p. 226.

92. Robert F. Turner, *Vietnamese Communism: Its Origins and Development* (Stanford: Hoover Institution, 1975), "Appendix H: Agreement on the Cessation of Hostilities in Viet Nam and Final Declaration of the Geneva Conference," pp. 365–93; *Pentagon Papers*, I, pp. 108–79; Dwight D. Eisenhower, *Mandate for Change, 1953–1956* (Garden City, NY: Doubleday, 1963), pp. 353–75; R. B. Smith, *An International History of the Viet Nam War: Revolution vs. Containment* (New York: St. Martin's Press, 1983), pp. 28–31.

93. Fall, *Two Viet Nams*, p. 229.

94. Bodard, *Quicksand War*, p. 61.

95. Fall, *Two Viet Nams*, p. 223.

96. Thomas C. Thayer, *War without Fronts: The American Experience in Viet Nam* (Boulder, CO: Westview, 1986), p. 9; Douglas Pike, *Viet Cong: The Organization and Techniques of the National Liberation Front of South Viet Nam* (Cambridge, MA: MIT Press, 1966), p. 49n.

97. Fall, *Street without Joy*, p. 45.

98. Ibid., p. 136.

99. O'Ballance, *The Indochina War*, p. 249; Pike, *Viet Cong*, p. 49n.

100. PP, vol. 1, p. 385.

101. PP, vol. 1, p. 83.

102. PP, vol. 1, p. 386.

103. PP, vol. 1, p. 385.

104. PP, vol. 1, p. 386.

105. PP, vol. 1, p. 362.

106. PP, vol. 1, p. 55.

107. Samuel Fugg Bemis, ed., *The American Secretaries of State and Their Diplomacy*, vol. 16, *Dean Acheson* (New York: Cooper Square, 1972), p. 312.

108. PP, vol. 1, p. 77.

109. Stephen E. Ambrose, *Eisenhower: The President* (New York: Simon and Schuster, 1984), p. 175.

110. PP, vol. 1, p. 79.

111. Richard Nixon, *The Memoirs* (New York: Grosset and Dunlap, 1978), p. 152.

112. Lloyd C. Gardner, *Approaching Viet Nam* (New York: Norton, 1988), p. 53.

113. Dwight D. Eisenhower, *Mandate for Change* (Garden City, NY: Doubleday, 1963), p. 372.

114. Ronald Spector, *Advice and Support: The Early Years, 1941–1961* (Washington, DC: U.S. Army Center of Military History, 1983), p. 203.

115. Eisenhower, *Mandate*, p. 341.

116. Richard Nixon, *No More Viet Nams* (New York: Arbor House, 1985), p. 31.

117. PP, vol. 1, pp. 461–62.

118. Ibid., p. 443.

119. Ibid., p. 89.

120. Ibid., p. 471.

121. Ibid., p. 511.

122. Ibid., pp. 482–83.

123. Eisenhower, *Mandate*, pp. 341, 350–51.

124. Robert A. Divine, *Eisenhower and the Cold War* (New York: Oxford University Press, 1981), pp. 49–50.

125. Ambrose, *Eisenhower*, p. 181.

126. Nixon, *Memoirs*, p. 154.

127. PP, vol. 1, p. 92.

128. Divine, *Cold War*, pp. 46–47; PP, vol. 1, p. 503.

129. Divine, *Cold War*, pp. 41–44.

130. Ambrose, *Eisenhower*, p. 177.

131. Divine, *Cold War*, p. 45.

132. Nixon, *Memoirs*, p. 152; this remarkable statement certainly reveals the Brit-

ish government's assessment of the relative weight of imperialist versus "Free World" interests in Indochina.

133. George C. Herring, *America's Longest War: The United States and Viet Nam, 1950–1975*, 2d ed. (New York: Knopf, 1986), p. 42.

134. Tanham, *Communist Revolutionary Warfare*, p. 7.

135. See William J. Duiker, *The Rise of Nationalism in Viet Nam, 1900–1941* (Ithaca, NY: Cornell University Press, 1976); and criticisms of this book in Huynh Kim Khanh, *Vietnamese Communism, 1925–1945* (Ithaca, NY: Cornell University Press, 1982). For skepticism about the Viet Minh as the true embodiment of a potent Vietnamese nationalism see Duncanson, *Government and Revolution*, passim.

136. Duncanson, *Government and Revolution*, Chapter 4.

137. Duiker, *Communist Road to Power*, Chapter 5.

138. Anthony James Joes, *The War for South Viet Nam, 1954–1975* (New York: Praeger, 1989), Chapters 8 and 13.

139. Fall, *Two Viet Nams*, p. 35; Hammer, *Struggle for Indochina*, p. 73; Duncanson, *Government and Revolution*, p. 103; McAlister, *Viet Nam: Origins*, passim.

140. On this important question see Vilfredo Pareto, *The Mind and Society* (New York: Dover, 1963); and especially Pareto's *I sistemi socialisti* (Turin: U.T.E.T., 1963); Richard Pipes, *The Russian Revolution* (New York: Knopf, 1990), Chapter 4; Jacques Sole, *Questions of the French Revolution* (New York: Pantheon, 1989).

141. McAlister, *Viet Nam: Origins*, pp. 300–301 and 74.

142. Samuel P. Huntington, *Political Order in Changing Societies* (New Haven: Yale University Press, 1968), Chapter 5. On this important topic see also Chalmers Johnson, *Peasant Nationalism and Communist Power* (Stanford, CA: Stanford University Press, 1961); Eric Wolfe, *Peasant Wars of the Twentieth Century* (New York: Harper and Row, 1969), and John Womack, *Zapata and the Mexican Revolution* (New York: Vintage, 1969).

143. For this insight, as for much else, I am indebted to Professor Richard Shultz of the Fletcher School of Law and Diplomacy.

144. McAlister, *Viet Nam: Origins*, p. 47.

145. Duiker, *Communist Road to Power*, p. 130.

146. O'Ballance, *Indochina War*, p. 198.

147. Lancaster, *Emancipation of French Indochina*, p. 267; Fall, *Street without Joy*, p. 257.

148. Ely, *Lessons of the War in Indochina*, p. 44.

149. Patrick O'Brian, Introduction to Bodard, *Quicksand War*, p. vi.

150. Davidson, *Viet Nam at War*, p. 275.

151. Bodard, *Quicksand War*, p. 14.

152. Ibid., p. 164.

153. Davidson, *Viet Nam at War*, p. 51 and passim.

154. Ibid., pp. 35–36.

155. O'Ballance, *Indochina War*, p. 254.

156. Tanham, *Communist Revolutionary Warfare*, p. 63.

157. Sir Robert Thompson, *No Exit from Viet Nam* (New York: David McKay, 1969), p. 133.

Chapter 5

South Viet Nam: Defeat Out of Victory

Perhaps the major lesson of the Vietnam war is: do not rely on the United States as an ally.

Sir Robert Thompson, *Peace Is Not at Hand*

In Viet Nam, the United States abandoned the indirect approach that had proven so successful in Greece and the Philippines and for the first time in its history undertook to confront directly a Communist insurgency. This conflict soon became the most controversial war Americans have fought in this century, and the controversies have not concluded.

THE EMERGENCE OF SOUTH VIET NAM

On June 18, 1954, Pierre Mendès-France became premier of France, ready to make the best deal with the Viet Minh that he could get. That same day, Ngo Dinh Diem announced in Paris that Emperor Bao Dai had appointed him prime minister of Viet Nam, with full emergency powers.

Born in 1901 at Hue, the son of a Mandarin, a Christian like Chiang Kai-shek and Syngman Rhee, Diem graduated first in his class from the French-run School of Law at Hanoi. Before he was 25, Diem was governor of Binh Thuan province. Bao Dai made him minister of the interior in 1933, but Diem's nationalism antagonized the French so much that he had to resign. In 1944–1945, as the Pacific War drew to its painful conclusion, Diem received offers of the premiership first from the Japanese, then from

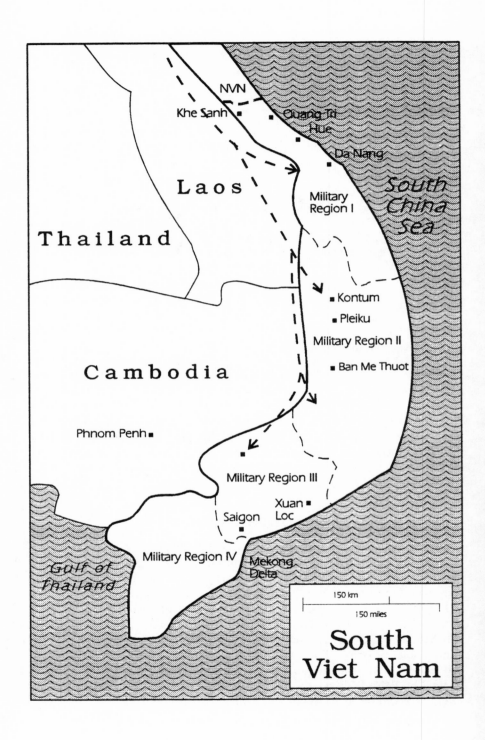

NVN

Khe Sanh

Quang Tri
Hue

Da Nang

Laos

Thailand

Military
Region I

South
China
Sea

Kontum

Pleiku

Military Region II

Cambodia

Ban Me Thuot

Phnom Penh

Military Region III

Xuan
Loc

Saigon

Gulf of
Thailand

Military Region IV

Mekong
Delta

150 km

150 miles

South
Viet Nam

the French and then from Bao Dai; in 1946 Ho Chi Minh wanted to make him minister of the interior of his new revolutionary regime.[1] Each of these offers had too many strings for Diem, and so he declined them all.

By 1950, the Viet Minh had put a price on Diem's head. The French would not pledge to protect him, so Diem left the country, journeying to Rome, the United States, and France.

Three more times Bao Dai offered Diem the premiership, but each time Diem insisted that he should run the war against the Viet Minh, and the French refused to allow this. By these multiple refusals of high office, Diem had demonstrated to Vietnamese nationalists his "perfect integrity, competence, and intelligence."[2]

At last in 1954 Diem became prime minister with the full powers he had so long demanded. But in the first days, Diem controlled hardly more than a few square blocks of downtown Saigon. Bao Dai, the French, and his own generals conspired against him, Binh Xuyen pirates ran the Saigon police, southern Communist cadres awaited their chance, religious sects with their private armies were entrenched not far from Saigon, a million refugees were about to flood into the country from the north, and the Politburo of Hanoi, backed by the Soviet Union and China, glared down upon him with undisguised malice. Even his private office was accessible to any group of assassins who might choose to burst in.

In the midst of this hostility and chaos, Diem had to establish the authority of his government, free South Viet Nam from the vestiges of French colonialism, overcome the powerful centrifugal forces in southern society, and—not least—devise a scheme whereby to defeat Ho Chi Minh's plans to swallow up his state. Few expected him to last more than a few months.

The first order of business was to set up security for Diem, and this was accomplished with the help of the legendary Edward Lansdale and Philippine army Colonel Napoleon Valeriano, fresh from the victorious struggle against the Huks. After some hesitation President Eisenhower, fearing the effects on the rest of Southeast Asia of the fall of Saigon, decided to back Diem, who also picked up support from influential members of Congress, among them Senators Mike Mansfield, Hubert Humphrey, and John F. Kennedy.

Within two years of taking office, Diem had thwarted all his enemies. He secured American assistance. He brought Saigon, the army, and the sects under his control. He attacked malaria, extended education, and settled almost a million northern refugees. He wrote a new republican constitution and got himself elected first president of the Republic of Viet Nam. And he sanctioned the Strategic Hamlet program, a basically sound plan for separating the peasants from the guerrillas.

THE VIET CONG

After the partition, many thousands of Viet Minh cadres did not withdraw to the north as they were supposed to, but instead remained behind in South

Viet Nam to prepare the overthrow of the government. The methods of the stay-behind revolutionaries ranged from agitation to assassination: by the end of 1958, they had murdered 20 percent of southern village chiefs. Schoolteachers were another favorite and frequent target.[3]

Nevertheless, by 1959, the Politburo in Hanoi realized that propaganda and assassination would not overthrow Diem. On the contrary, he was busily uprooting the southern Communist apparatus. The Party history calls 1958–1959 "the darkest period."[4]

Hanoi did not want a non-Communist Vietnamese state with which it could be negatively compared; South Viet Nam must be destroyed. Hence Hanoi directed and fueled what became the Viet Cong insurgency, taking great care that its own role in the insurgency be hidden.[5]

Who joined the Viet Cong, and what motivated them? Common sense might suggest that the primary motives were a desire for reunification and a rebellion against poverty. Yet little evidence supports this response. Rather, the heavy-handedness of agents of the Saigon government and the chance for upward mobility offered by the Viet Cong seem to have been much more important in building the ranks of the guerrillas.[6] Communist agitators hammered away at the government's corruption, arbitrariness, and urban middle-class flavor and the often-indiscriminate punishments handed out to peasants by the army during sweep operations.

To be an officer in the South Vietnamese army (ARVN) one had to possess a high school diploma. This limited officership almost exclusively to the urban middle classes. No peasant lad, no matter how brave or ambitious or patriotic, could realistically aspire to hold a post of leadership in ARVN. The Viet Cong, in contrast, made lack of formal education a virtue; the untutored but dedicated could hope to become officers, teachers, administrators.

It was not difficult to recruit teenage farm boys to the exciting life of the guerrilla. After the Americans appeared in large numbers, the Viet Cong could also tap the powerful Vietnamese vein of xenophobia in the form of anti-Americanism. They often forced prisoners to join their ranks, tying their good conduct to the fate of their families.

As the war went on and American presence increased, life for the guerrillas became much harder. The Viet Cong had to rely more and more on forced recruitment of younger and younger boys. The VC also obtained recruits by abducting boys or young men and forcing them to commit a criminal act in public, thus cutting them off from normal society. Even so, growing numbers of northerners received assignments to nominally Viet Cong units. By end of 1968, most so-called Viet Cong units consisted primarily of northerners.[7]

THE OVERTHROW OF DIEM

In his search for reliably anti-Communist and personally loyal helpers, Diem surrounded himself with members of his family and filled his government with those who shared his aims. Thus, in the mainly Buddhist, peasant, and xenophobic south, the Diem government became disproportionately Catholic, urban, northern, and European educated.

The Americans had looked for a true nationalist to set up against Ho Chi Minh. They found him in Diem but were not happy. Diem proved to be a difficult ally. He had overcome enormous obstacles to get where he was, and this achievement, along with his deep religious commitment, no doubt increased his self-confidence. He did not always take the advice the Americans lavished upon him. He had refused to bend to the French, the Japanese, Bao Dai, or Ho Chi Minh, and he "had considerable reason to doubt the superior judgment of transient Americans concerning the ability and reliability of men with whom he had spent most of his life."[8] Diem did not want his country taken over or torn up by what he saw as naive and technology-happy Americans. But in Washington this was (in more senses than one) the Camelot era: the Kennedy Administration saw South Viet Nam as the place in which to prove wrong the theorists of People's Revolutionary War in Peking and to show Nikita Khrushchev that Kennedy was really tough. Washington began to doubt Diem's zeal to win the war.

Many in the American press corps in Saigon hated Diem. They saw little connection between Diem's difficulties and Viet Nam's long, complex, and troubled history: everything was Diem's fault. Pierre Salinger has testified to the hostility American correspondents showed toward Diem, and Ambassador Maxwell Taylor wrote of their "full-scale vendetta" against him: "To me, it was a sobering spectacle of the power of a few relatively young and inexperienced newsmen who, openly committed to 'getting' Diem . . . were not satisfied to report the events of foreign policy but undertook to shape them."[9]

The hostility of the press bore its fruit when in the summer of 1963 a dispute arose between local officials in Hue and some Buddhist monks over who could fly what flags on Buddha's birthday. In a very confused episode several demonstrators were killed. Diem tried to calm tempers. Nevertheless, the affair escalated into an effort by a group of highly politicized and ambitious Buddhist monks, thoroughly infiltrated by Communist agents, to overthrow him. American correspondents eagerly provided the breakfast tables of Washington with photographs of monks immolating themselves. No effort was made to help the American electorate put these events into the context of traditional Buddhist practice and belief or of a country riven by terrorism and insurrection. The increasingly sensationalist publicity from Saigon shook President Kennedy's confidence in Diem.[10]

Both Ambassador Henry Cabot Lodge in Saigon and Averell Harriman in Washington thoroughly disliked the insubordinate Diem. The Buddhist crisis was their opportunity. Under their prodding, President Kennedy announced cuts in aid to ARVN in September 1963. ARVN interpreted this as a signal that Diem should be thrown out, even though Defense Secretary Robert McNamara, CIA Director John McCone, Vice President

Lyndon Johnson, and Kennedy's previous ambassador to Saigon, Frederick Nolting, opposed such a move. On November 2, after an attack on the presidential palace, ARVN generals captured Diem and his brother Ngo Dinh Nhu, and murdered them both.

Hanoi and the Viet Cong saw these events as heaven sent.[11] The killing of Diem put the country in the hands of less-than-inspired generals whom the world viewed as completely dependent on the Americans. Diem's death also quite predictably opened the floodgates of instability: coup followed coup, purge followed purge, the Strategic Hamlet program fell by the wayside. The Buddhist immolations, allegedly caused by Diem's repression, did not stop, but instead increased. Less than a year and a half after Diem's murder, with South Viet Nam in mortal peril of Communist conquest, President Johnson would find it necessary to inundate the bleeding country with American troops.

President Kennedy had repeatedly stated that a main purpose of United States involvement in South Viet Nam was to reassure its allies about the reliability of American guarantees. How American involvement in the overthrow of Diem was supposed to advance this purpose is not entirely clear.[12] By its complicity in the killing of a legitimate and friendly head of state, the Kennedy Administration saddled the United States with complete responsibility for the fate of South Viet Nam. Years later, William F. Colby called the removal of Diem the first great American mistake in Viet Nam.[13]

THE ARVN

The foundations of the Army of the Republic of Viet Nam (ARVN) were the scores of thousands of Vietnamese who had fought against the Viet Minh either in the French forces or in Bao Dai's Vietnamese National army. When the French army left South Viet Nam in 1956, American officers arrived to assist in training an expanding ARVN.[14]

American advisers did not develop armed forces of the type that had proved so effective against subversion in Malaya and the Philippines. Instead, they strove to build an ARVN that would have been able to repel the North Korean invasion of 1950. ARVN became roadbound like the French army and overreliant on heavy firepower like the American army. Nobody paid much attention to the elements that are most crucial in the early stages of an insurgency, namely the police and the militia (called in Viet Nam the territorial forces). Most U.S. advisers were competent, well-trained, and well-meaning, but they served only one-year tours, did not speak the language or dialects, and taught and learned disappointingly little.

The United States gave ARVN inferior equipment. It did not get the M-16 rifle, for instance, until 1968; before then it had found itself completely outclassed by the Communist forces armed with excellent automatic weapons (and some experts and veterans claim the M-16 was not as good as the

Communists' AK-47). Even as late as the 1970s, ARVN's American-made M-41 tank was inferior to the Soviet T-54.[15]

The Romans created armies that were small and well trained. ARVN was just the opposite. Owing to the demands of combat and a chronic shortage of good officers, an average ARVN unit had less than two hours' training a week and received hardly any political education.[16]

ARVN was always short of officers, especially those of the middle grade. Commissions required a high school education, which excluded the peasant class almost entirely. ARVN had one of the world's best-educated officer corps: in the mid-1960s, 5 percent of generals, 13 percent of colonels, and 15 percent of field-grade officers held Ph.D.s. In 1967, one-fourth of ARVN officers were northern born, and one-fifth were Catholics, twice the Catholic proportion of the general population.[17]

Politicization of the officer corps had gone far under Diem (and resulted in his death). Under President Nguyen Van Thieu, political considerations became even more central, because the ARVN had become the principal nationwide institution holding the country together. In general, political and personal connections were the key to advancement; good field commanders were left in the field.

In spite of these grave problems, the South Vietnamese Marine Division and the Airborne Division had no equals among the North Vietnamese (NVA).[18] In 1974 a noted British authority placed ARVN second only to the Israeli army among free-world land forces.[19] ARVN did its best fighting when its back was to the wall, in the disastrous spring of 1975: for example, Xuan Loc, the last bastion between Saigon and the conquering Communists, was held by the 18th ARVN Division, nobody's idea of a prize unit. To subdue it, the NVA eventually had to commit four of its best divisions.

DESERTION IN ARVN

ARVN desertion rates were high, and some American journalists interpreted this as proof that the South Vietnamese people did not want to fight against the north. But the causes of ARVN desertion were mainly sociological, not political. In rural South Viet Nam, desertion carried no social stigma for the offender or his family; nor did the government search out and punish deserters with any vigor. Much more importantly, government policy assigned peasant draftees to posts far from their home provinces. This practice was deeply at variance with the values of rural society (one result of having an officer corps drawn overwhelmingly from educated urban sectors). "Few steps the [Communist] Party could have taken," writes one student of the war, "would have been so effective in crippling the morale and effectiveness of the government's military forces as was the government's own decision to adopt a policy of nonlocal service."[20] This ill-considered sending of young peasant draftees far from home accounts for the high desertion rates among first-year soldiers at harvest time and around the supremely important Tet holidays.

Some who deserted ARVN later rejoined; other deserters joined territorial units (called Regional Forces/Popular Forces: RF/PF or Ruff-Puffs) close to home. In vivid contrast to both ARVN and the Viet Cong, desertion rates among the Ruff-Puffs, whose units defended their native province or village, and whose casualty rates were higher than ARVN's, were close to zero. And here is a most crucial point: desertion from ARVN hardly ever meant defection to the Communists. In contrast, among the Viet Cong, desertion rates were not only as high as in ARVN, but 200,000 Viet Cong defected to South Vietnamese forces as well.[21]

It may help to put ARVN desertion into some perspective by recalling that a month before Gettysburg, the largest battle ever fought on the continent of North America, the principal force defending the Union, the Army of the Potomac, was down to half-strength because of desertions. During the American Civil War the general desertion rate in the Federal forces was 330 per 1,000 and among the Confederates 400 per 1,000.[22]

ARVN CASUALTIES

One of the most grotesque of the myths about the Viet Nam conflict is that the South Vietnamese did not fight very much. In fact, however, ARVN paid a very high price in blood. Some statistics will underline exactly how high that price was.

In Viet Nam, during the entire conflict from 1954 to 1975, 57,000 Americans lost their lives, a number almost exactly equaled by highway fatalities in the United States in the year 1970 alone—neither of these small or desirable figures to be sure. Between the beginning of the Kennedy buildup in 1961 and the fall of Saigon in 1975, the Americans incurred an average of 4,000 military deaths a year. Calculating only from 1965 (the Johnson buildup) to 1972 (when the last U.S. ground combat units left South Viet Nam), the figure becomes 8,000 military deaths a year. During the Korean War, the comparable figure is 18,000 per year and in World War II, 100,000 per year.

Every year from 1954 to 1975, ARVN combat deaths were higher than those of the Americans.[23] In all, about 200,000 ARVN personnel were killed; some authors give higher figures, and these numbers include neither territorials nor civilians.[24]

But to say that the South Vietnamese regular army forces took higher casualties than the Americans only touches the surface, because the population of South Viet Nam was many times smaller than that of the United States. If American military fatalities had been in the same proportion to the population of the United States as ARVN's were to the population of South Viet Nam, they would have numbered not 57,000, but rather 2.6

million. How is one to comprehend this figure? What does it mean to say that if American losses were proportionate to South Vietnamese losses, they would have amounted to 2.6 million military deaths? It means this: total American military fatalities in all the wars the Americans fought during 200 years—from the American Revolution through Viet Nam, including World War I and World War II and both sides in the Civil War—amount to less than 1 million. In relation to population, ARVN alone (excluding the militia, whose rates were higher) was suffering more than forty times as many fatalities as the Americans.

TET

In the early months of 1967, after two years of large-scale American presence in South Viet Nam, the Communists were taking enormous losses. In fact, the Hanoi regime imposed casualties on its people at a rate about twice as high as that suffered by the Japanese in World War II. General Giap told a European interviewer in 1969 that between 1965 and 1968 alone, Communist military losses totalled 600,000.[25] By way of comparison, from 1960 to 1967 13,000 Americans died in Viet Nam, fewer than the Americans who died in that period from falling off the roofs of their houses.[26]

Hanoi had little to show for these losses. The Thieu government had clearly stabilized itself, while morale among the Viet Cong was sinking. In response to these depressing conditions, Hanoi began to make plans for a great offensive, to coincide with the Tet holidays of 1968. In these plans, the Communists had two main objectives: to disorganize the ARVN and to provoke a great popular uprising in cities, especially Saigon. If all went according to plan, the Americans would find themselves in effect without a country to defend, and they would go home. The Tet Offensive was the acknowledgment by Hanoi that its guerrilla campaign against the south had failed.

Because South Viet Nam was not a police state but a relatively open society, it was easy for the Viet Cong/NVA to infiltrate numerous small groups into the cities. Allied commanders in Saigon were aware well before January 1968 that something big was coming, but for the most part they simply could not believe that the Viet Cong/NVA would throw aside the guerrilla tactics that were serving them well and instead suicidally rise to the surface to be confronted by allied firepower. This incredulity on the part of the Americans was a major element producing the surprise of Tet. Like the events immediately preceding the Japanese attack on Pearl Harbor, American skepticism about the likelihood of a major Viet Cong offensive illustrates a severe weakness of even the best intelligence system: human beings are loath to believe any information that seems to contradict common sense.

On January 30, with half the ARVN on leave during the traditional holiday truce, which the Communists had pledged to respect, the Communist offensive exploded. Viet Cong units attacked cities and military installations all over South Viet Nam. In Saigon, they attempted to take over the presidential palace, army headquarters, the airport, and the radio station. A suicide squad of fifteen managed to penetrate the outer grounds of the United States Embassy.

For a few days, the fate of South Viet Nam seemed to hang in the balance. But ARVN held together. The Viet Cong were stunned at the total lack of response for their calls for urban uprisings, and they suffered devastating casualties.

For the Communist side, Tet was a calamity of unparalleled dimensions. Of 84,000 Viet Cong involved in the offensive, something like 30,000 were killed.[27] "In truth, the Tet offensive for all practical purposes destroyed the Viet Cong."[28] In the aftermath of this bloody debacle some, including former Viet Cong, have suggested the Tet offensive was a plot by Hanoi not only to destabilize and discredit ARVN, but also to engineer a massacre of the Viet Cong, "killing two birds with one stone" and thus removing all obstacles to an eventual total takeover by Hanoi.[29] Whatever the truth of these allegations, henceforth the guerrilla conflict would fade into the background, as NVA regular units openly took up the burden of a conventional war of conquest. More than four years were to go by before the Communists felt strong enough to mount another offensive.[30]

Communists and their apologists tried to explain away the failure of the large and growing urban population of South Vietnam to rise up against the government by saying that ARVN was too strong for the civilians. This is not convincing. Louis XVI and Nicholas II maintained large armed forces in their capital cities, but those two monarchs nevertheless suffered dethronement and death. The Hungarian army did not prevent the popular earthquake in Communist Budapest in 1956; the superbly equipped Iranian army did not save the Shah in 1978; nor did well-armed and well-indoctrinated troops stop the revolutions in East Germany, Czechoslovakia, and Romania in 1989. Even in April 1975, during what were obviously the last days of the Saigon government, the South Vietnamese did not rise. It is hard to escape the conclusion that the people in the urban south never rose up in support of a Communist conquest because they did not wish to.

Tet transformed the war politically as well as militarily. All over South Viet Nam, wherever the Viet Cong had achieved temporary control, they committed atrocities against civilians. The massacres at Hue were especially grisly. In the aftermath of the offensive, survivors and relatives exhumed thousands of bodies in that city: students, priests, low-level government employees and their families, many with hands tied behind their backs and apparently buried alive.[31] Such events thoroughly alarmed the bulk of the southern population and steeled their determination to resist a northern conquest.[32] The Thieu government distributed arms to hundreds of thousands of militia members.

Before the Tet Offensive, 18-year-old villagers would lie and say they were 13 to get out of the draft; after the Tet Offensive, 13- and 14-year-olds would lie and say they were 18 to get into the draft before the Communists got to them. The perception of the craziness of what the Communists were doing was increased, and the idea that they were inevitable winners was so deflated that people changed very much how they felt.[33]

The Communists launched Tet because of the unacceptably heavy losses they were taking, and it turned out to be a devastating reverse for them, so much so that southern Communists would soon accuse Hanoi of having plotted to be rid of them. Yet in an irony of stupefying magnitude, the Tet Offensive was the beginning of the end of both the Johnson Administration and American commitment to the South.

VIETNAMIZATION: FROM INSURGENCY TO INVASION

The Tet Offensive produced the "Vietnamization" program, badly misnamed because it implied that the Americans would now get ARVN to do its share of the fighting, when of course ARVN had been doing at least its share for years. Vietnamization had two major aspects: first, the long-overdue upgrading of American equipment delivered to ARVN and second, the reduction of U.S. combat troops in Viet Nam—also overdue.

The great test of the success of Vietnamization occurred during the 1972 Easter Offensive. In the spring of that year General Giap threw in the entire NVA, the "most efficient fighting machine in all Asia,"[34] against the south, from which nearly all American ground-combat units had been evacuated. For practical purposes, on the ground the South Vietnamese stood alone.

The Communist attack was four pronged, across the egregiously misnamed Demilitarized Zone and through Laos and Cambodia. The offensive began on March 30; before mid-May it was clearly a failure. As ARVN had withstood the best efforts of the Viet Cong in 1968, so it withstood the best efforts of the North Vietnamese Army in 1972—or, in the quaint language of General Creighton Abrahms: "By God, the South Vietnamese can hack it."[35] And—once again—insistent Communist calls for the southern urban population to rise against their oppressors had fallen on ears quite deaf. ARVN had demonstrated that if it could count on replacement parts for its equipment and on U.S. air support, especially the all-powerful B-52s, it could stand up against Hanoi indefinitely.

THE TERRITORIAL FORCES

The bedrock of any plan to resist the Communist conquest of South Viet Nam should have been militias of peasants organized to protect their homes from the guerrillas. But from the beginning, such territorial forces had been ignored by Diem and scorned by the Americans. They received no training and few weapons, and those of poor quality.

The 1964 reorganization of these elements into the Regional Forces and Popular Forces looked like an improvement. Popular forces were organized on the hamlet and village level, Regional Forces on the provincial level. The task of the PFs was to resist guerrillas trying to enter the village just long enough for RF units to come to their assistance. But the PFs had no pay, no ranks, and no system of recognition or reward. Their guns, when they had any, were castoffs; their training, when they got any, was sketchy. Even if the PFs in a certain village were lucky enough to possess a radio, the Regional Forces often lacked the mobility to respond in time to a plea for help.

The Tet Offensive changed everything. Many RF/PF units performed exceptionally well during the crisis, and Saigon responded by finally giving them good weapons, although they did not receive the M-16 until 1970.[36] Between 1968 and 1972, ARVN suffered 37,000 killed; the Territorials, 69,000.[37] RF units gave especially good accounts of themselves at the siege of Hue and in other battles during the Eastern Offensive against regular NVA forces. By 1973, when the last U.S. combat units were long out of South Viet Nam, territorial forces numbered over half a million.[38] The heavily populated Mekong Delta provinces were mostly under control of Ruff-Puffs.

South Vietnamese Territorial forces, while receiving only from 2 to 4 percent of the war budget, accounted for 30 percent of VC/NVA combat deaths. They were "the most cost-efficient military forces employed on the allied side."[39]

THE UNITED STATES AND VIET NAM

The effort to assign exact responsibility for the outbreak of the Cold War has provided employment for two generations of American historians, and will certainly continue for a long time. But no one can hope to achieve any real understanding of the intervention of the United States in the conflicts in Viet Nam without a keen awareness of the Cold War context in which that intervention took place.

The outbreak of the Cold War between the West and the Soviets and the outbreak of the hot war between the French and the Viet Minh occurred almost simultaneously. Communist-led insurgencies were threatening the governments of Greece, Malaya, and the Philippines, all allies of the United

States. Along with these disturbing events came Stalin's effort to force the Western Allies out of Berlin, the subversion of Czechoslovakia, the Maoist takeover of mainland China, the invasion of South Korea, and the United Nation's resistance to it. When Ho Chi Minh fatefully declared that he and his regime were at the side of Stalin and Mao in their titanic conflict with the Western democracies, an American reaction was inevitable.

Against the background of these alarms Presidents Eisenhower and Kennedy adopted the concepts known as the Domino Theory (or Domino Principle). In its simplest form, the Domino Theory held that the Communist conquest of South Viet Nam would most probably be followed eventually by the takeover of Laos and Cambodia, and perhaps Thailand, Burma, and other Southeast Asian states.[40] In its broader implications, the Domino Theory indicated that South Viet Nam was the testing ground of the credibility of the United States as an ally in the Cold War. The fears of Eisenhower and Kennedy and their advisers received confirmation from no less than Lin Biao, Mao's confidant and defense minister, who proclaimed that revolutionary guerrilla war was the indeflectible weapon by which the Communists would first isolate and then dominate the West.[41]

Eventually, many Americans would conclude not so much that the Domino Theory itself was false but that the cost of preventing the fall of the dominoes was excessive. One reason they reached that conclusion was because of the mistakes the Johnson Administration made in fighting the war. Another reason was the information and analysis they received from the media.

THE MEDIA AND THE WAR

The American war in Viet Nam was the first uncensored press war. Uncensored, that is, for the allied side; the North Vietnamese and the Viet Cong did not permit foreign news personnel to film whatever they wished and question whomever they pleased. But nobody seemed very disturbed by this asymmetry.

The American news industry provided the American people with some memorable photographs. It also presented President Diem as the source of most of the trouble in South Viet Nam and interpreted the Tet Offensive as a great Communist victory. Indeed, the treatment of events during and after Tet by reporters who knew little of war, less of Leninist tactics, and nothing of Vietnamese society represents perhaps the professional nadir of American journalism.[42] The American press forgave Hanoi and the Viet Cong everything and Saigon nothing. It completely ignored the South Vietnamese contribution to the common effort: throughout the entire conflict, apparently not a single major newspaper in the United States ran even one positive story on the fighting qualities of a single ARVN unit.[43] Too much of what was presented as news by leading newspapers and news

weeklies came from Communist agents posing as journalists, or from the
Hanoi Politburo.[44]

The Viet Nam conflict revealed profound flaws in the American news
media; it is not at all clear that these have been corrected, or even admitted.
Remarkably, many accounts of the war by journalists were no worse than,
and some were considerably superior to, those produced by academicians,
then and for many years thereafter.

Misinformation via the airways and the pages of the slick news weeklies
inexplicably encountered no serious effort by President Johnson to inform
the American electorate of the real meaning of events in Viet Nam. The
devastating combined failure of both the media and the administration to
provide an accurate analysis of the war, and especially of the Tet Offensive,
shook the faith of many ordinary citizens in the competence of their armed
forces and the truthfulness of their government.[45]

In the last analysis, while journalists sensationalized or obfuscated the
most distressing aspects of the war, they did not create them. However
grave the errors of omission and commission of the media, these would
not have had a decisive impact on the American public and Congress if
there had not been in fact another set of grave errors, committed not by
journalists but by politicians and soldiers in Washington and Saigon. No
single one of these errors "lost the war" for the United States, but their
cumulative effect was disastrous. Among these errors were:

• Americanization of the war;

• the strategy of attrition;

• the bombing campaign against North Viet Nam; and

• acceptance of the permanent invasion of the south by way of the Ho Chi Minh
  Trail.

AMERICANIZATION

In 1965 the South Vietnamese, like the French before them, appeared to
be on the brink of defeat by the Communists. The response of the Johnson
Administration was to commit a major rupture with the policy of President
Eisenhower by sending a huge army to Viet Nam. This fateful decision
occurred in a remarkably offhanded manner, and against the advice of CIA
Director John McCone.[46] As in 1963 the Americans decided to jettison
President Diem without any clear idea of what was to follow, so in 1965
they decided to take over the war.

The Americans believed that despite the failure of the French in Viet
Nam, they themselves would be successful. The United States was much
richer, much stronger, much more united than the Fourth Republic. Equally
important, in the last analysis the French had been fighting to hold onto a

colonial position; in contrast, the Americans would be fighting not for the subjugation but for the independence, stability, and prosperity of South Viet Nam.

When President Eisenhower left office in 1961, there were 875 U.S. military personnel in Viet Nam. At the death of President Kennedy that number had multiplied twenty times, to more than 16,000. Two years after President Johnson's inauguration there were 184,000, and two years after that there were half a million.

The American armed forces that arrived in South Viet Nam knew little about Vietnamese society or—incredibly—about the French experience there.[47] Far worse, they knew little about guerrilla warfare, and the army's policy of one-year tours of duty insured that hardly anybody learned anything.[48] Even assuming that this large American force were to achieve success, however defined, how long would it or could it remain in Southeast Asia? Meanwhile, the presence of so many young, unattached, and, by Vietnamese standards, fabulously rich foreign males contributed greatly to the disruption and corruption of Vietnamese society.

The commitment of a huge American force did not even provide the great numerical preponderance that successful counterguerrilla war requires. When the Americans increased their forces in South Viet Nam by any given number, Hanoi could counter it by increasing its own forces there by merely a fourth or even a tenth that number.

In fact, the numerical superiority enjoyed by the allies over the Communists existed on paper, not in the field. The American forces, and the ARVN whom they had trained, had a very big "tail": only a very small percentage of allied troops in South Viet Nam were actual combat infantry (a mere 80,000 out of 536,000 American servicemen in Viet Nam at the end of 1968).[49] The rest mainly provided support for the combat troops. Thus, where it counted, in the number of fighting men prepared to contest control of the countryside, the allies most of the time had a very small advantage over their enemies, or none at all. This is not the way to defeat guerrillas, or anybody. By sending a huge army to the other side of the Pacific Ocean, the Johnson Administration prevented an immediate victory of the Communists but also opened up a fissure in American society which it did not know how to close or even contain.

THE BOMBING OF NORTH VIET NAM

Air power was supposed to be the big ace in the American hand. The Johnson Administration viewed bombing the north as a substitute for stopping the invasion of the south on the ground. Quite probably it would have proven impossible through air interdiction alone to dissuade or prevent Hanoi from flooding South Viet Nam with troops and munitions. Yet the Johnson Administration so badly conceived and executed the air campaign that the bombing not only failed to accomplish its purpose but also became a weapon in the hands of opponents of the war, and of the United States, at home and abroad.

The United States never bombed North Viet Nam the way it had bombed Germany or Japan. The Johnson Administration did not use bombing as a method to break North Vietnamese civilian morale. Instead, it took great pains to avoid unnecessary damage to civilian areas in Hanoi and to the dikes that were essential to food production. The crucial port of Haiphong remained untouched. The bombing campaign aimed at only a limited number of targets, often selected in the White House thousands of miles away.

The administration punctuated the air war with pauses—ten of them— that were somehow supposed to convince Hanoi of American "goodwill" but instead provided the North with opportunities to repair damage, improve defenses, and increase its infiltration of the south. Johnson told his successor that "all the bombing pauses were a mistake."[50]

In spite of the Johnson Administration's laudable self-restraint, critics of American involvement at home and overseas leveled charges of barbarism against the United States; they even employed the term genocide, as if they actually lacked the wit to distinguish between Lyndon Johnson and Hitler or Stalin. A United States senator from Massachusetts dismayed many Americans and delighted their enemies with his false charges that the Americans were deliberately bombing dikes.[51]

The constrained air war against the North Vietnamese damaged their morale and interfered with their war effort. But it did not prevent them from obtaining more than enough replacement equipment from the Soviets and the Chinese.[52] Thus it did not decisively impair North Viet Nam's warmaking capacity. At the same time, approximately one out of twenty American bombs dropped in Viet Nam were duds, whose high-quality metal was recovered by enterprising NVA to make ammunition and booby traps.[53]

The Johnson Administration's haphazard, ineffective use of American air power against North Viet Nam prolonged the war, increased American casualties, contributed to growing disunity in American society, and provided valuable ammunition to foes of democracy all over the globe. Conventional wisdom identifies the middle course as the right one. Yet in the bombing of North Viet Nam, as indeed in the whole war, Lyndon Johnson chose the middle course, and it destroyed him.

ATTRITION

Neither the bombing of the North nor the sending of an overly large and cumbersome American army to South Viet Nam would have in itself undone the American purpose, if American forces in the South had pursued an effective strategy there. But they did not. The Americans assumed major responsibility for fighting the guerrillas; this was a profound error. The Americans then compounded their error by choosing to fight the guerrillas the wrong way.

The core concept in classic (and successful) counterguerrilla warfare is to provide security to the peasantry, separating the guerrillas from the civilians among whom they operate and from whom they draw sustenance.

General William Westmoreland rejected such a strategy as a basically defensive one that would negate the advantages possessed by the American fighting forces. He wished to capitalize on U.S. superiority in firepower by pursuing aggressive tactics against the enemy. Hence the development of what is usually called the strategy of attrition. The essence of the strategy was to employ superior technology to kill the enemy in numbers greater than could be replaced. Thus the war would eventually simply peter out.

Since attrition did not aim at holding territory or increasing the number of peasants living in secure villages, there was no way to measure its progress but the notorious "body count": adding up the number of Vietnamese corpses remaining after an encounter. This way of measuring progress may have been the biggest public relations disaster in American history. (Nobody wanted to remember that Clausewitz wrote: "Casualty reports on either side are never accurate, seldom truthful, and in most cases deliberately falsified"; and "that is why guns and prisoners have always counted as the real trophies of victory.")[54]

Attrition failed to achieve its objectives in time, before key groups in the United States had run out of patience with the war. Among the reasons for this failure are the following.

First, for attrition to work, the enemy must fight. But in Viet Nam, the tempo of fighting was in fact controlled by the Communists, who could fight or not, as they chose. And when they did fight, they often "hugged" American units so closely that they rendered American artillery and air power ineffective. True enough, the allies, with their superior firepower, were able to break the back of the Viet Cong for good during the Tet Offensive, but here again it was the insurgents who chose the confrontation, not the Americans, and their choice violated the most elementary principals of sound guerrilla tactics. That is, Tet was a great victory for the allies, but it was handed to them on a platter.

Second, attrition ran up against the brutal fact that the Hanoi party-state was willing and able to impose enormous sacrifices on its own people. Years before, Ho Chi Minh had declared that the Viet Minh would suffer ten times as many deaths as the French and still win. And General Giap offered the revealing observation that "every minute, hundreds of thousands of people die all over the world. The life or death of a hundred, a thousand, or tens of thousands of human beings, even if they are our compatriots, represents really very little."[55]

Third, the Johnson-McNamara policy of gradualism, whereby Washington would force Hanoi to abandon the struggle by slow increments of military pressure, meant that Hanoi had time to absorb each blow before the next was delivered. Partly based on the fear of a Chinese intervention on the Korean model, Johnson's gradualism included repeated assurances to Hanoi, public and private, that the United States would not attack North Viet Nam on the ground. Johnson never threatened, that is, the existence of the North Vietnamese party-state. This of course enabled Hanoi to employ every possible ounce of strength against the attrition strategy in the South. Gradualism worked against attrition, in the end exhausting not the North Vietnamese but the Americans.

American forces in Viet Nam expended enough bullets, bombs, rockets, and shells to destroy all the soldiers in all the armies that ever existed in the history of the world.[56] Some have estimated that at certain points in the war the United States was spending $400,000 to kill each enemy soldier.[57] This unprecedented use of American military technology killed many of the enemy; it also killed many neutral and friendly civilians. The American way of combat was exceedingly destructive: no American would wish his home or neighborhood to be "liberated" in the style of the American forces in the Viet Nam war. The side effects of American combat tactics made many converts for the Viet Cong.[58]

The attrition strategy hurt the Communist enemy severely; this was the reason for the launching of the disastrous Tet Offensive. And United States forces in Viet Nam never lost a significant battle, a military record unparalleled in history. Yet the combination of growing American casualty lists, an increasingly negative presentation of the war by the American news media, and the seemingly endless nature of the struggle caused Americans at home to question the value of the war and for all this the attrition strategy, more than anything else, was responsible.[59]

ACCEPTANCE OF PERMANENT INVASION

To one degree or another, the three errors already mentioned had their roots in the failure to stop Hanoi's invasion of the South through Laos. President Eisenhower had warned President Kennedy that Laos was the key to South Viet Nam, and General Taylor told him as early as 1961 that the insurgents could not be beaten as long as infiltration via their Laotian sanctuary went unchecked.[60] Begun in 1959, the Ho Chi Minh Trail through Laos had by the 1970s become a network of roads down which poured thousands of troops and trucks every month. *If the troops who had infiltrated South Viet Nam from the North in small numbers between 1958 and 1965 had all come in at the same time, it would have looked like a Korean-style invasion.* Instead, the Trail confronted American and ARVN troops with a sort of slow-motion Schlieffen Plan, by which they were constantly being outflanked.[61]

General Westmoreland and others wanted to cut the Trail on the ground by sending several divisions across Laos to the border of Thailand, a distance roughly equal to that between Washington and Philadelphia. The Johnson Administration forbade this; they planned to stem the tide of men and supplies from the air. The Americans carried out the most intensive bombing campaign in the history of warfare—to no avail; traffic was slowed but not stopped.

Failure either to close the Trail or to adopt an alternative strategy that would have neutralized its effects meant that Hanoi not only could retain the offensive but could also fight on interior lines, an enormous advantage. It meant that attrition would take longer than key segments of the American public would accept. Indeed attrition, with all its negative side effects for the Americans, was like the bombing of the north: a substitute strategy forced on the Americans through their failure to interrupt the Ho Chi Minh Trail. But "it was impossible to defeat North Viet Nam decisively in South Viet Nam without stopping the invasion" via the Trail.[62] Since the fall of Saigon, many in Hanoi have expressed the conviction that the Trail was the key to their success.[63]

Not surprisingly, the escalating involvement in Viet Nam generated escalating protest at home. The antiwar movement attracted some noble spirits and had some powerful points to make. As the war went on, however, exhibitionist and destructive personalities came to dominate its public image, and it became less an antiwar than a pro-Hanoi movement.

Some protestors heaped venom upon Viet Nam veterans, including nurses, for two decades. They turned many university campuses from bastions of reason and research into whirlpools of fanaticism and groupthink. While poll after poll, as well as the 1968 and 1972 national elections, showed that a thumping majority of Americans did not identify with the protestors, they nevertheless came close to disrupting the 1968 presidential selection process, a chilling reminder of what implacable minorities can do in a democracy. After the war Hanoi acknowledged the contribution that the antiwar movement had made to its cause; during the 1980s, several prominent figures in the movement publicly repented their participation.

"PEACE IS AT HAND"

After four years of negotiations, Washington and Hanoi signed the Paris Agreements on January 27, 1973. The principal effect of the so-called peace accords was that the United States withdrew its remaining fighting forces from South Viet Nam and ceased all air attacks on the North. The agreements implicitly recognized the right of North Viet Nam to maintain almost one quarter of a million troops in South Viet Nam, with another 50,000 in Laos.

The profound asymmetry of the pacts—the Americans leave, the North Vietnamese stay—caused President Thieu to refuse his assent. President

Nixon pressured Thieu with threats of a unilateral American signature but also assured him in writing that if Hanoi resumed its effort to conquer the South, it would call down upon itself U.S. air power.[64]

The cessation of American air strikes allowed the North, in complete violation of the peace, to greatly increase the number of its troops inside the South.[65] Nevertheless, South Viet Nam was in generally good shape in 1973, much better than it had been on the eve of the Tet Offensive. In the cities, the Viet Cong had never had any real strength, a fact that accounts for the failure of the urban population to carry out the general uprisings so ardently predicted by the Communists during both the Tet and the Easter offensives. One source very friendly to the Communists estimates that in 1974 there were about 500 activists in Saigon, a city of 2.5 million people.[66] In the countryside, Communist support had long been waning, in part because of heavy combat losses, in part because in the early 1970s Saigon had carried out "the most extensive land reform program yet undertaken in any non–Communist country in Asia."[67] In the mid-1970s, most estimates put support for the Communist side at well below one third of the South Vietnamese population.[68]

Catholics, northern refugees, members of the powerful southern religious sects, army officers and their families, the urban middle class, all were determined to resist a northern conquest. The Territorial forces (Ruff-Puffs) had the heaviest casualty rates and the lowest desertion rates. Most of all, the ARVN had stood firm both in 1968 and in 1972 against the best the Communists could do to it. As an army it could stand comparison to that of Israel.[69]

THE AMERICANS DESERT THE
SOUTH VIETNAMESE

When the Paris Agreements went into effect, President Thieu refused to yield another square inch of territory to the Communists inside South Viet Nam, no matter how exposed and vulnerable to attack a village, province, or ARVN strongpoint might be. This hold–everywhere policy was extremely unwise. It allowed the Communists to pursue their familiar tactic of amassing great numerical superiority at the point of attack, while ARVN was stretched so thinly that it possessed neither a strategic reserve to rush to the point of danger nor troops to interdict Communist movements in Laos and Cambodia.

In these extremely perilous circumstances, South Viet Nam's American ally began openly to turn against it. On July 1, 1973, Congress forbade any combat in or over Viet Nam after August 15, 1973. This repudiation of President Nixon's promises to President Thieu gave Hanoi an unmistakable green light for invasion. The Congress also slashed assistance to Saigon: after 1973, the South Vietnamese were receiving less than one-third the dollar amount of aid they had obtained in 1972, in inflated dollars. By 1974, the United States had spent $150 billion (perhaps $400 billion in 1993 values) on the war. Only 1 percent of that total was what the Saigon government was asking for. But Congress slashed aid to South Viet Nam to only $700 million, not nearly enough for ARVN to keep the equipment it had in working order. From 1976 to 1980, however, Congress would distribute close to $15 billion to Israel and Egypt alone.

These actions of Congress "seriously undermined South Vietnamese combat power."[70] ARVN had to cut its radio communications by 50 percent. Many Saigon fighter aircraft ceased to fly for lack of replacement parts. Artillery batteries in the Central Highlands could fire only four shells per day. By the summer of 1974 each ARVN soldier was receiving 85 bullets a month. It became necessary to wash the bandages of soldiers who had died and use them again. At the same time the Soviets were supplying Hanoi with great quantities of oil, heavy weapons, and ammunition.[71]

Because NVA divisions were infinitely more vulnerable to air attack than VC units had ever been, the cessation of American air strikes had been a priceless boon to the North. Now, on top of this, the drastic reductions in American aid to the South convinced Hanoi that "a fundamental turning point" had been reached in the conflict.[72] Thus in December 1974, North Vietnamese Army units attacked and captured Phuoc Long province. To this dramatic and open violation of the peace agreements, the United States made no response; indeed, in his first State of the Union address, President Ford did not mention Viet Nam even once. The Hanoi Politburo now had absolute proof that it could do as it wished, Paris peace agreement or no.

THE DESTRUCTION OF SOUTH VIET NAM

On March 11, 1975, NVA forces seized Ban Me Thuot. Hanoi had publicly ripped up the Paris peace accords and defied the United States. By way of response, the Democratic Caucus of the House of Representatives rejected President Ford's plea for emergency aid for South Viet Nam. Thereupon President Thieu announced to his generals a plan for military retrenchment: with the exception of enclaves at Hue and Danang, ARVN would withdraw from Military Regions I and II, falling back to consolidated positions in MR III (around Saigon) and MR IV (the Mekong Delta).

In itself, retrenchment was a good idea. The majority of ARVN's 13 divisions were in MR I and II, which contained only 20 percent of the south's population. Thieu had not previously carried out a consolidation of ARVN forces toward the densely populated southern provinces because he had always believed that the United States would not desert South Viet Nam. When Thieu at last decided on a pullback, the South was without American advisers, without fuel and replacement parts, without even the goodwill of its mighty onetime ally across the broad Pacific. But Thieu and his staff had done little serious preparation for such a massive operation. Many key ARVN officers and civil officials did not know what was happening. Often the roads and bridges designated for retreat to the south were impassable.

Most damaging of all, when the civilian population in the northern provinces realized that ARVN was retreating, memories of the Communist massacres of civilians at Hue in 1968 unloosed a torrent of refugees who clogged the roads to Hue and Danang, making both movement and defense almost impossible. Many soldiers added to the chaos by leaving their units to search for their families and ensure their escape toward the south; here was the most disastrous result of the ARVN policy of assigning draftees far from their home villages. The resulting panic and rumors were fed by the numerous Hanoi agents inside the Saigon civil service and army.

The retreat turned almost overnight into a collapse. Most of the ARVN forces that had been holding Military Regions I and II simply disintegrated. On March 24, the North Vietnamese captured the ancient, symbolic city of Hue. Six days later Danang, where the U.S. Marines had landed ten years before, in the first days of President Johnson's Americanization of the war, fell to the invader amid scenes of indescribable suffering. The disaster that overtook the South Vietnamese retrenchment of 1975 had been foreshadowed by the fate of French evacuations during the 1950s, especially the fall of Cao Bang and Lang Son.

Nevertheless the Southern government still held the entire Mekong Delta: of its 16 provincial capitals, and the scores of district capitals, every single one was in Saigon hands. Between Saigon and the Cambodian border many ARVN units were fiercely holding back the NVA. Some units had broken out of the encirclement at Xuan Loc and were headed for Saigon. At Lai Khe, 30 miles north of Saigon, the 5th ARVN Division was fighting to get to the city. There was no uprising or disturbance inside Saigon. By late April, plans were being made to turn Saigon into a second Stalingrad. And with the whole NVA around Saigon, the ever-expected B–52s could break Northern military power for a decade.

And the rains were coming, the tropical inundations that would halt the NVA's tanks in a sea of mud and give beleaguered Saigon the chance to repair its position. But on April 30, President General Duong Van Minh, one of Diem's assassins, announced the surrender. Halfway through his speech, the heavens opened and the rains poured down. Saigon fell twenty-five years to the day after President Truman first authorized assistance to the French war effort in Viet Nam.

REFLECTIONS: HOW TO LOSE A WAR

Guerrilla insurgencies will undoubtedly continue to be a major characteristic of politics in those areas of the world which have neither industrialized nor democratized. The United States may well find itself involved in one or another of them. But the prospect of the United States engaging in a conflict that reproduced even just a few of the peculiarities of Viet Nam approaches the point of inconceivability. In that conflict, the Americans confronted a well-disciplined Communist organization that had been able to secure something of a monopoly on the cause of national independence in a successful conflict against a major European power; to say the least, this has been a rare circumstance in world politics.[73] The Americans vastly escalated their ground commitment to the war without the assistance or even the approval of their principal allies. They permitted the country that they were trying to defend to be subjected to continuous invasion through the territory of two officially neutral neighboring states. During the conflict, the White House developed a policy of Americanization/attrition/gradualism almost perfectly calculated to arouse that impatience for which the American people are notorious. Finally, major powers avowedly hostile to the United States openly sent its adversaries great quantities of essential munitions.

It is hard to imagine a future American administration allowing itself to sink into a similar strategic swamp. Nevertheless, careful reflection on the Viet Nam wars may yield up some insights, although they may turn out to be unpalatable.

The debacle at Saigon in 1975 turned one of the most important "lessons" of the Viet Nam conflict into the most overlooked: people's revolutionary war—that invincible Communist weapon of the 1960s—failed. The United States, of all the industrialized democracies, is probably the most culturally alien to underdeveloped countries; nevertheless, however expensively and destructively, the Americans and their allies beat the Viet Cong guerrillas, despite the fact that the latter enjoyed sanctuaries and outside help. In any list of the causes of the defeat of the Viet Cong, American firepower, land reform, determined South Vietnamese resistance, and the abandonment of classical guerrilla tactics in the Tet Offensive must rank very high.

Then why did South Viet Nam fall? In discussions about the conquest of South Viet Nam, one sometimes hears the observation that the United States should never again become involved in a war on behalf of a government that does not enjoy the support of its own people. This is another way of saying that the fall of South Viet Nam was the fault of the South Vietnamese: the final and total defeat of the Saigon government is taken as proof that the South Vietnamese people did not truly desire, and perhaps were not really worthy of, independence. Hence there was nothing that the Americans could have done.

It is easy to understand why many Americans should wish to shift the blame for the conquest of South Viet Nam primarily or solely onto the South Vietnamese. But the conquest of South Viet Nam by the NVA in 1975 does not prove that its people desired the Communist victory anymore than the conquest of South Korea by the North Korean army in 1950 or the defeat of the Spanish Republic by Francisco Franco's forces in 1939 prove that the populations of either of those places desired those outcomes.

In Communist Hungary in 1956, in Fulgencio Batista's Cuba in 1958, in PDPA Kabul in 1980, in Nicolae Ceausescu's Romania in 1989, the armed forces of these tightly controlled police states broke apart under remarkably, even ridiculously, little pressure.[74] In contrast, even under the ferocious blows of Tet and the Eastern Offensive, the South Vietnamese army did not break up. On the contrary, along with the territorial militias, it sustained huge casualties year after year after year. The steadfastness of the fighting forces, the wide distribution of arms by the Saigon government to the population after Tet, the failure of the inhabitants of Saigon to rise up against their government in 1968 and in 1972 and even in 1975, the consequent necessity for the whole North Vietnamese Army to fight its way through to Saigon, the constant flow of refugees southward even in the weeks of collapse in 1975, the tragic epilogue of the Boat People—none of this indicates that a majority of the South Vietnamese people desired conquest by Hanoi. No, South Viet Nam did not fall because the South Vietnamese were morally inferior or avid for Communism. The truth is much more embarrassing than that.

By 1973, South Viet Nam was becoming what the Americans always said they wanted it to be, a country with a stable government and at least some of the external attributes of democracy. The war also had become what the Americans always said they wanted it to be, not an ostensible guerrilla conflict but a clear-cut conventional campaign of conquest by Hanoi. In such a war the ARVN needed only American supplies and air support to stand up to the best efforts of the NVA, as the 1972 offensive had demonstrated. And precisely at the conjunction of all these favorable developments, precisely when South Viet Nam was in the best shape it ever had been, the United States Congress decided to repudiate and abandon its ally. The Americans slashed their aid to the South while the Soviets continued theirs to the North. It was in these circumstances that President Theiu attempted the retrenchment that turned into disaster.

Then the Americans watched while North Viet Nam proceeded to trample on a peace agreement that the United States had signed a scant two years before and launched perhaps the largest conventional invasion Asia had seen in thirty years. In the face of this invasion, South Viet Nam's American-trained and American-equipped armed forces ground to a halt for lack of American supplies. In Hanoi's 1972 Easter Offensive, the South Vietnamese, bolstered by U.S. air power and supplies, repulsed General Giap's best efforts. In Hanoi's 1975 offensive, the South Vietnamese, deprived of promised U.S. support, were destroyed.

But that was not the whole of the United States legacy to South Viet Nam. For years, what had passed for American strategy had permitted

Hanoi to construct through so-called neutral neighboring states a complex of major military highways like a noose around South Viet Nam. When the Americans abandoned their allies, the outflanked South Vietnamese fell victim to the geography of Indochina that enabled Hanoi to substitute invasion for subversion.

The South Vietnamese could not have preserved their independence without long-term American assistance; but the same was once true of the West Europeans and the Israelis. The South Koreans, under U.S. protection for decades, today live in independence and prosperity. And since the American impact was much greater on South Vietnamese than on South Korean society (it was, in fact, more comparable to the U.S. impact on Japan by 1946), the South Vietnamese, whatever their political frailties, would by today probably have made significant advances toward some recognizable kind of liberal democracy. But they never got the chance. Even the Soviets, when they pulled their troops out of Afghanistan, did not abandon their allies so utterly, although they might have done so with much justification.

There are those who say that the struggle to preserve South Viet Nam was not totally in vain. It provided other countries in Southeast Asia with sobering evidence of what Communism really meant, and time—two decades—to get their economic and political houses in order. This is probably not much consolation to the South Vietnamese people, who dwell in Asia's most mismanaged economy and most efficient police state, and whose fate has been inexpressibly sad.

APPENDIX: AN ALTERNATIVE STRATEGY FOR DEFENDING SOUTH VIET NAM

There is no easy way to defeat a true guerrilla insurgency. The Johnson policy in Viet Nam, however, stands out as a model of what not to do. Sending a huge American army to Viet Nam for active campaigning ignored the essence of antiguerrilla war by seeking to kill rather than to isolate the guerrillas. It neutralized American technological advantages, caused needless American casualties, inflicted tremendous hurt on friendly civilians, alarmed our friends, gratified our enemies, and wore out the American public.

A valid alternative strategy would have been one that avoided Americanization, maximized American firepower, minimized American and friendly civilian casualties, diminished the effects of the Ho Chi Minh Trail, denied the bulk of the population to the VC/NVA, and placed the main responsibility for counterinsurgency where it belonged.

Harry Summers, Norman Hannah, and others have forcefully presented the case that the proper strategy for the United States was to stop the slow invasion of South Viet Nam by blocking the Ho Chi Minh Trail. In their scenario, American and ARVN forces would have deployed along a roughly

east-west axis across Laos to the border of Thailand.[75] The following discussion of an alternative strategy, however, begins with the assumption
that the Johnson Administration would not sanction such a move into Laos,
on the grounds that it would widen the conflict, invite an NVA attack
through northeastern Thailand, put too many Americans on the ground
too far from blue water, and so on. A second assumption is that President
Johnson would continue to forbid an invasion even of the southern provinces
of North Viet Nam because he and his advisers feared a Chinese intervention
on the Korean model (this fear had little basis in reality but was not un-
reasonable, given the experiences of the decision makers in Washington).
A third main assumption concerns clear-and-hold counterinsurgency operations of the type so ably advocated by Sir Robert Thompson.[76] These
produced excellent results in Malaya and are probably the best response to
insurgency in any country where the guerrillas are essentially lacking a
sanctuary. In South Viet Nam, however, such tactics would not in themselves have been sufficient because the insurgency was only one arm of the
campaign to destroy the Saigon government, the other being a slow-motion
invasion from the north.

In South Viet Nam, geography was destiny. Had South Viet Nam been
a peninsula, like South Korea or Malaya, or an archipelago like the Philippines, its defense would have been incomparably easier. But it was neither
of these things. Instead, the country was too big, too poorly shaped, too
exposed to flanking attacks from Laos and Cambodia to defend in its entirety
at a cost the American electorate would be willing to bear over the long
term. Since the allies would neither invade the enemy's base (North Viet
Nam) nor prevent him from coming to them (the Ho Chi Minh Trail), in
order to succeed they would have had to remake the geography of South
Viet Nam to their own advantage: to redefine the shape of *political* South
Viet Nam. That is the essence of the following strategy: a demographic
frontline plus counterinsurgency.

A demographic map of South Viet Nam would have revealed that the
overwhelming majority of the population lived in greater Saigon and the
Mekong Delta (Military Regions III and IV), plus a few urban centers along
the coast. The defense of these areas is the heart of the alternative strategy
here proposed. The northern boundary of Military Region III constituted
a rough "demographic frontier" dividing the heavily populated from the
sparsely populated provinces. In this alternative strategy, most U.S. and
some ARVN forces would deploy along that line and along the border
between MR III and Cambodia, supported by mobile reserves. Behind the
allies holding the demographic frontier, ARVN units and the Territorial
Forces would deal with remaining Viet Cong elements, with units modelled
on the Combined Action Platoons (CAPs) in highly exposed districts. Some
carefully selected and highly trained South Vietnamese guerrilla units might
remain behind in the highlands. Above this deployment of forces would

be the air power of the allied states, with the United States committed to maintaining a decisive superiority over the North Vietnamese air arm.

In addition, allied forces supported by the U.S. Navy would hold Hue and Da Nang in MR I. Hue had enormous symbolic importance for the Vietnamese, and both places would serve as potential launching areas for seaborne flanking attacks. (Da Nang would be the Inchon of South Viet Nam, except that the Americans would already be there.) These two coastal cities would become swollen with refugees from MR I and II; many of them could and should be evacuated to the south. Also, naturally, all those civilians above the demographic front line who wished to come into allied territory would be assisted.

Creating a real front line, with the enemy on one side and the civilians on the other, would give free play to superior American firepower. The United States would deploy in Viet Nam not a part-conscript army of half a million, but a much smaller professional force that by pursuing conservative tactics would incur far fewer losses: no more chasing of the enemy, no more search and destroy, no more body counts, no more booby-trap casualties. The bombing of North Viet Nam would become unnecessary; the Ho Chi Minh Trail would become irrelevant. Faced with such a front line, the enemy would have to abandon the struggle, in effect accepting a new partition militarily much more advantageous to the South, or else seek a decisive confrontation in the teeth of overwhelming allied fire superiority.

Besides greatly decreasing the size of the American force in South Viet Nam and directing its firepower toward the enemy and away from civilians, this strategy, by creating a true rear area, would both have made possible a thorough clear-and-hold cleanup in the regions of dense population and would also have allowed time for serious social and economic reforms to take hold in those same areas.

Next to reducing American and South Vietnamese casualties, one may consider the supreme advantage of the demographic strategy to be that under it the debacle of 1975 could not have occurred. In January 1975, most of the ARVN was in the sparsely populated Central Highlands and the dangerously exposed First Military Region below the 17th parallel. President Thieu's decision to remove the bulk of these forces to positions north of Saigon was a very good one and should have been put into effect years before. The 1975 retrenchment turned into a catastrophe for two main reasons. One was hasty planning. The second was the presence of the families of ARVN soldiers in the Central Highlands and other exposed areas. The understandable desire of ARVN soldiers to see to it that their relatives did not fall into Communist hands resulted in disintegration of many ARVN units and the conquest of the South.

Those families were present in the path of the retreat because ARVN considered it too much of a hardship on draftees to send them far away from their relatives for a long period. Instead of stationing soldiers far from their home areas and letting their families follow them, the government should have let the families stay put in their true homes and deployed the soldiers to defend them. If ARVN had been previously concentrated further south, in an orderly manner, with their families on one side of them and the Communists on the other, not only would a retrenchment have been unnecessary, but retreat or desertion would have become hardly thinkable. Nobody ever considered the 18th ARVN Division to be worth very much, but in the last days of the war it put up a ferocious defense at Xuan Loc after its dependents had been evacuated southward.[77]

Some serious objections to this strategy may come to mind.

First objection: A demographic strategy is defensive, giving the initiative to the enemy.

Response: So what? The Ho Chi Minh Trail put General Westmoreland's forces on the defensive anyway (and on exterior lines), but they refused to acknowledge this and thus could not take advantage of it. Clausewitz wrote that "it is easier to hold ground that to take it" and "the defensive form of warfare is intrinsically stronger than the offensive."[78] Under this demographic strategy, if the enemy "took the initiative," so much the better for the allies: NVA/VC forces mounting major attacks against one or more points on the frontier would pull down on top of themselves everything from B-52s to the 16-inch guns of the *New Jersey*, while confronting highly mobile allied forces operating on interior lines. One should never forget what happened to Giap's forces during the Easter Offensive, when they were attacking under the most favorable conditions.

Second objection: How could the South Vietnamese be induced to abandon large sections of their territory?

Response: They did it anyway, in 1975, only under the worst possible circumstances. There was nothing sacred about the 17th parallel; the *French* had made it a border, not the South Vietnamese. South Viet Nam had no obligation to defend indefensible territory, and neither did the United States. The trading of territory for survival is a venerable stratagem: the Russians retreated before Napoleon and Hitler, the Chinese before the Japanese; Lee defended Virginia, not Arkansas.

Third objection: Such a strategy would require the commitment of American forces for too long a time.

Response: How long is too long? United States forces have been standing guard in Germany, Japan, the Philippines, and Korea for two generations. The important question is not "how long," but "how many U.S. casualties," which a demographic strategy would have greatly reduced.

NOTES

1. Bernard Fall, *The Two Viet Nams* (New York: Praeger, 1967), p. 240.

2. Philippe Devillers, *Histoire du Viet-Nam de 1940 à 1952* (Paris: Editions du seuil, 1952), p. 63.

3. Fall, *Two Vietnams*, p. 281; Jeffrey Race, *War Comes to Long An: Revolutionary Conflict in a Vietnamese Province* (Berkeley: University of California, 1972), p. 83; William J. Duiker, *The Communist Road to Power in Viet Nam* (Boulder, CO: Westview, 1981), p. 180.

4. Duiker, *Communist Road*, pp. 183–84; Ronald Spector, *Advice and Support: The Early Years, 1941–1960* (Washington, DC: U.S. Army Center for Military History, 1983), pp. 315–16 and 326. Quotation is from Spector, p. 326.

5. Duiker, *Communist Road to Power*, pp. 99 and 186–88; Fall, *Two Viet Nams*, p. 316; Timothy J. Lomperis, *The War Everyone Lost—and Won: America's Intervention in Viet Nam's Twin Struggles* (Baton Rouge: Louisiana State University Press, 1984), p. 57; Douglas Pike, in *Viet Nam as History*, ed. Peter Braestrup (Washington, DC: University Press of America, 1984), p. 73; Guenter Lewy, *America in Viet Nam* (New York: Oxford University Press, 1978), p. 40 and passim; Robert F. Turner, *Vietnamese Communism: Its Origins and Development* (Stanford, CA: Hoover Institution, 1975), pp. 229–32; "Viet Nam: We Lied to You," *Economist*, February 26, 1983; Van Tien Dung, *Our Great Spring Victory* (New York: Monthly Review Press, 1977), p. 206 and passim; R. B. Smith, *An International History of the Vietnam War: Revolution versus Containment, 1955–1961* (New York: St. Martins, 1983), pp. 16–17 and 213.

6. John C. Donnell, *Viet Cong Recruitment: Why and How Men Join* (Santa Monica, CA: Rand Corporation, 1975); Nathan Leites, *The Viet Cong Style of Politics* (Santa Monica, CA: Rand Corporation, 1969).

7. Duiker, *Communist Road to Power*, pp. 250, 276.

8. Maxwell Taylor, *Swords and Plowshares* (New York: Norton, 1972), p. 235.

9. Ellen Hammer, *A Death in November: America in Viet Nam, 1963* (New York: Dutton, 1987), p. 45; Taylor, *Swords and Plowshares*, p. 300.

10. See Dennis J. Duncanson, *Government and Revolution in Viet Nam* (New York: Oxford University Press, 1968), pp. 327–41; Robert Scigliano, *South Viet Nam: Nation under Stress* (Boston: Houghton Mifflin, 1964); and Hammer, *Death in November*, are also revealing.

11. Hammer, *Death in November*, p. 309.

12. Duncanson, *Government and Revolution*, pp. 339–41; Tran Van Don, *Our Endless War* (San Rafael, CA: Presidio, 1978), pp. 107, 112; Hammer, *Death in November*, pp. 293 and 299; *The Pentagon Papers: The Defense Department History of United States Decisionmaking on Viet Nam* (Boston: Beacon Press-Gravel, 1971), vol. 2, p. 269; Denis J. Warner, *Certain Victory: How Hanoi Won the War* (Kansas City: Sneed, Andrews and McKeel, 1978), p. 129.

13. William Colby, *Lost Victory* (Chicago: Contemporary Books, 1989).

14. Spector, *Advice and Support*.

15. Phillip B. Davidson, *Viet Nam at War: The History, 1946–1975* (Novato, CA: Presidio, 1988), p. 660.

16. Thomas C. Thayer, *War without Fronts: The American Experience in Viet Nam* (Boulder, CO: Westview, 1986), p. 71.

17. Allan E. Goodman, *An Institutional Profile of the South Vietnamese Officer Corps* (Santa Monica, CA: Rand Corporation, 1970).

18. Olivier Todd, *Cruel April: The Fall of Saigon* (New York: Norton, 1990), p. 438.

19. Sir Robert Thompson, *Peace Is Not at Hand* (New York: David McKay, 1974), p. 169.

20. Race, *War Comes to Long An*, p. 164n.

21. Thayer, *War without Fronts*, p. 202; Douglas Pike, *PAVN: People's Army of Viet Nam* (Novato, CA: Presidio, 1986), p. 244.

22. Bruce Catton, *Glory Road* (Garden City, NY: Doubleday, 1952), pp. 102, 255; Allan Nevins, *The War for the Union: The Organized War, 1863–1864* (New York: Scribners, 1971), p. 131.

23. Thayer, *War without Fronts*, p. 106.

24. Todd, in *Cruel April*, says 250,000 ARVN were killed from 1960 to 1974 (p. 234).

25. *Washington Post*, April 6, 1969.

26. Don Oberdorfer, *Tet!* (Garden City, NY: Doubleday, 1971), p. 81.

27. Taylor, *Swords and Plowshares*, p. 383.

28. Davidson, *Viet Nam at War*, p. 475.

29. See, among others, Truong Nhu Tang, *A Viet Cong Memoir* (New York: Harcourt, 1987); and A. Charles Parker, *Viet Nam: Strategy for a Stalemate* (New York: Paragon, 1989).

30. For the magnitude of the Communist disaster, see Tran Van Tra, *Concluding the 30-Years War* (Roslyn, VA: Foreign Broadcast Information Service, 1983), p. 35; Duiker, *Communist Road to Power*, p. 269; Lewy, *America in Viet Nam*, p. 76; Thayer, *War without Fronts*, p. 92; Robert Shaplen, *Bitter Victory* (New York: Harper and Row, 1986), pp. 188–89; Douglas Blaufarb, *The Counterinsurgency Era: U.S. Doctrine and Performance* (New York:: Free Press, 1977), pp. 261–62.

31. Oberdorfer, *Tet!*, p. 201; Alan Dawson, *55 Days: The Fall of South Viet Nam* (Englewood Cliffs, NJ: Prentice-Hall, 1977), p. 92.

32. Some estimate that after the conquest, the Communists killed at least another 65,000 South Vietnamese; Todd, *Cruel April*, p. 427.

33. Samuel Popkin, "The Village War," in *Viet Nam as History*, ed. Peter Braestrup, p. 102.

34. *Economist*, April 15, 1972, p. 15.

35. Bruce Palmer, Jr., *The Twenty-Five-Year War: America's Military Role in Viet Nam* (Lexington: University Press of Kentucky, 1984), p. 122.

36. Colonel Hoang Ngoc Lung, *The General Offensives of 1968–1969* (Washington, DC: U.S. Army Center of Military History, 1981), p. 150.

37. W. Scott Thompson and Donaldson B. Frizzell, eds., *The Lessons of Viet Nam* (New York: Crane, Russak, 1977), pp. 256–61; General Ngo Quang Truong, *Territorial Forces* (Washington, DC: U.S. Army Center of Military History, 1981), p. 77.

38. William E. Le Gro, *Viet Nam from Cease-fire to Capitulation* (Washington, DC: U.S. Army Center of Military History, 1981), p. 330; James Lawton Collins, *The Development and Training of the South Vietnamese Army* (Washington, DC: Department of the Army, 1975), p. 151.

39. Thomas C. Thayer, "Territorial Forces," in Thompson and Frizzell, eds., *Lessons of Viet Nam*, p. 258.

40. Norman B. Hannah, *The Key to Failure: Laos and the Viet Nam War*, says,

Of course nations don't roll over with the inevitable automaticity of a row of dominoes. Nor did President Eisenhower mean that when he applied the expression to Southeast Asia. The essential meaning of the domino concept is that in international power politics, as in physics, a force once moving in a given direction will continue until deflected or stopped by a greater force. Moreover, such a force tends to gain momentum as it gains mass from sequential victories. As a result, the longer that counter-action is postponed, the greater the resistance needed to stop the force. The moral underlying the domino concept is derived from the historical observation that nations (especially democracies) tend to put off setting up the necessary counter-force until the initial threat has attained a momentum at which it can openly be stopped by a massive and destructive effort—for example, World War II.

([Lanham, MD: Madison Books, 1987], pp. 154–55)
41. Lin Biao, *Long Live the Victory of People's War* (Peking: 1965).
42. Peter Braestrup, *Big Story* (Boulder, CO: Westview, 1977).
43. Alan Goodman, "The Dynamics of the United States–South Vietnamese Alliance," in *Viet Nam as History*, ed. Peter Braestrup, p. 90.
44. Todd, *Cruel April*, pp. 253, 398; Lewy, *America in Viet Nam*, pp. 400–404.
45. Braestrup, *Big Story*.
46. *Pentagon Papers*, vol. 3, p. 480.
47. Donald Vought, "American Culture and American Arms: The Case of Viet Nam," in *Lessons from an Unconventional War*, eds., Richard A. Hunt and Richard H. Schultz, Jr., (New York: Pergamon, 1982).
48. Andrew F. Krepinevich, Jr., *The Army and Viet Nam* (Baltimore: Johns Hopkins University Press, 1986).
49. Sir Robert Thompson, *No Exit from Viet Nam* (New York: David McKay, 1969), p. 53; Krepinevich, *Army and Viet Nam*, p. 197. Edward N. Luttwak, *The Pentagon and the Art of War* (New York: Simon and Schuster, 1984), p. 32.
50. Richard M. Nixon, *RN: The Memoirs of Richard Nixon* (New York: Grosset and Dunlap, 1978), p. 431.
51. Douglas Pike, "Masters of Deceit" (Berkeley: University of California, unpb. ms), p. 31.
52. Thayer, *War without Fronts*, p. 85.
53. *Pentagon Papers*, vol. 4, pp. 56, 116–20, 137, 168, 184, 223–24; see also Mark Clodfelter, *The Limits of Air Power: The American Bombing of North Viet Nam* (New York: Free Press, 1989).
54. Karl von Clausewitz, *On War*, Book IV, Chapter four.
55. Thompson and Frizzell, eds., *Lessons of Vietnam*, p. 77.
56. Luttwak, *Pentagon and the Art of War*, p. 42.
57. *New York Times*, December 7, 1967.
58. The destructiveness of the American way of war unfortunately antedates Viet Nam. Consider Sherman's campaigns in the Civil War, the bombing of nonmilitary targets in Europe and Japan in World War II, or the thorough liberation-devastation of Seoul.
59. Lewy, *America in Vietnam*.
60. Taylor, *Swords and Plowshares*, p. 247.
61. This was the concept for the German invasion of France, developed by Alfred von Schlieffen, chief of the German General Staff from 1891 to 1905. Under the Schlieffen Plan, the French Army would be outflanked and then destroyed by a vast wheeling movement of the German Army's massive right (northern) wing across neutral Belgium.

62. Norman B. Hannah, *The Key to Failure: Laos and the Viet Nam War* (Lanham, MD: Madison Books, 1987), p. xxv.

63. Shaplen, *Bitter Victory*, pp. 148, 157; Douglas Pike, "Road to Victory," in *War in Peace*, vol. 5 (London: Orbis), 1984.

64. See Nguyen Tien Hung and Jerrold Schechter, *The Palace File* (New York: Harper and Row, 1986).

65. Le Gro, *Viet Nam from Cease-fire to Capitulation*, p. 78.

66. Gabriel Kolko, *Anatomy of a War* (New York: Pantheon, 1985), p. 482.

67. Charles Stuart Callison, *Land to the Tiller in the Mekong Delta* (Lanham, MD: University Press of America, 1983), p. 111.

68. See Robert A. Scalapino, "We Cannot Accept a Communist Seizure of Viet Nam," in the *New York Times Magazine*, December 11, 1966, V1, p. 46; the CBS survey quoted in Wesley Fishel, Viet Nam: *Anatomy of a Conflict* (Itasca, IL: Peacock, 1968), pp. 653, 659; Kolko, *Anatomy of a War*, p. 250; Thompson, *No Exit from Viet Nam*, p. 65; Race, *War Comes to Long An*, p. 188; Howard R. Penniman, *Elections in South Viet Nam* (Washington, DC: American Enterprise Institute, 1972), p. 199; Duncanson, *Government and Revolution*, p. 13, estimates that the Communists had the support of one in four South Vietnamese.

69. Thompson, *Peace Is Not at Hand*, p. 169.

70. Le Gro, *Viet Nam from Ceasefire*, p. 88.

71. Lewy, *America in Viet Nam*, p. 208; Van Tien Dung, *Our Great Spring Victory*, pp. 17–18; General Dong Van Khuyen, *The RVNAF* (Washington, DC: U.S. Army Center of Military History, 1980), pp. 287–88; Le Gro, *Viet Nam from Ceasefire*, pp. 84–87; Lomperis, *The War Everyone Lost*, p. 75.

72. General Vo Nguyen Giap, *How We Won the War* (Philadelphia: Recon, 1976), p. 24.

73. Chalmers Johnson has made this summary:

In terms of revolutionary strategy, communism has succeeded only when it has been able to co-opt a national liberation struggle, and it has failed whenever it was opposed to or isolated from a national liberation struggle, such as those in Israel, Algeria, Indonesia and Burma. Needless to add, even when supporting a war of national liberation, the communists have occasionally been defeated, as in Greece, Malaya, the Philippines, and Venezuela. (*Autopsy on People's War* [Berkeley: University of California, 1973], p. 10).

74. Anthony James Joes, *From the Barrel of a Gun: Armed Forces and Revolutions* (Washington, DC: Pergamon-Brassey's, 1986).

75. See Harry Summers, *On Strategy: A Critical Analysis of the Viet Nam War* (Novato, CA: Presidio, 1982); and Hannah, *Key to Failure*.

76. Sir Robert Thompson, *Defeating Communist Insurgency: The Lessons of Malaya and Viet Nam* (New York: Praeger, 1966).

77. According to Liddell Hart:

Man has two supreme loyalties—to country and to family. And with most men the second, being more personal, is the stronger. So long as their families are safe they will defend their country, believing that by their sacrifice they are safeguarding their families also. But even the bonds of patriotism, discipline and comradeship are loosened when the family itself is menaced. (B. H. Liddell Hart, *Strategy* [New York: Praeger, 1954], p. 153).

78. Clausewitz, *On War*, Book VI, Chapter one.

Chapter 6

Afghanistan: The End of the Red Behemoth

We have never rejected terror on principle and we can never do so.

V. I. Lenin

There are only two things Afghans must have: the Koran, and Stingers.

Ahmad Shah Massoud

In the 1980s the world witnessed "the largest single national rising in the twentieth century," the revolt of the Afghan people against Soviet occupation.[1] The war in Afghanistan was the longest military conflict the Soviets ever experienced: direct Soviet involvement extended from December 1979 to mid-1988. During the struggle Soviet troops reached Qandahar, the southernmost expansion of Russian power since the days of Peter the Great. The conflict turned into a textbook study on how a major power should not wage a counterguerrilla war. In the end, the Soviets withdrew their army from Afghanistan, and that was to be only the beginning of such withdrawals.

THE COUNTRY

Afghanistan lies at the point of intersection between the Middle East and East Asia and lies astride the principal routes between Persia and India. The country is roughly the combined size of France, Belgium, the Netherlands, and Switzerland; or of Illinois, Ohio, Michigan, Wisconsin, and Indiana. There are no railways and few real roads (Norway, another mountainous

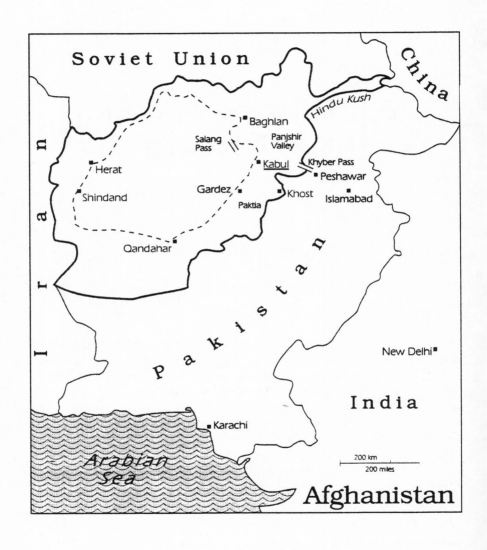

country, with half the area of Afghanistan, had about twenty times the paved road mileage).

The pre-invasion population was about 16 million. Kabul, with 600,000 inhabitants, was by far the largest city. The population is highly diverse ethnically and linguistically, with the 6,000,000 Pushtuns being politically the most important. The lingua franca is a dialect of Persian that some scholars call Dari.

Before the invasion, Afghan society was overwhelmingly rural, made up of independent farmers. Large landholdings were relatively rare. Afghanistan was a poor country: per capita income on the eve of the Soviet invasion was about $168, the literacy rate was 10 percent. But by Asian standards the people were well fed. Everyday life revolved around local affairs and religion.

Among the fiercely independent Afghans the basic unifying force has been the adherence of 90 percent of the population to Sunni Islam. "The ideal male personality type in Afghan society is the warrior-poet."[2] The Pushtun moral code included a prohibition on killing women or children or musicians, or anyone who had asked for mercy or was found in a mosque. "Quite possibly the Afghans are the most hospitable people in the world."[3] During World War II, Afghanistan provided a refuge for numerous Jews seeking to escape the European holocaust.

A SKETCH OF PRE-INVASION AFGHAN HISTORY

When the author of these lines was a boy, Afghanistan was a word (like Timbuktu) used to denote utter remoteness. But the historian Arnold Toynbee described Afghanistan, lying athwart the trade route from the Mediterranean to China, as one of the two great crossroads of cultural dispersion from prehistory to the Renaissance.

The written history of Afghanistan begins in 329 B.C. with the invasion of Alexander the Great, who found himself a bride there, Roxanne. Islam reached Afghanistan in the seventh century A.D., although it took several hundred years to establish its dominance. In 1219, Genghis Khan invaded and conquered the area. This was a true catastrophe, because the conquerers systematically destroyed irrigation systems, turning much good land to desert. More Mongol invasions occurred between 1370 and 1500. By the end of this period, Afghanistan was prostrate. Its only hope of recovery lay in the revival of trade, but new sea routes had opened up between Europe and the East, and thus Afghanistan sank to the status of a remote area.

The nineteenth century saw the gradual establishment of Afghanistan's present borders. This was the era of the Great Game between the Tsarist and British empires for control of the Indian frontier regions. Afghanistan was able to establish and maintain what independence it possessed in part because it provided a convenient buffer between the two contending empires. But being a buffer meant that its borders were artificial, embracing a hodgepodge of tribes, religions, and tongues. As a result, most Afghan peoples have ethnic brethren across the borders in former Soviet Central Asia and Pakistan. The mountainous terrain, poor communications, and linguistic diversity kept Afghanistan administratively decentralized, with little national consciousness. Presiding over this diverse population was a monarchy with hardly any bureaucratic apparatus and usually no real program except survival. Political life was mainly local.

The modern world burst in upon Afghanistan in the form of a British invasion during the First Afghan War (1839–1842). That conflict showed, not for the last time, how much easier it was to overrun Afghanistan than to control it. A principal event of this incursion was the annihilation of the British garrison at Kabul, the greatest British defeat in modern history until the fall of Singapore. It is very important to note, in light of contemporary events, that the Afghanistan that inflicted this bloody repulse on a waxing British imperialism lacked both the structure of a modern state and access to modern weapons.

The end of World War II was the beginning of the British retreat from empire. Thus the traditional counterweight to Russian domination of Afghanistan disappeared; India, successor to the Empire, was too weak, and the United States was too preoccupied elsewhere, to replace the British in the Great Game. The United States did not grant diplomatic recognition to Afghanistan until 1934, and it was not until 1942 that the first U.S. representative arrived in Kabul.

THE SAUR REVOLUTION

The constitution of 1964 placed almost all power in the hands of the king, the diffident Zahir, born in 1915. Zahir ruled with the support of a conservative parliament. During the 1960s the Afghans held national parliamentary elections, with secret balloting and woman suffrage. Nevertheless, on July 17, 1973, while the king was in Italy, a bloodless coup in Kabul proclaimed his rule at an end and a republican government in force. Mohammed Daoud, a cousin and brother-in-law of the king, had been prime minister from 1953 to 1963. He was the instigator of the coup and proclaimed himself president and prime minister. This first Afghan experiment with republicanism, a political form unfamiliar to the people and their leaders, was not off to a propitious start. Thus Daoud set the stage for his own personal tragedy.

This 1973 coup was not Communist-inspired, although the Communists were no doubt glad to see the end of the monarchy, one unifying institution in a multilingual, multiethnic society.[4] King Zahir went into reclusive exile in Rome; he proclaimed his intention to return to his country as king only if a plebiscite called him back. Some in Afghanistan later blamed Zahir for all their subsequent sufferings, saying that the Communists were able to take over the country because Zahir had done nothing to move it out of its backwardness.[5]

Daoud came into power with some big ideas about developing the country. In need of large-scale financial assistance for economic and military development, he looked to the United States, but Washington expressed no interest in helping Afghanistan. Daoud then turned to the Soviet Union, which was more receptive. By 1976, however, Daoud apparently had come to regret the degree of his dependence on the Soviets, seeking to counterbalance their influence by turning more closely to India (a pale reflection of the old Anglo-Russian Great Game). In the beginning of his rule Daoud had the support of the Afghan Communists, called the People's Democratic Party of Afghanistan (PDPA), and its numerous members and sympathizers in the army officer corps. His attempts to edge away from the Soviet Union antagonized these groups. In April 1978, the PDPA organized a large demonstration in Kabul. Alarmed, Daoud ordered the arrest of the principal party leaders—but not their friends in the army. This turned out to be literally a fatal mistake. Communist elements in the armed forces apparently feared that Daoud, after he had arrested and perhaps killed the leadership of the PDPA, would turn on them. Leftist officers thereupon organized a coup against Daoud. After some bitter fighting with Daoud's guards on April 27–28, they killed him, as well as all the members of his family they could get their hands on.

Afghan Communists have mythologized the murder of Daoud as "the Great Saur [April] Revolution," but it was in fact "an urban coup d'état against an unpopular, autocratic government" carried out by a relative handful of military officers.[6] The coup, however, was shortly followed by the installation of a completely PDPA cabinet. How the PDPA managed to take over so quickly and easily is not clear.[7] Neither is it clear to what degree the coup was Communist engineered from the beginning. Certainly the timing of the move against Daoud itself was fortuitous, being triggered by Daoud's orders to arrest leaders of the PDPA. The Soviet Union apparently knew about, and approved, the coup against Daoud and supported the new PDPA cabinet. But Soviet participation in the coup, both the instigation and the actual deed, seems to have been minimal. Part of the explanation for the PDPA takeover of power from Daoud lies in the fact that for years he had allowed their members to infiltrate the officer corps and the bureaucracy; indeed Daoud himself had appointed many PDPA members and sympathizers to office.

In any event, former U.S. Ambassador Robert Neumann advised the Carter Administration to cut off all U.S. aid to the new PDPA regime. Neumann later stated that the mild American reaction to the killing of Daoud contributed to the subsequent Soviet invasion. President Carter's former national security adviser Zbigniew Brzezinski agrees with this assessment.[8]

THE PDPA REGIME

The Afghan Communist party had existed only since January 1965. All the founding members of the organization were from the educated elite of Afghan society; there were no workers or peasants, and the party won only two parliamentary seats (out of over 200) in the 1969 elections. There is some evidence that founding father Babrak Karmal, one day to play a leading role in the tragedy that engulfed his country, was as early as 1965 an agent of the Soviet KGB.[9] The party soon split into irreconcilably hostile factions, the Parcham ("Banner") and the Khalq ("the masses"). Ideological differences seem to have been less important than sociological and personal ones. Members of the Parcham were overwhelmingly Kabulis, relatively sophisticated and Persian-speaking, and thoroughly subservient to the Soviets. Khalq supporters tended to be from the provinces, and heavily Pushtun. Khalqis predominated in the officer corps of the military, while Parchamis eventually controlled KhAD, the secret police.

With President Daoud out of the way, the new PDPA government included Nur Mohammed Taraki as president, Hafizullah Amin as foreign minister and most important figure in the cabinet, and Babrak Karmal as deputy prime minister. All had been founders of PDPA, and they would be, respectively, the first, second, and third presidents of Communist Afghanistan.

Nur Mohammed Taraki is the first known member of the Afghan Communist party. He studied English in Bombay, where he allegedly joined the Indian Communist Party in 1937. He worked in the U.S. aid mission in Kabul and in the U.S. Embassy in the 1950s and 1960s. By the time of his selection as president, he was an alcoholic. Hafizullah Amin was the son of a government employee and a graduate of Kabul University. He earned an M.A. in education at Teachers College of Columbia University in the 1950s and unsuccessfully sought a Columbia Ph.D. Babrak Karmal, founder of the Parcham faction of the PDPA, was born in 1929, the son of an army general. He attended Kabul University in the early 1950s after having previously failed his entrance examinations.

The new Taraki-Amin dictatorship first purged followers of Daoud from the bureaucracy, then turned against members of the Parcham faction. One result of this intraparty strife was that young and inexperienced Khalqis were put into sensitive offices, where they soon made a mess of government programs.

The regime also turned its wrath against the non-Communist intelligentsia and the religious leadership. During 1978 and 1979, the new government admitted killing 12,000 political prisoners. Some estimates run much higher. The Taraki-Amin regime encouraged factionalism within the PDPA and ignored political organization within the army. Most of all, they alienated vast strata of the population with a program badly conceived and worse administered. For example, Khalqi reforms required that women achieve equality with men, and this meant first of all making women literate. Hence women would be dragged out of their homes and made to sit in literacy classes, where the lessons often contained attacks against religion.

Against religion, Bad Move

Mullahs (Islamic religious teachers) who opposed such practices were often simply shot by enlightened young Kabuli PDPA types, with no trial or other ceremony. In 1978 there were perhaps 320,000 mullahs in the country, and the regime thoroughly alienated this strategic group. Growing numbers of Afghans viewed the policies of the clique in Kabul as "repulsively anti-Islamic."[10]

The Kabul regime also believed in land redistribution, as a prelude to collectivization. Nobody in the Afghan government seemed to know how much land would be available for or distributed by government land reforms. In the villages, land was taken away from arbitrarily defined "rich landlords" and handed over to "poor peasants" on the Leninist model. Such reforms cut tenant farmers off from the age-old village social security system provided by patronage from larger landowners and offended traditional Islamic ideas of legal propriety.[11]

Many servants of the PDPA regime undoubtedly wanted to raise the status of women in Afghan society; they also viewed literacy as a great boon that they would bestow on the population. Westerners may find these ideas laudable. But the tiny PDPA and a somewhat larger circle of sympathizers provided a very slender political base for the new and illegitimate regime. When, therefore, the government launched headlong attacks on the whole Afghan way of life, treating any who resisted such attacks (which eventually included the majority of Afghans) as enemies to be crushed, it was provoking disaster. The whole PDPA approach to governing suggests not naive sympathy, but profound hostility toward the people. It was not liberation but modernization that PDPA intended to impose, modernization at any cost, no matter how destructive: a true Central Asian Stalinism. "It was the attempt by a minority regime to drastically alter the existing Afghan value system and social structure, and the brutality associated with this attempt, that finally provoked large-scale resistance."[12] Thus this tiny minority, urban, foreign educated, religion-hating, peasant-despising, and teacher-killing (reminiscent of the Greek Communists) enkindled the wrath of the population against it. In March 1979, nearly a year before the Soviet invasion, furious crowds demonstrated in the streets of Herat, killing hundreds of Afghan Communists and scores of the numerous Soviet personnel in their city. The regime restored its control in Herat at the cost of between 3,000 and 5,000 civilian deaths. By the eve of the Soviet invasion, perhaps as many as 23 provinces (out of 28) were under guerrilla control.[13]

The egregious incompetence displayed by their protégés in Kabul alarmed the leaders in Moscow. President Taraki, who found himself more and more pushed into a figurehead role, journeyed to the Kremlin, where he apparently received orders to get rid of Amin, the radical force in the Kabul regime. In September 1979, Taraki attempted to arrest or kill Amin at government headquarters, whereupon an authentic shoot-out occurred. The unexpected result of this palace gunfight was that Amin threw Taraki into prison and took the presidency for himself. A few weeks later the regime announced that ex-president Taraki had "died of a serious illness."

THE SOVIETS INVADE

In retrospect, it is clear that the Kremlin was giving signs as early as the spring of 1979 that it had decided an invasion might be necessary. Among these signs were the visits to Kabul by numerous high-ranking Soviet officers, including General Ivan Pavlovskii, who had commanded the invasion of Czechoslovakia in 1968.

Indeed the invasion of Afghanistan was modeled upon the Czechoslovakian scenario: subversion of an unreliable Communist regime and its replacement, after Soviet troops had taken control of the capital city in a lightning move, by pliant stooges.

In the last weeks of December, in preparation for the coming invasion, Soviet advisers began removing the batteries from Afghan army tanks for "winterization" and gathering up antitank ammunition for "inventory." Afghan army officers invited to a Soviet reception got drunk and found themselves locked up. On December 24, Soviet airborne troops, flight after flight, began to descend upon Kabul, occupying key positions and buildings. At the same time ground troops poured across the border, heading for Kabul and Herat. On December 27, special Soviet units attacked the palace where Amin was living; after a fierce fight, during which they sustained numerous casualties, Soviet troops killed Amin and members of his family.

The Kremlin brazenly explained all this to the world by saying that the Afghan government had requested Soviet aid. A request for assistance—invasion—was in fact made, but by Babrak Karmal; this Central Asian Quisling asked, from a radio station inside the Soviet border, that Moscow send assistance to his country—after 20,000 Soviet troops had already crossed the frontier.[14] No invitation ever came from Amin, an invitation that would have given the Soviet invasion the figleaf of legality; Amin was dead, killed by his erstwhile Soviet patrons who had come to "assist" him.[15] Indeed, the Soviets were later to claim that Amin was a CIA agent.[16] In return for his services, the Soviets installed Babrak Karmal as president.

The Soviet takeover was a masterpiece of its kind, better planned and executed even than the Czech invasion; Brezhnev knew that practice makes perfect. Conceivably, Amin could have organized resistance around Kabul, called for a popular rising, or requested foreign assistance. "But Amin could do [none of these things] because the first move of the Soviet invasion was an airborne coup de main [by elite Soviet airborne troops] which suppressed any attempt at resistance."[17] The timing seemed good too: the Carter Administration was reeling from both foreign and domestic setbacks, the American polity was still punchdrunk from Viet Nam and Watergate and distracted by the upcoming presidential election and the Iranian hostage crisis. But the invasion, technically a success, did not work out as it was intended. Instead of quenching popular resistance to Kabul, it enflamed it. Seizing Kabul was the easy part; enforcing the authority of a Russian puppet regime over the rest of the country was to prove a greater challenge.

REFLECTIONS ON THE INVASION

Many observers at the time expressed the belief that the Soviets invaded Afghanistan in order to prevent the overthrow of a Communist regime; that is, the main reason for the invasion was to enforce the Brezhnev Doctrine. But this explanation is problematical. From an ideological standpoint, the Afghanistan that the Soviets invaded in 1979 was not a Communist or even a socialist state; it was merely a state ruled by Communists.[18] Besides, there are other, much more historically rooted explanations.

Afghanistan's geography, including its thousand–mile border with the Soviet Union, made it inescapably interesting to its northern neighbor. Tsarist Russia had long cherished ambitions to move toward the shores of the Indian Ocean. Leon Trotsky said in 1919 that "the road to Paris and Berlin lies through the towns of the Punjab and Afghanistan." (Of course, history has shown Trotsky to be dead wrong about this, as about many other things, but that is beside the point: he and other Communist leaders probably believed it.) In the infamous Hitler–Stalin Pact of 1939, the future area of Soviet territorial loot was identified as being "south of the Soviet Union in the direction of the Indian Ocean" and "in the general direction of the Persian Gulf."

Occupied as he was with digesting and imposing socialism on his new Eastern European subjects, Stalin displayed little interest in what we once called the Third World. Khrushchev, on the other hand, who had emerged as supreme leader by 1957 at the latest, had other ideas. His neo–Trotskyite interest in the underdeveloped world as the weak link in the defenses against Soviet expansionism manifested itself partly in the attention he gave to neighboring Afghanistan. There is much ethnic overlap between Soviet Central Asia and Afghanistan's northern, Soviet-contiguous provinces, which also contain most of its natural resources. Impressive mountain chains divide these northern provinces from the rest of the country, and for decades there has been sentiment in favor of at least regional autonomy in the area.[19]

Besides, a Sovietized Afghanistan would have made a perfect base from

which to propagate the independence of "Baluchistan" and "Pushtunistan."
The success of this policy would achieve the dismemberment of Pakistan,
ally of the United States and China, and the establishment of a group of
pseudo-independent Soviet protectorates from the Soviet border down to
the Indian Ocean.

Beginning in the 1950s, therefore, the Soviet Union lent Afghanistan
money, delivered MiG-15 fighters, and built three air bases in the country.
Many Afghan army and air force officers and cadets went to the Soviet
Union for training.[20] Most of these officers who had been exposed to the
Soviet Union came back to Afghanistan profoundly impressed with the
military might of their northern neighbor. The king, suspicious of these
returnees, would not let them rise to the highest ranks. Here was one of
the roots of the coup that destroyed the monarchy and eventually brought
the country to its subsequent catastrophe. Another was that the educational
reforms of the 1950s began to produce an element in the population cut off
from both the traditional power wielders and the conservative masses. Embarrassed by their country's position in the world, and their own position
within their country, these new would-be elites turned to the Soviet Union
for inspiration. Thus, the Brezhnev Doctrine quite aside, "the invasion
appears as the logical culmination of decades of Soviet [and Tsarist] policies
aimed at achieving ever-greater control of Afghanistan."[21] On the other
hand, if the Soviets had not invaded in 1979, and the result had been the
overthrow of a friendly regime in Kabul and its replacement by a militantly
anti-Communist and Islamic Afghanistan, the effects on the millions of
Muslims living in Soviet Central Asia could have been profound.[22]

We should also recall, finally, that the Afghanistan invasion occurred in
a context of increasingly bold Soviet international behavior. Article 28 of
the Brezhnev constitution of 1976 proclaimed that "the foreign policy of
the USSR shall aim at . . . supporting the struggle of peoples for national
liberation." Soviet submarines were making repeated incursions into Swed-
ish waters; Soviet aircraft wantonly downed a Korean airliner in 1983, and
so on.[23] The invasion of Afghanistan merely underlined in red the fact that
the world was "confronted by clear evidence of an utterly novel boldness
on the part of the Soviet military leaders, and of an equally new confidence
on the part of the Kremlin leaders in the professional competence of their
military colleagues."[24]

THE UPRISING

Not long after the April (Saur) coup, armed risings occurred in several
provinces. These were revolts against government policies, but not necessarily intended to precipitate or end in the fall of the government itself;
armed resistance to unpopular Kabul policies was a venerable exercise. But
the PDPA in Kabul responded with such violence that it drove the resisters

to real civil war.[25] Then came the Soviet invasion, the first true foreign occupation of Afghanistan in modern times. Now dissatisfaction with government policies would be overshadowed by the explosive, elemental power of outraged religion.

The Afghan freedom fighters, as President Ronald Reagan called them, faced truly tremendous odds. These included the enormous disparity in size, wealth, population, and technological capacity between Afghanistan and the Soviet Union, the proximity of the invading power, the geographical and political isolation of Afghanistan, a widespread tendency in world capitals to write off Afghanistan as being "within the Soviet sphere of influence," and finally, but not least, internal disunity within the insurgent ranks approaching fragmentation. As one keen and sympathetic observer put it, "the Afghan Resistance is not an army but rather a people in arms; its strengths and weaknesses are those of Afghan society."[26]

Traditionally, local leadership had been independent of national or even provincial control; in this conflict, the first loyalty of a guerrilla in Afghanistan was usually to his commander, often a tribal or provincial figure of importance. The localism, individualism, and readiness to defend one's honor so characteristic of the Afghan people made them excellent prospects for guerrilla war but also worked against them in that this individualism and localism hindered unity within the resistance. Indeed, explosive rivalries riddled the insurgency: among the various religious, regional, and tribal groups inside Afghanistan; among the exiled party politicians in Pakistan; between these politicians and the guerrilla commanders inside Afghanistan; and among the guerrilla commanders themselves.

Tribal and ethnic divisions made it possible for the Kabul regime to recruit here and there local militias, composed of tribes or clans different from those in the area that supported the resistance.[27] "The majority of them [members of these militias] are simply mercenaries attracted by the substantial pay (about £30 per month)", and "throughout the war, the militia's willingness to take Communist money has far exceeded their willingness to fight."[28]

Gérard Chaliand, visiting Afghanistan in 1980, observed that the resistance was vastly popular but politically weak. Unlike many other post–World War II guerrilla movements, the Afghan resistance was overwhelmingly conservative in its political orientation (resembling the Spanish guerrillas that fought Napoleon's occupation). But the old pre-coup establishment was largely absent from the leadership of the resistance; this was especially true of army officers and professional politicians of the old regime. The former, pre-Saur political structure of Afghanistan appears to have been completely shattered. In its place was rising a new leadership group, including many non–Pushtun elements. But the lack of unity (and worse) within this group presented an unattractive picture to the outside world. The resistance movement divided into many different parties, each with its headquarters in Pakistan. These parties funneled supplies to particular guerrilla bands associated with them inside Afghanistan. They also sought to represent the resistance to the outside world.

Some students of the war saw tribal divisions or the influence of some outstanding personality as much more important than ideology as an explanation for fragmentation within the resistance.[29] There was undoubtedly much truth in this view. Nevertheless, the parties can be usefully, if crudely, divided into two main groups. The moderates, friendly to the West, professed to seek a new government based on democratic elections, possibly with former King Zahir playing an important if symbolic role. The so-called fundamentalists, often devoted to the Iranian Ayatollah Ruhollah Khomeini, wished to establish a postwar Islamic republic and expressed profound hostility to King Zahir and the West as well. Indeed, in the Hazara area of central Afghanistan, some elements declared they were fighting for eventual incorporation into a "Greater Iran."[30]

As a result of all these centrifugal forces, during the anti-Soviet conflict the Afghan resistance never established a true governmental infrastructure, like that of Unitá in Angola. The insurgency lacked central coordination, and this meant that there was never a general strategy. Lack of coordination of effort often allowed the Soviets to operate against one group at a time. There has even been bloodshed between different guerrilla groups.[31]

After 1984, the disarray inside the resistance ranks abated to a degree. Significant moves toward at least formal unity among most of the different groups resulted in a unified delegation being sent to the Fortieth Anniversary celebration at the United Nations. In January 1987, leaders of the resistance parties in Peshawar proclaimed a united program consisting mainly of two points: (1) the necessity of complete Soviet withdrawal from Afghanistan and (2) the resistance mujahideen (mujahideen means warriors of God) to govern the country until free nationwide elections.[32] Early in 1988, resistance leaders established a provisional government, with a supreme council including the leaders of the seven main parties.[33]

Lacking unity, the resistance also lacked weapons. For years Afghan guerrillas were poorly equipped, much more so than their contemporaries in El Salvador or Angola. Most guerrilla units were self-supporting; they captured their guns from Soviet and Kabul forces. Defectors from the Kabul army and from ostensibly pro-Kabul local militias were another major source of weapons and ammunition. Foreign arms shipments did not assume any importance until well after the Soviet invasion.[34] Pakistan, Egypt, Saudi Arabia, China, and Kuwait sent arms, while particular types of modern weapons supplied by the United States became especially crucial in the mid-1980s (see below).

In the early years, nothing seemed to be going well for the resistance. The dominant theory of guerrilla warfare holds that as the fish move in the water, so the guerrillas move among the civilian population, receiving life-giving sustenance and life-saving intelligence from it. But in fact, by 1984, because of the dreadful depradations of the Soviet invaders and their murderous marionettes in Kabul, the impoverished civilians in many areas were not able to provide the guerrillas with food, so that the freedom fighters had to carry their own. In fact, in many instances the guerrillas themselves had to provide food for starving villagers.[35]

Infiltration by the enemy also afflicted the resistance. Both the KGB and KhAD, Kabul's East German–trained intelligence/secret police, penetrated the various resistance groups inside Afghanistan, in Pakistan, and also in Europe. That some KGB agents were from Soviet Central Asia facilitated this infiltration. (This is one area where the fragmentation within the resistance did not have entirely negative consequences, because it limited what KhAD and the KGB could discover.) KhAD operated with some effect in the refugee camps in Pakistan, spreading rumors and dissension and occasionally killing a resistance leader. These agencies also took Afghan children to the Soviet Union, where they were trained in the use of explosives and sabotage and then sent them back to infiltrate resistance units.[36]

These activities bore fruit. There were a few spectacular defections from the resistance to the Kabul-Soviet side, most notably that of Ismatullah Achekzai, who took more than 100 guerrillas with him.

The regime also sought to win over tribes and clans with cash donations and privileges such as exemption from the draft. These overtures were not always rejected, although most such alliances between local leaders and Kabul turned out to be tactical and temporary.

THE RESISTANCE: STRENGTHS, STRATEGY, AND TACTICS

Clearly, the resistance ledger was not all debits, or the war would have come to an end years ago with a Soviet victory. The fragmented nature of Afghan society made resistance unity impossible, especially since no truly charismatic leader appeared who could transcend tribal, regional, and religious divisions among the freedom fighters. But it also deprived the Soviets of a target against which to launch a major, decisive attack. The resistance was amorphous, therefore almost impossible to destroy. It might be a good thing to recall that it was a loosely organized, multilingual Afghan commonwealth that inflicted a serious defeat upon the mighty British Empire in the First Afghan War.

The rugged mountainous terrain of most of Afghanistan is well suited to guerrilla warfare. Most of the guerrillas came equipped with hardy physiques and stoic attitudes, bequeathed to them by many centuries of Spartan living. The resistance also enjoyed the truly priceless asset of a sanctuary in Pakistan. Pakistan served not only as an area in which guerrillas could leave their families in relative safety; it was also an irreplaceable conduit for outside assistance, especially sophisticated American weapons. The years of combat against the Soviets also helped forge a new sense of Afghan nationality.[37]

But above all, the strength and basis of the resistance was Islam. Western analysts are uncomfortable with the subject of religion and tend to ignore the fundamental place of Islam in the resistance movement. But from the first days of the Soviet invasion the guerrillas were fighting not only for national (or more accurately, provincial) freedom but also—and most especially—for the true religion. The one weapon, therefore, that was never lacking to the resistance, the most important weapon in any army, was high morale; after all, as the freedom fighters would ask, if God is with us, who shall prevail against us?

No one has ever been able to be sure how many active guerrillas there were at any one time. Estimates vary from 80,000 to 150,000, with the latter figure probably much too high. Arrayed against these were, by 1985, 115,000 Soviet troops, backed up by 30,000 regular Afghan army troops (down from a pre-invasion force of 100,000), and perhaps 50,000 in other Kabul units.

From the beginning the Communist forces controlled the cities and large towns, and the resistance controlled the countryside. The basic insurgent tactics were mining roads and ambushing convoys. The paucity of good roads magnified the effects of these tactics, so that the tasks of sending supplies to and maintaining communications between regime-held urban centers became especially difficult and dangerous. From time to time the resistance would succeed in literally isolating a city or regime fortress, necessitating supply by aircraft, sometimes for years.

The mujahideen were most active at night, attacking small fortified posts, blowing bridges, and launching rocket attacks. "Sniper fire from the insurgents was a particular headache for the Soviets."[38] The insurgents also increasingly carried out assassinations of government figures, notorious collaborators, and Soviet officials and soldiers.

During the first five years of the war, Soviet and Kabul forces would emerge from the cities to carry out large "sweeps" of the surrounding guerrilla-infested territory. In the face of these major efforts, the resistance fighters often simply faded into the hills. Villagers, abandoning their homes and their scanty possessions, would also disappear. The troops would arrive in a designated area and find no one to kill, little to loot, and nothing to eat. Unable therefore to live off the land, they would have to bring in supplies by convoy—always a danger—or else retreat back to their strongholds. When the troops went away, the villagers would return. This was the general pattern of repeated Soviet-Kabul campaigns in the strategic

Panjshir Valley.[39] Sometimes, however, the insurgents would not retreat in the face of an attack. Such attacks would usually have Kabul troops in the lead, with Soviet soldiers behind them. Typical insurgent tactics let the Kabul forces pass and then concentrated fire on the Russians. In the meantime, many of the Kabul soldiers would have run away or defected to the insurgents. Sometimes a freedom fighter would strap a homemade gasoline bomb to his body and leap onto a Russian tank.[40] Neither side took many prisoners.

The basic strategy of the insurgents was not to defeat the Soviets, a task that their superior firepower and discipline would have been impossible. It was instead to make the war so expensive for them that they would eventually negotiate or just get out altogether. Stalemate was the objective of the resistance, and stalemate was what it achieved before the end of 1985.

THE KABUL REGIME

Most PDPA leaders, activists, and members were urban or urban oriented, admirers and imitators as far as possible of Soviet experience and policies and therefore full of impatient and embarrassed contempt for traditional Afghan society. In no area of state activity did these characteristics show as clearly, or with such disastrous consequences, as in the dealings of the Kabul regime with the Afghan peasantry, the overwhelming majority of the population the PDPA claimed to rule. There is no doubt, for example, that many small farmers and landless peasants were quite poor and could have benefited from land reform, a principal plank in the PDPA program. But many country people were reluctant to participate in land reform programs that seemed to them unnecessarily punitive and confiscatory, violating local custom and Islamic law. PDPA activists sent to stir up class feeling in the rural areas made the peasants march together in formation through the streets of their villages, shouting strange slogans and denouncing unknown enemies ("American imperialists"). This sort of behavior was considered by the local people to be immodest and demeaning.

No opportunity was lost, it seems, to annoy, offend, or shock the peasants. For example, PDPA activists in rural areas often forbade dancing at weddings and set very low maximums for how much food could be served at these celebrations, all of which offended peasant ideas of propriety and hospitality.

Since a Marxist-Leninist revolution requires a proletariat, and since such a class was hardly visible in Afghanistan, PDPA activists dreamed up the idea of creating a "Proletariat of Women," who presumably would be glad to support radical social change. As anybody but PDPA zealots could have predicted, village women were not interested in fulfilling the role of historic substitute for the Petrograd proletariat; besides, the government made few efforts to follow up on this idea (it faced more explosive problems). The whole project collapsed, but not before additional strata of the Afghan rural population had been further alienated.[41]

Things weren't much better in Kabul itself. Many reports described government or party agents entering a private home on the pretext of searching for rebels and weapons and then simply looting the place.[42]

Since the PDPA and its programs attracted few supporters, the party resorted to the time-tested Leninist expedient of the front organization. The "National Fatherland Front" was supposed to provide an umbrella group for people who would not join the PDPA but might be induced to support the government because they disliked or feared the resistance. This front, like all the other programs of the PDPA, came to nothing.

Meanwhile, Parcham-Khalq hostility within the PDPA continued and even increased, in spite of the fact that the party-regime was fighting for its very survival. After the murder of Amin, President Babrak Karmal freed his fellow Parchamis from prison. They immediately turned on their Khalqi persecutors, humiliating or even killing many. The split within the party was beginning to take on aspects of a traditional Afghan blood feud, but it also reflected some serious policy differences. The Parcham side was totally pro-Soviet, and in favor of "softening" the PDPA revolutionary program in order to attract more support or at least calm some of its opponents. The Khalqis, however, grew ever more bitter and intransigent toward the resistance, indeed toward the whole Afghan population: many of them insisted on total, immediate revolution. Correctly perceiving the Kremlin as being in favor of a "softening" policy, the Khalqis, many of them, displayed increasing suspicion and hostility toward their Russian mentors.

Afghan civil society began to crumble even before the Soviet invasion, and the process accelerated over the years. During the first year after the invasion (1980), many among the Afghan elites either defected to the resistance or escaped to foreign countries: diplomats, athletes, airline crews, almost everybody who was in a position to get out of the country.

Afghan education suffered mortal wounds. The PDPA put intense pressure on schoolteachers to join the party; those who refused lost their jobs, often their freedom, and sometimes their lives. Higher education was totally disrupted: almost the entire pre-invasion faculty of Kabul University had been purged or had fled by the end of 1981; their posts were filled by Russians or unqualified PDPA members.[43] One authority estimates that by 1985 from 50 to 70 percent of the pre-invasion university faculties had been thrown into prison, driven into exile, or killed.[44]

Despairing of finding real support for Communism in a country like Afghanistan, the Soviets took 10,000 Afghan children to the Soviet Union to educate them into the nucleus of a new communist state.[45] In November 1984 alone, nearly 900 Afghan children under ten years old were sent to the Soviet Union for ten years of schooling.[46]

But the principal result of the PDPA's war against Afghan civil society and the Soviet invasion and campaign to destroy the resistance was depopulation. More than a million civilians lost their lives, out of a pre-invasion population of 16 million; other millions fled across provincial or national lines, so that whole areas of the country became in effect uninhabited.[47] PDPA activists were not upset by these disasters, this massive killing and destruction. On the contrary, one official commented that even if only one million Afghans were in the end left alive, that would be sufficient to build a new socialist society.[48]

THE KABUL ARMY

As the Soviets were invading Afghanistan, most of the Afghan army allowed itself to be disarmed by Russian advisers and troops. There were exceptions: the Afghan 8th Division put up very stiff resistance and suffered heavy casualties as a consequence. Predictably, the post-invasion military performance of Kabul troops was so miserable that to their dismay the Soviets soon found themselves assuming a greater and greater share of the fighting.[49]

A major contributing factor in the poor showing by the puppet army was the condition of the officer corps. The post-invasion officer corps consisted mostly of new men. What had happened to the 8,000 officers of the pre–1978 army? The Taraki-Amin government had killed great numbers of experienced officers because they were not Communists, or they belonged to the wrong PDPA faction. (Even as late as September 1982, General Wodud, commander of the Central Corps, was found shot dead in his office.)[50] Many of the rest had gone into exile, accepted work in other government agencies, or joined the resistance.[51] Political interference with promotions and assignments also weakened and demoralized the officer corps. Most of the officers who belonged to the PDPA were Khalqis, but the Babrak Karmal regime, as well as the Russians, distrusted them and therefore gave them politically less critical assignments wherever possible.

As the fighting escalated, the standard training period for officers was cut from three years to two. Some officers who deserted to the resistance claimed that they had had only three months of training.[52] Conditions among enlisted men were comparably bad.

Aside from poor preparation and humiliating subservience to the Russian invaders (see below), the Kabul troops were often improperly used. The 444th Commando Brigade, perhaps the best of the regime units, was decimated when it parachuted into the Panjshir Valley in the summer of 1985, in one of the interminable efforts to sweep the area.[53]

Most of all, the army of the Kabul regime was being destroyed by the unwillingness of its members to remain in its ranks. Most of those who deserted just went home, but significant numbers wound up in the ranks of the resistance, often bringing their invaluable weapons with them. Of the 80,000 men in the Afghan army on the eve of the invasion, over half either deserted or else defected to the resistance.[54]

The unreliability of the Kabul forces assumed alarming proportions even before the Soviet occupation. In May 1979, on the road between Gardez and Khost, the motorized brigade of the Afghan 7th Division—the whole unit, 2,000 officers and men, plus armored vehicles and heavy weapons—surrendered to the guerrillas without a fight. Mutinies among Kabul units, including the killing of officers, were common. Outside the defense perimeter of the capital city, Kabul troops during most of the war were completely unpredictable.

Soviet officers planned most, if not all, operations by Kabul forces.[55] Suspecting members even of the highest ranks of the Kabul army of collaboration with the insurgents, the Soviets forced any Afghan, even a general officer, to submit to a search before entering the precincts of the Ministry of Defense. They eventually deprived their allies of what tanks and heavy weapons the resistance had not destroyed, for fear that these also would eventually fall into insurgent hands. So great became the distrust on the part of the Russians for the Kabul forces that the latter were not allowed to have on hand at any one time more than a week's supply of materiel.[56] Conditions within the Kabul army eventually sank to such depths that the soldiers were required to turn in their weapons when not fighting. The Russians tried to increase the reliability of the Afghan army by training officers in the Soviet Union, but many of these also deserted or defected.[57]

The PDPA regime used several methods to induce men to join its forces and not to desert or defect. It sent conscripts to serve away from their home areas. The minefields that surrounded regime garrisons and forts served both to keep the mujahideen out and the troops in. Another method was accelerated promotion: one defecting officer told the mujahideen that of 400 men in his unit, no less than 20 were brigadier generals. Army pay for officers was much higher than for comparable civilian jobs. Young men who joined the Kabul paramilitary forces were paid more than what a deputy minister received before the 1978 coup. Any tenth grader who volunteered for the army would receive a twelfth grade diploma after completion of his military service. Any eleventh grader who volunteered would be guaranteed admission to any institution of higher education without having to take entrance examinations.[58]

These inducements were not enough. Hence the draft age was lowered to 16 in 1984, and eventually the government declared liable to conscription all males between the ages of 14 and 50.[59] These moves by the regime, as well as an increase in conscripted service from three years to four, contributed to mutinies and defections even in the Kabul area.[60] When the insurgents captured young Kabul conscripts, they usually either paroled them to their homes or incorporated them into the ranks of the resistance.

By the end of 1986, the Kabul armed forces consisted of about 30,000 regular troops, with 10,000 in the air force, and perhaps another 40,000 in paramilitary units, secret police, and militia organizations.[61] Relatively few new officers joined the PDPA, and often they did so because the resistance had requested them to infiltrate the party.[62] And in the midst of these dangers and calamities, hostility between Khalq and Parcham raged unabated.[63]

RUSSIAN WARS IN CENTRAL ASIA

The Afghanistan imbroglio was of course not the first time that Russians found themselves fighting a determined Islamic foe in mountainous terrain. The Russian conquest of the Caucasus between 1820 and 1860 provides a similar scenario, allowing an opportunity to study the classic Russian manner of dealing with this kind of military challenge.

Like Afghanistan, the Caucasus was inhabited by many tribes. The mountains provided excellent possibilities both for guerrilla warfare and for guerrilla disunity. European visitors to the area described the inhabitants as brave, handsome, deeply religious, and punctiliously hospitable. "Every man was a born rider, a keen swordsman, a good shot."[64]

The Russian method for defeating Central Asian peoples was perfected in these struggles. It had three components: isolate the insurgent region, destroy the insurgent leadership, devastate the local economy so that it cannot sustain the guerrillas.[65] To these ends, the Russians advanced slowly into the Caucasus, building roads and bridges before them, constructing lines of forts, laying waste to settlements, driving off or killing cattle, and—most important of all—bringing in enough troops to make all of these policies effective. Even so, from time to time forts in the Russian line would be overrun with heavy losses: for example in 1845, near Dargo, insurgents killed or captured 4,000 Russian soldiers, including three generals.[66]

The internal and external dimensions of the struggle to subdue the Caucasus grew complex. In later phases of the conflict, Christian populations in Georgia and Armenia supported the Russians against Muslim guerrillas. The resistance, on the other hand, received encouragement and sometimes weapons from the Turks and the British.[67]

During the 1920s and 1930s the Soviet regime faced a serious rising in its Central Asian provinces, which it called the Basmachi Revolt. This was in essence an outright struggle between Russian Communism and Central Asian Islam. Predictably, tribal rivalries weakened the Basmachi insurgents, but their revolt was prolonged, in part because the kingdom of Afghanistan allowed them to cross the border at will. Soviet troops also crossed into Afghanistan several times.

The Russians sought fairly successfully to further the fragmentation of their Central Asian subjects by encouraging the cultivation of local languages and dialects, with Russian as the sole linqua franca. The Tsarist army would normally not accept Central Asians for service. But the huge losses suffered by the Russian army in World War I led to the imposition of the draft in Central Asia, a move that provoked massive and persistent riots. During World War II, the Germans were able to recruit many soldiers from the ranks of their Central Asian prisoners.

In the 1980s, most Central Asian subjects of the Soviet Union had inferior educations and hence were found in the lower ranks of the Soviet army and in the less technical and noncombat branches of the service. This situation encouraged many ethnic Russians to believe that the blood cost of the war inside Afghanistan was being borne in undue proportion by young Russians.[68]

SOVIET STRATEGY IN AFGHANISTAN

From one perspective, the invasion of Afghanistan by the Soviets was a great success and an operational model. But the Soviets were surprised and thrown off course by two factors upon which they had not calculated: one was the widespread and determined internal opposition to their occupation of the country; the other was the amount of foreign help to this resistance.

When the Soviets invaded their southern neighbor, they expected that Kabul forces would do most of what fighting needed to be done. By January 1980 there were only about 50,000 Soviet troops in Afghanistan, many of them Central Asian reservists recently mobilized; the invasion of Czechoslovakia a decade earlier had been on a much larger scale.

But the intensity of popular resistance, as well as the reluctance to fight and the tendency to desert shown by the Kabul troops, made it clear that the Soviets were going to have to carry a much bigger share of the fighting than originally planned. They were never able to do this effectively because Moscow, for reasons that have not become clear, never committed enough troops to Afghanistan to do the job.

By the end of 1984, the Soviets had 115,000 military personnel in Afghanistan, raised to 120,000 by 1987, with perhaps 30,000 immediately over the Soviet border in support. Some 22,000 of these troops were holding down Kabul.[69] These numbers amounted to a mere 4 percent of the total Soviet ground forces.[70] Only perhaps 6 of 194 Soviet combat divisions were in Afghanistan on a full-time basis. Admittedly, over 50 percent of these forces were combat troops, a much higher ratio than the Americans ever reached in Viet Nam. But after subtracting garrison security forces, the Soviets were left with only about one battalion in each province for offensive operations.[71] Even with their Kabul allies, the Soviets never remotely approached the 10-to-1 ratio of government troops to insurgents that many students of guerrilla warfare believe essential to victory.

The Soviets consequently had to adopt a strategy dictated by the inadequate number of their troops in the field. They eventually settled on a modified enclave strategy. In essence it consisted of five elements:

- holding Kabul and other main cities in sufficient force to prevent expulsion;
- protecting communications between these cities (Soviet supply lines were long: from the Soviet border to Kabul is well over 400 km; from Qandahar to Herat is 600 km. Control of the roads was so tenuous that Soviet bases and even the garrisons in big towns had to be supplied mainly and sometimes exclusively by aircraft.);
- clearing the northern Afghan provinces of guerrillas in order to safeguard supply routes to Soviet forces in Kabul and to prevent any spillover of fighting from northern Afghanistan into the Muslim provinces of the USSR;
- launching periodic sweeps to break up mujahideen concentrations or seize their strongholds; and
- interdicting infiltration from Pakistan and Iran.

As the conflict dragged on, Soviet strategy expanded to include:

- building up a Sovietized Afghan elite that would one day take over the war and run the country, and
- destroying systematically the economy of those provinces that they did not control.[72]

THE SOVIET ARMY AGAINST THE PEOPLE

The tenacity of the resistance plus the inadequacy of Soviet and Kabul force levels led inexorably to the most appalling aspect of the entire war: the Soviet policy of depopulating the main resistance areas, what the anthropologist Louis Dupree has called "migratory genocide."[73]

Before the invasion of Afghanistan, the Soviet army had a great reputation as a fighting force, mainly because of its size and its impressive achievements against Germany in World War II. But in fact between the surrender of Nazi Germany in May 1945 and the invasion of Afghanistan in December 1979, the Soviet army had had less combat experience than the armies of Britain, China, Egypt, France, India, Israel, Pakistan, Portugal, or the United States. Probably for this reason the Soviet army sought to give as many of its officers as possible a "turn" at the Afghanistan combat, a policy similar to that pursued by the United States in Viet Nam, and probably with the same negative effects on making progress in the war. The so-called "Afghan Brotherhood" inside the Soviet army might have replaced the dominance of those who served in "the West" (World War II) with those who served in "the South."[74]

Not only was the Soviet army that invaded Afghanistan a force untested in real combat for decades, but it had been built (much like the American army) to fight World War III, to fight NATO forces in Europe, not Central Asian mountaineers armed with antique rifles.[75] In the 1940s and early 1950s the Soviet army had waged a fierce campaign to exterminate guerrillas in the Ukraine, but since this struggle was a "secret," even a non-event, there were no serious studies on the topic for wide use by the Soviet armed forces. Modern Soviet counterinsurgency doctrine was thus woefully underdeveloped.[76] Nor were their troops experienced in mountain warfare. Consequently, "the overall counterinsurgency capabilities of the average Soviet conscript [were] unimpressive."[77] This is why the Soviet army did well in the invasion itself, but not well at all in the long campaign to subdue the recalcitrant rural population.

For many years the Soviets sought to assist Third World governments fighting against guerrillas. Almost everywhere—not only in Afghanistan, but also Angola, Cambodia, Ethiopia, and Mozambique—Soviet assistance has produced disappointing results. The unimpressive Soviet record on counterinsurgency in the Third World had several causes. First, and most obviously, there is the absence of good counterinsurgency doctrine. Second, the Soviets were generally unsuccessful in denying the guerrillas outside assistance and sanctuaries. Third, they sought to have the army of the local regime which they were assisting do most if not all of the real fighting; this is a good idea, but Soviet efforts to build up forces capable of carrying out such a charge were disappointing, Afghanistan being merely the most egregious case. Finally, but by no means least in importance, the Soviets, and the states they controlled or influenced, would not address the root causes of the local insurgency: unpopular or disastrous government policies.[78] The Soviet method, the "socialist" prescription, for dealing with Third World societies (or any society in their grip) was centralized political control and a bureaucratized, collectivized economy, including agriculture. These policies aggravated rather than alleviated the conditions that helped produce the insurgency.

The typical Western method of fighting guerrillas is to try to separate them from the civilian population and to win the goodwill of the latter. That was not the Soviet way. In Afghanistan they made some efforts at winning over the religious leaders (mullahs) by preaching the compatibility of Marxism and Islam, by helping to repair mosques, and so forth. But this was not their dominant approach. They did not seek to "win the hearts and minds" of the peasantry. Their method, rather, was to drain the water in which the guerrillas might swim: to destroy any civilian population friendly to, or even close by, the guerrillas.[79] To this end the Soviets sought with much success to empty the provinces along both the Soviet and the Pakistan borders by forced migration. But since virtually the whole country rose against the Soviets and their Kabul puppets, this policy of devastation was eventually employed in almost every province.

According to the report of the human-rights organization Helsinki Watch, the Soviets waged a campaign of deliberate terror against the civilian population.[80] They systematically bombed villages, attacked columns of refugees, chopped down orchards, and killed or maimed animals.[81] In October 1981, when the resistance captured a noted Soviet geologist and offered him in exchange for 50 Afghan hostages, the Soviets simply killed all the hostages.[82] A report issued by the United Nations in the fall of 1982 suggested that the Soviets had used chemical weapons, and they apparently used poison gas campaigning in the Panjshir Valley in the spring of 1984.[83] They trained children to act as saboteurs and even assassins.[84] Responsible observers have accused them of the deliberate and repeated bombings of hospitals.[85] Finally, numerous witnesses have declared that Soviet aircraft often dropped explosive devices in the shape of toys and pens; "their main targets are children, whose hands and arms are blown off."[86]

By the first anniversary of the Soviet invasion, this policy had created 1.5 million Afghan refugees. Within a few more years over 4 million Afghan men, women, and children had become refugees (nobody knows how many were simply killed). In 1985, perhaps one Afghan in three was an internal or external refugee.[87] Soviet claims that this disaster, this "migratory genocide," resulted from the machinations of native reactionaries and CIA troublemakers were embarrassing in their poverty. The world, for the most part, tried to ignore this crime. But justice—elementary justice—demands the recognition of the fact that the refugees, inside Afghanistan, in Pakistan, and in Iran were not an accidental or unavoidable consequence of war; they were an intended, an engineered, result, "a part of Soviet warfare strategy."[88]

Lacking good counterguerrilla doctrine, employing the most brutal policies conceivable toward the civilian population, the Soviets' experience in Afghanistan was far from what they had expected at the time of the invasion. By 1986 "the performance of the average conscripted Soviet soldier remain[ed] unimpressive."[89] It is not hard to account for this. Many Soviet privates arrived in Afghanistan with less than a month's training.[90] Even noncommissioned officers (NCOs) often had little experience or training. The Soviet army had tried to prepare for mountain warfare youths who had probably never even seen a real mountain. Brutality by older soldiers against younger ones, even against NCOs, was common.[91] Increased Soviet combat activity after 1982 meant increased casualties. Many of the soldiers were young conscripts who had been told that they were in Afghanistan to save the people. What they encountered must have severely shaken them, accounting to a large degree for the increasing incidents of theft and sale of military equipment to the resistance in return for drugs, including heroin.[92] Naturally, the Soviet army reflected in many ways the larger society from which it was drawn: centralization, rigid discipline, and punishment for failure discouraged initiative among the junior officers, a really fatal handicap in fighting guerrillas, where so much depends on small-unit action.

Eventually the Soviets learned to give up their costly and ineffective valley sweep operations. They placed more emphasis on such classic counterinsurgency tactics as using the ambush against the guerrillas, having convoys be preceded by tanks without turrets and with mine-detecting rollers on the front, and rapidly airlifting small, well-trained detachments of Special Purpose Forces (Spetsnaz), of which perhaps 5,000 were in Afghanistan in 1986.[93] Nevertheless, at the end of the fighting, as at the beginning, the bulk of Soviet forces—motorized rifle units—were roadbound.

Things would certainly have been much worse for them if it had not been for the helicopter gunship. In February 1980, and again in April, anti-regime and anti-Soviet riots gripped Kabul. The Soviets strafed the crowds with their helicopter gunships, killing hundreds.[94] But it was against guerrillas, not against civilian rioters, that the Soviets found the best use for the helicopter. Indeed, it proved to be their most effective weapon.[95] The number of helicopters in use in Afghanistan rose from 60 in mid-1980 to over 300 by the end of 1981.[96] Helicopter gunships provided the Russians with the kind of firepower normally obtainable only from tanks, but in the mountains, where tanks cannot operate. Gunships escorted convoys passing along especially vulnerable sections of mountain roads. But helicopters are relatively slow and not very maneuverable, and they can be easily hurt, especially their rotor blades, as the Americans learned to their great cost in Viet Nam. In January 1982, freedom fighters in Paktia province were able to down a helicopter whose crash resulted in the death of a Soviet lieutenant general.[97] Nevertheless, until the resistance was able to obtain heavy machine guns in 1983, there was little defense against the gunships. In 1986 the Russians introduced new machines with armored bottoms almost totally immune to machine-gun fire.

The period of nearly complete Soviet domination of the battlefield through the helicopter was coming to an end, however. In 1983, using surface-to-air (SAM) missiles, resistance fighters shot down several helicopters near Khost. The introduction of SAMs sent waves of panic throughout the Soviet establishment in Afghanistan. Nobody knew how many of these SAMs the freedom fighters had, but knowledge that any at all were in their hands forced helicopter pilots to fly higher than was effective.

The United States began providing the resistance with the excellent Stinger missile apparently in the latter half of 1986. The Stingers neutralized the effectiveness of the helicopter gunship. "The Stinger missile has robbed the Soviet forces of their command of the air."[98] Indeed, "the [mujahideen's] acquisition of surface-to-air missiles (SAMs) was critical to their ability to counter . . . Soviet tactics. Since late 1986, when SAMs were used in significant numbers, the mujahideen were able to move without constant fear of Soviet helicopter attacks."[99]

THE COURSE OF THE WAR

The revolt against the Kabul regime began in October 1978, more than a year before the Soviet invasion. In the following March, serious fighting in Herat, the country's third-largest city, took the lives of hundreds of Afghan Communists and Soviet personnel. Thousands of civilians died during the restoration of regime control.[100] By November 1979, a month before the Soviet invasion, insurgent forces dominated Badakhshan province (the link with China) and most of the Hazarajat (the center of the country).

During 1980, demonstrations and strikes rocked Kabul. Because Afghan soldiers often refused to fire on student demonstrators, Soviet troops were called in and did much killing.

Because of the Soviets' very conservative strategy—holding key cities and the roads between them—and their lack of confidence in the Kabul army, there were few sizable operations during the first year of Soviet occupation and for much of 1981. The road-bound, mountain-hating Soviet army thus failed to take advantage of mujahideen disunity, lack of equipment, and inexperience with modern guerrilla techniques. More than half of the country was under insurgent control by the end of 1980.[101] In April 1981, mujahideen killed the deputy head of KhAD in Kabul. That same month and again in September insurgents briefly overran Qandahar, the country's second-largest city. By the end of 1981 every single Afghan province was experiencing some form of armed resistance.

The year 1982 witnessed much more elaborate "pacification" efforts. The Panjshir Valley lies about 60 miles northeast of Kabul; in resistance hands it would threaten the capital, the vital Bagram air base, and road communications between Kabul and the Soviet Union. About 14,000 Soviet and Kabul troops attacked the 5,000 insurgents there under Ahmed Shah Massoud. After campaigning hard for six weeks and suffering 3,000 casualties and 2,000 defections, the Soviet-Kabul forces withdrew.[102]

During 1983, the insurgents extended their control to about two-thirds of the territory and three-quarters of the populations.[103] The Soviets again bombed the city of Herat, killing several thousand civilians. The insurgents in turn carried out increasingly frequent and deadly attacks inside Kabul; they hit the Soviet Embassy and assassinated numerous Kabul regime officials and collaborators.[104] As the fourth year of the Soviet occupation drew to a close, resistance casualties totaled between 50,000 and 100,000, and regime casualties between 50,000 and 60,000.[105]

In 1984, the Soviets greatly increased their operations. For big offensive movements they no longer used mainly conscripted units but trained mountain fighters. They again attacked the Panjshir Valley, this time with 20,000 Soviet troops, 500 armored vehicles and thousands of Kabul soldiers—and again they failed. In June the Soviets launched a massive effort around Herat, forcing some insurgent groups to retreat into Iran.[106] High altitude saturation bombing was a common feature of these campaigns, and Soviet forces also looted the city of Qandahar twice during the month of October.[107]

Concerted efforts were made to assassinate key insurgent leaders. Radio Kabul announced the death of Ahmed Shah Massoud, the "Lion of the Panjshir," a onetime engineering student who now led the resistance in the Panjshir Valley. The announcement turned out to be quite premature. Many of these assassination attempts, especially by KhAD, failed because the targets of the attacks were tipped off in time. Massoud and his forces would survive no less than nine Soviet-directed offensives against them.

After five years of occupation, close to 10,000 Soviets and their wives (no children) lived in a special ghetto in Kabul, surrounded by barbed wire, armed guards, and great danger.[108] Life in Kabul had never been secure, but during 1984 conditions deteriorated. In March alone, 15 PDPA officials were killed by the resistance in just one area of the city.[109] On August 31, a bomb was set off at Kabul International Airport; less than a month later another action inside the capital destroyed a dozen Soviet armored vehicles and killed numerous Kabul regime troops.[110]

The year 1985 opened with the disruption of the PDPA's anniversary celebration by a mujahideen rocket barrage. The arrival of a new Soviet commander, General Zaitsev, heralded a series of major offensives in Kunar and Paktia provinces and the much fought-over Panjshir Valley. The Paktia operation, employing 15,000 Communist troops, including at least three Soviet regiments, ended in defeat. By closing down many roads and destroying bridges, the insurgents were thwarting the basic Soviet strategy of maintaining communications between the occupied cities. The insurgents were now acquiring heavy weapons; above all, they improved their air defense. With Soviet air power reduced, ambushes of convoys increased in effectiveness.[111] The resistance enjoyed some less strategic but quite spectacular successes in 1985; in June, for instance, under the leadership of the celebrated Ahmed Shah Massoud, they attacked the 500-man fort at Pechgur, capturing almost all the troops and many weapons. Life in the capital became even more dangerous, with attacks on the airport and the Soviet Embassy, even stabbings of Soviet citizens in the streets. At the end of the sixth year of Soviet occupation, the war in Afghanistan, at a higher level of fighting than ever before, had clearly become a stalemate.

In January 1986, the Kabul regime proclaimed a six-month cease-fire, but neither their troops nor the Soviets reduced their operations against the resistance under this or subsequent so-called cease-fires.[112] Looking for a scapegoat, the Soviets dumped their puppet Babrak Karmal and replaced him as boss of the PDPA with the head of the secret police, Najib. The Soviets were improving their tactics; in the spring they occupied and destroyed the resistance complex at Zhawar, a grave blow.[113] Mass defections by Kabul troops had practically ceased; sometimes they would actually stand

and fight and even win an engagement. The insurgents still had not learned to specialize (for example, after all these years there were still no skilled sappers among them); they had not yet held an entire provincial capital for any length of time; and KhAD agents had penetrated their organizations.

But the guerrillas had even more thoroughly penetrated the regime: it was very difficult for Kabul or the Soviets to mount surprise attacks because of the omnipresence of resistance agents and sympathizers. A government fort at Ferkhar fell to the resistance in September, with 300 government troops killed or captured.[114] The security situation in Kabul continued to deteriorate.[115] Very significantly, Massoud was now deploying units of up to 120 men who were willing to fight anywhere in the entire north, not just in their local areas. This development greatly increased the ability of the guerrillas to concentrate against sizable targets.

By the beginning of 1987, the insurgents were growing stronger: they were receiving better equipment from abroad, they now had permanent bases in strongly defended mountain areas, and their various leaders were cooperating more closely. In Paktia province (a key area on the Pakistan border) a major Soviet-Kabul operation, including air strikes, heavy artillery, and assaults by elite Spetsnaz commandos was repulsed with heavy casualties; the cooperation of several different resistance groups, enhanced by good logistics and buoyed by the participation of political leaders from Peshawar, made the difference.[116] A major Soviet effort to open the road between Gardez and Khost, closed by the guerrillas since 1979, also failed.

The resistance demonstrated increasing willingness to target Soviet forces and operate in Soviet-controlled areas during 1987. Mortar shells continued to hit the Soviet Embassy in Kabul and rockets often fell on Bagram Airbase (north of the capital, the most important Soviet base in the country).[117] Because the resistance increasingly used long-range artillery, the Soviets had to expand the security perimeter around Kabul. During the summer, Soviet garrisons abandoned several outlying posts, leaving most of the country without any Soviet presence at all. In July insurgent units stormed Kalafgan, less than fifty miles from the Soviet border, seizing priceless artillery. For the first time the Soviets acknowledged that the resistance had raided the territory of the Soviet Union itself,[118] although reports of such forays into the Soviet Union had appeared in the Western press years earlier.[119] *Izvestia* provided an interesting indicator of the growing power of the resistance by charging that the mujahideen were being trained by instructors from Pakistan, France, Saudi Arabia, the United States, China, Egypt, Iran, Britain—even Japan.[120]

But most important of all was the growing availability of the American Stinger, a one-man surface-to-air missile launcher. The first of these priceless weapons were delivered to the insurgents in the fall of 1986. It had always been very dangerous for the resistance to stand and fight against Soviet and Kabul forces because of the possibility of air attacks. The Soviets had been relying more and more on their total control of the air to surprise resistance forces and devastate the civilian population. Now painfully aware that the resistance possessed Stingers, Soviet and Kabul pilots began to fly at inefficiently high altitudes; daylight airlifts of supplies and troops became rare. By diminishing the value of Soviet airpower, the Stinger changed the course of the war.

THE WORLD WATCHES THE WAR

Late in 1988, diplomats and international relief workers estimated that 1.3 million Afghan men, women, and children had died as a direct result of the war. Three-quarters of Afghanistan's villages were destroyed or abandoned. Tens of thousands of inhabitants have been maimed for life. One third of the prewar population of 16 million fled across one or another border, producing the world's largest refugee mass.[121] "Moscow," said the *Washington Post* "[was] committing one of the world's great crimes."[122]

Yet the world's response to this genocide was astoundingly low-key. "The discrepancy between the magnitude of the tragedy and the international attention it receives works very much to Moscow's advantage."[123] The Soviets counted on being able to carry out this genocide in relative secrecy, with the world simply forgetting about Afghanistan. The Soviets from time to time issued threats against foreign journalists captured in the company of mujahideen,[124] but the lack of concern on the part of the world's press greatly assisted Moscow in its actions.[125]

The most essential foreign supporter of the freedom fighters was Pakistan. Corrupt Pakistani officials siphoned off some of the aid flowing through Pakistan from the outside world; sometimes old weapons replaced new ones.[126] Yet without the support of the Pakistani government, it is not easy to see how the Afghan resistance would have survived.[127] Pakistan provided a home to millions of Afghan victims of war, and all the important Afghan political parties made their headquarters in Peshawar. Most of all, Pakistan allowed its territory to be used for transshipment of aid into Afghanistan. The 1,400-mile-long Afghanistan-Pakistan border, with its hundreds of mountain passes, was the lifeline of the resistance.

Pakistan took big risks to assist the Afghan resistance. Many ethnic groups overlap the border between Pakistan and Afghanistan, and the Soviets promised to punish Pakistan by stirring up Baluchi and Pushtun nationalism, a menace to the country's very survival.[128] If the Soviet Union had decided to make an all-out effort against the huge resistance infrastructure over the eastern border, Pakistan would have been in mortal peril. But the Soviets held back from a major blow, no doubt influenced by the hostility toward its Afghanistan policy of all the world's other great powers, from the United States to China, from West Germany to Japan. In June 1981, the Chinese premier paid a significant visit to a refugee camp near Peshawar;

two years later U.S. Secretary of State George Shultz told refugees in Pakistan: "We are with you." Even so, many Pakistanis paid with their lives for the policy of assisting the insurgency: in 1984 alone, Soviet air and artillery "errors" killed 200 Pakistanis.[129]

Other Muslim states supported the resistance. In January and again in May 1980, conferences of foreign ministers of Islamic countries condemned the Soviet invasion. Aside from Pakistan, Saudi Arabia was the first and for a while the only country to give aid to the mujahideen. President Anwar Sadat of Egypt supplied weapons that he had received from the Soviets before his break with them in 1972.[130] Resistance leaders were invited to various Islamic Conferences. On the other hand, in 1987 the infamous Saddam Hussein received the Kabuli prime minister in Baghdad, up to that point the highest level reception for a member of the puppet government outside the Soviet bloc.[131] Soviet clients and semiclients such as Syria, South Yemen, and the PLO gave at least verbal support to the Kabul regime. And the vaunted and ludicrously named Non–Aligned Movement accomplished absolutely nothing for the suffering millions of Afghanistan.

In Iran, the postrevolutionary leadership was more bitter against the United States than against the Russians. Even after the Soviet genocide in Afghanistan became well known, the Iranians gave most of their attention after September 1980 to their murderous conflict with neighboring Iraq. Nevertheless, Teheran included mujahideen leaders in its own delegation to the May 1980 Islamic Conference (from which Kabul's representatives were banned) and supplied arms to particular resistance groups, almost exclusively drawn from Afghanistan's Shia minority. More than once Soviet units in pursuit of fleeing insurgents crossed into Iran.[132]

China steadfastly supported Pakistan, its only friend in the region. The leadership in Beijing saw the Soviet occupation of Afghanistan as another move in a gigantic Soviet encirclement of China including Viet Nam, India, and Mongolia. Beijing repeatedly declared the withdrawal of all Soviet forces from Afghanistan to be a precondition for improved relations between the two Communist behemoths.[133] The Chinese sent rocket launchers, heavy artillery, and assault rifles into Afghanistan, but no one outside the Chinese government knows the quantities.

Various European governments, parties, and private groups reacted with hostility to the invasion. Italian Communist Party leaders were so bitter about events in Afghanistan that they were not permitted to address the 26th Soviet Party Congress in Moscow in 1981. But of all the Europeans, the French were the most interested in and sympathetic to the Afghan resistance. French medical personnel provided significant help, often at the peril of their lives. French groups helped found Radio Free Kabul in 1981 (which the Kabul regime identified as "a Jewish radio station.")[134] And in 1987 the French foreign minister met with resistance leaders in Pakistan.

Soon after the invasion, the United Nations began voting year after year by big margins that all "foreign troops" should leave Afghanistan. In 1986, the vote was 122 to 20; it is not clear exactly how these votes assisted the Afghan people, whose villages, whose society, was being destroyed. Meanwhile UNICEF—in September 1986!—presented an award to the puppet regime in Kabul for its literacy campaign, a campaign that in part sparked the insurgency in the first place because women were forced to attend classes in which religion was ridiculed.[135]

And then there was India. At the Emergency Session of the United Nations General Assembly in January 1980, the Indian representative criticized the General Assembly for presuming even to discuss the Soviet invasion of Afghanistan. India consistently refused to condemn the Russian occupation and recognized the Kabul regime and extended aid to it. In 1987, when the United Nations voted that "foreign troops" should leave Afghanistan by a vote of 123 to 19, India abstained. On May 3, 1988, the president of the Kabul regime visited New Delhi, the only non–Communist capital that accorded him full honors as head of state.

THE UNITED STATES AND AFGHANISTAN

In 1953, the Joint Chiefs of Staff informed President Dwight Eisenhower that "Afghanistan is of little or no strategic importance to the United States."[136] This statement encapsulates the traditional American approach to that country. The United States refused Afghan requests for military aid in 1948 and 1951 (under President Truman) and in 1954 (under President Eisenhower).[137] Policymakers in Washington did not view Soviet moves to increase their influence in Afghanistan as a threat to this country, and besides there was little the United States could do about the situation. The Americans looked upon Afghanistan as being in the "Soviet sphere of influence" and believed that no matter how much aid they might give to Afghanistan, nothing would ever be able to pull that country out of the Soviet orbit.[138] In 1956, the National Security Council determined that arms transfers to Afghanistan might provoke the Soviet Union into strong countermeasures.[139] Besides, Pakistan would have objected to any plans for American assistance to Afghanistan in view of their age-old border dispute, and Pakistan was Washington's ally in the Baghdad Pact, which Afghanistan had declined to join. Most of the time the U.S. Embassy in Kabul contained nobody who could speak Dari adequately.[140] Hence, it may be distressing but not surprising that the word "Afghanistan" does not appear even one time in the index of the first volume of Eisenhower's presidential memoirs. For that matter, it does not appear at all in the memoirs of President Truman, or Secretary of State Dean Acheson, or the theorist of containment George F. Kennan.

Faced with Secretary of State Dulles's support for Pakistan in its border disagreements with Afghanistan, Daoud turned to the Soviets. The Russians built the Bagram airport north of Kabul, and the Salang Pass through the mountains near the Soviet-Afghan border (both of these projects proved very useful for the invasion of 1979).

It appears almost certain that Moscow expected little trouble with the United States over its invasion of Afghanistan.[141] The Americans in the end had done nothing about the Soviet invasions of Hungary (1956) and Czechoslovakia (1968). Still wallowing in its "Viet Nam syndrome," the United States did not try to block Soviet activities in Angola and Ethiopia. By 1979, the Carter Administration was in an obvious and apparently irreversible downward spin. The Kremlin also expected no effective response from the Americans because it expected no effective response from the Afghans.[142]

In fact, however, the invasion thoroughly alarmed the Carter Administration. With notable hyperbole, the excited American president called the Soviet move "the greatest threat to peace since the Second World War." Washington viewed the invasion as extremely ominous: it was not only the first-ever Soviet military movement outside the Soviet bloc, but it also carried Soviet armed forces perilously close to the source of major Western and Japanese oil supplies. "If the Soviets could consolidate their hold on Afghanistan," Carter wrote later, "the balance of power in the entire region would be drastically modified in their favor, and they might be tempted toward further aggression."[143]

President Carter's response to the invasion was wide-ranging. He postponed consideration of the Salt II treaty by the Senate (where in light of the invasion it was doomed anyway). He proclaimed a U.S. boycott of the 1980 Moscow Olympics, in which he was joined by China, Japan, West Germany, and 50 other countries. He imposed an embargo of wheat sales to the Soviet Union, sought a condemnation of the invasion by the United Nations, and initiated legislation aimed at a reintroduction of the draft. Most importantly from the Soviet view, perhaps, Carter called for greatly increased aid to Pakistan, Secretary of Defense Harold Brown journeyed to Beijing, and military and financial assistance began to flow to the mujahideen.[144] And, in case the Soviets should have ideas about further advances toward the Persian Gulf, in his State of the Union message on January 23, 1980, President Carter issued a warning:

Let our position be absolutely clear: An attempt by any outside force to gain control of the Persian Gulf region will be regarded as an assault on the vital interests of the United States of America, and such an assault will be repelled by any means necessary, including military force.[145]

In the early years of the conflict, even during the first Reagan Administration, the flow of American arms to the resistance was not great. There was no large Afghan ethnic element in the United States to put pressure on Congress to act, and U.S. news media coverage of the fighting and destruction inside Afghanistan was scanty. One observer wrote that only about 20 percent of resistance weapons came from foreign sources.[146] Nevertheless, as the brutality of the Soviets and the determination of the mujahideen to resist became ever clearer, American commitment to the resistance deepened.

At the time of the Greek Civil War, President Truman declared it to be the policy of the United States to render assistance to "free peoples" resisting subversion or subjugation by Communist forces; this declaration, the essence of the Cold War Containment Policy, came to be called the Truman Doctrine. As the war in Afghanistan grew ever more desperate, President Reagan enunciated what became known as the Reagan Doctrine: this extended the principle of assistance to include not only "free peoples" resisting the Communist yoke but also "subjugated peoples" seeking to escape from it. Observers at the time viewed this Reagan Doctrine as a repudiation of and challenge to the so-called Brezhnev Doctrine, which declared that once Communists had acquired governmental power in a country, by whatever means, the Soviet Union and other fraternal socialist states would never permit that country to have any other kind of government. (This of course had been the doctrinal basis for the Warsaw Pact invasion of Czechoslovakia in 1968.) President Reagan received a delegation of mujahideen leaders in the Oval Office in May 1986.[147]

By the end of 1984 the United States was providing perhaps only $80 million worth of aid to the resistance. This amount grew to something like $470 million in 1986 and $700 million in 1988. A great deal of this aid never made it from Pakistan to Afghanistan, a fact that American policymakers will have to consider in any similar future conflict.[148] The Central Intelligence Agency was given charge of assistance to Afghan insurgents, and this turned out to be the largest covert CIA operation since Viet Nam.[149] Fearing that too-open provision of U.S. aid would provide a good excuse for serious Soviet retaliation against Pakistan, the CIA often supplied the insurgents with Soviet weapons to mask their origin.[150]

THE SOVIETS DEPART

By mid-1987, the military situation from the Soviet point of view was a stalemate at best. The mujahideen could not capture the big cities because they could not overcome the combination of Soviet air and firepower, fortifications, and the mines that defended them (the Soviets laid down between 10 and 16 million mines in Afghanistan).[151] On the other hand, the Soviets and their Kabul allies had lost their complete air supremacy and controlled little of the countryside; they held only the largest cities, the key airports, and the north-south highway to Kabul.

Nothing the Soviets had done in Afghanistan seemed to work: on the contrary, after seven years of savage conflict the insurgents were better armed and more determined than ever before. Soviet efforts on the political and diplomatic fronts had failed as well. As a U.S. State Department paper summarized the situation, "by 1987 the mujahideen had fought the Soviet and regime forces to a stalemate: Moscow's Afghan policy had alienated it from the Islamic, Western and non-aligned countries; and the Soviets failed to find a client leader in Kabul who could capture the loyalty of the Afghan people."[152]

In the first eight years of the war, the Soviets suffered between 48,000 and 52,000 casualties, including some 13,000 to 15,000 deaths.[153] This amounts to approximately 35 deaths a week between December 1979 and December 1987. In view of the fact that the Soviets were combatting a resistance force of between 100,000 and 200,000, this was hardly an oppressive number. But it was certainly far more than anybody in the Kremlin was predicting in January 1980. So was the number of aircraft, including helicopters, downed by the resistance: something like 1,000 with perhaps 500 lost in 1987 alone (the Stinger effect).[154] The insurgents had also destroyed roughly 600 tanks, 800 armored personnel carriers, and several thousands of other military vehicles; Western correspondents sometimes reported seeing dozens of Soviet and Kabul army vehicles destroyed in just a single engagement.[155] And there was no end in sight.

The war was costing the Soviet Union around $3 billion a year by 1984. A lot of the expense was being recovered through Russian exploitation of Afghanistan's mineral resources.[156] The Soviets took vast quantities of natural gas out of Afghanistan by agreement with Kabul, but paid only a fraction of the world market price for it. "Robber and plantation economies [would have been] clearly indicated for Afghanistan's future if Soviet control there [had been] consolidated."[157]

The Afghan war, begun under Leonid Brezhnev, was imposing many other costs on Mikhail Gorbachev's Russia. By providing one of the levers President Reagan used to pry huge defense budgets out of his Congresses, by bringing Washington and Beijing closer together, by creating profound hostility among Islamic states, by dissipating the mystique of the invincible Soviet army—in all these ways the occupation of Afghanistan, instead of enhancing Soviet security, was undermining it.

Most menacing of all, perhaps, was a peculiarly Soviet variation of the venerable Domino Principle: the long-term effects of the endless Afghanistan campaign on the Soviet Union's Muslim population, 50 million strong and rapidly increasing.

The Muslims of Soviet Central Asia inhabited territories acquired by conquest and only recently. These peoples were held inside the Soviet Union not by the appeal of Marxism—"perceived not as an internationalist philosophy but as a technique devised by the Russians to protect their colonial rule"—but by the power of the Soviet army.[158] There is practically no intermarriage at all with ethnic Russians. The subject peoples of the British and French empires had shown relatively little inclination to challenge their imperial overlords until they saw these masters defeated at the hands of an Asian people in World War II. What did Russia's Central Asian Muslims make of the events in Afghanistan, where the Invincible Red Army had for years been hard pressed by the warriors of God, Leninism tamed by Islam, an Islam resurgent all over the world and nowhere more vigorously than on the southern borders of the Soviet empire? What if the international response to the war in Afghanistan had taught them that there is indeed a Muslim world community that stretches far beyond the borders of their less-than-invincible utopia?[159]

How had the Soviets become entangled in this predicament? What happened to the Soviets in Afghanistan can perhaps be best understood as the mutually aggravating effects of four basic circumstances.

First, their invasion confronted the Soviets with a forbidding terrain inhabited by hardy and high-spirited people who saw themselves as intolerably provoked into a defense of both their independence and their religion. In a word, Afghanistan was no Czechoslovakia.

Second, from the beginning the Soviets had greatly overestimated their ability to cut off supplies to the guerrillas by using modern weapons technology. Weapons got in, from Pakistan, from America, from Iran and China and Egypt and Saudi Arabia—surely one of the most heterogeneous coalitions ever seen, and daunting indeed in its implications for Moscow. The Soviets thus learned how very difficult it is to defeat a popular insurgency possessing secure sources of outside aid.[160] And very late in the war, but not too late, the foreign supporters of the mujahideen provided them with weapons that came close to driving the vaunted Red air force from the daytime skies. In analyzing the war, one cannot overestimate either the importance of the willingness of foreign powers to supply the insurgents with modern weapons or the failure of the Soviets to isolate the country from this assistance.

Third, the numbers of troops the Soviet Union committed to the conflict proved totally inadequate for the subjugation of the country, or even for the secure possession of major parts of it. This was the root of the Soviet terror campaign against the civilian population: lacking the manpower for pacification, they turned to depopulation. But the tremendous firepower of the Soviet armed forces, with apparently no limitations whatsoever on its use and enhanced by incursions into Pakistan and assassinations of resistance leaders in Peshawar, did not silence the insurgents. Instead, the Soviet terror policy actually constructed, among the millions of Afghans who fled across the borders into Pakistan and Iran, a vast support system and recruiting ground for the resistance. Thus had depopulation fatally backfired.

Fourth, by no means least, the various political formulas advanced by Moscow to solve the Afghanistan problem had all failed. In response to initial armed resistance in 1978–1979 the Soviets and their mannequins in

Kabul had pursued policies that only made their opponents more determined. Attempts to reverse these blunders, including engineering major leadership changes and launching a "national conciliation government," achieved nothing. The goal of establishing a pro-Soviet government in Kabul that would be popular and legitimate, or at least tolerated by the Afghan people, was revealed as an illusion.[161] It is nothing less than astonishing that in a country with such profound racial, ethnic, religious, tribal, and linguistic fissures, the Soviets should have proven incapable of developing effective divide–and–rule policies. In a profound sense the Soviet political failure produced the military failure.[162]

One possible response to all these negatives would have been to decide finally to win the war. But "the Soviet leadership recognized that there could be no military solution in Afghanistan without a massive increase in their military commitment."[163] There were approximately 200,000 mujahideen in 1987, with perhaps 100,000 of these being active fighters. To reach the standard 10–to–1 ratio of soldiers to insurgents generally believed necessary to wage conclusive counterguerrilla warfare, and assuming the ineffective Kabul forces remained at around 80,000 (an optimistic assessment), the Soviets would have had to put over 900,000 troops into Afghanistan—eight times their actual commitment. The logistical challenges of supplying such a force in the Afghan terrain were staggering. And by the middle of the 1980s the Soviet leadership had ceased trying to hide the fact that the Soviet Union was facing a systemic economic crisis with the most profound and alarming implications.

But even if the Soviet Union had bitten the bullet and decided on a massive increase of its troop levels there, that would not have guaranteed quick or even complete success. The Americans had sent to South Viet Nam, a territory one quarter the size of Afghanistan, an army five times the size of the Soviet forces there. Assisting the Americans in South Viet Nam was an indigenous allied force eventually numbering 1 million out of a population of 18 million, compared to the 80,000 men and boys the Kabul regime was able to scrape together out of a population of 15 million. Thus, although the Soviets had not suffered defeat in Afghanistan, they faced either continuous conflict or unacceptable escalation.

Against precisely what danger, for precisely what gain, and at precisely what internal and international costs was Gorbachev obligated to continue and perhaps greatly escalate the conflict? This Afghanistan mess was not even his creation; it was Brezhnev's. By 1988, Brezhnev was quite dead, and most of the members of the Politburo that had supported his invasion were also dead or retired. "In the final analysis, Moscow deemed the overall costs of pursuing a military solution to be too high."[164] And so the Kremlin chose the policy of withdrawal.

On April 14, 1988, Pakistan and the PDPA regime signed the Geneva Accords, to become effective May 15; the United States and the Soviet

Union were guarantors of the pact. "On May 15 [1988], in compliance with the Geneva agreement, the Soviets began to withdraw their troops from Afghanistan," monitored by UNGOMAP (United Nations Good Offices Mission in Afghanistan and Pakistan).[165] By February 1989, all or almost all Soviet troops had left Afghanistan, but substantial numbers of advisers and KGB personnel remained.[166]

FROM INSURGENCY TO CIVIL WAR

By the middle of 1988, the mujahideen controlled over three quarters of the national territory. They held the capitals of several provinces in the strategic northern and eastern parts of the country. The Soviets, who had directed the war, protected the key cities, policed the highways, provided air mobility to the Kabul army, and sent special forces to interrupt insurgent supplies, were leaving. The Americans therefore believed that the PDPA would soon find itself presiding over "Socialism in one City," and Kabul itself would quickly fall.[167] But as the conflict reached the decade mark, these expectations of Kabul's capture proved overly optimistic, for several reasons.

Well-suited to guerrilla warfare, the organization and tactics of the insurgents proved less successful in the siege of cities. The level of cooperation among the various mujahideen fighting groups had improved since the early days. Nevertheless, internecine rivalries and jealousies within the resistance—including assassination and even occasional open combat between various groups—continued to impede mujahideen success.[168]

At the end of 1988 the Kabul regime maintained armed forces equal in number to the active mujahideen. These included about 40,000 regular army troops, generally poor in quality and unreliable; 35,000 better-quality KhAD (intelligence and secret police) and Sarandoy (paramilitary police); and about 25,000 tribal militia, composed of men from ethnic groups different from that of the local mujahideen. Highly paid, of questionable loyalty, only nominally under the control of Kabul, nevertheless in their own areas the militia usually kept the insurgents out and the roads open.[169]

As the Russians withdrew, the minority of Afghans, mainly urban, that had for one reason or another supported the Kabul regime increasingly fought with an intensity born of desperation. Without their Soviet allies in the field, they feared that the collapse of the regime would mean wholesale massacre. Such fear was well founded. Certain foreign volunteers among the insurgents, especially Saudis, were accused of real brutality toward the civilian population, including rape and enslavement. Moreover, as the day of victory seemed to grow nearer, some insurgents sought vengeance for so many years of untold suffering. The *Far Eastern Economic Review* reported that "atrocities and revenge killings by the guerrillas after capturing small provincial capitals have not enhanced their reputation among civilians in the large Afghan cities."[170] In June 1988, the garrison of the capital of Badakhshan province (in the far northeast) handed the city over to the resistance, but after that event frequent massacres of soldiers who had surrendered brought defection by Kabul troops to almost a complete end.[171]

Thus, when in March 1989 the insurgents launched a major attack on Jalalabad, intending to make that city the capital of a countergovernment, the expected defection of the garrison did not occur; instead, regime air and artillery badly mauled the mujahideen. In the capital itself many who would never join the PDPA supported the government because of what seemed to them the needlessly indiscriminate shelling of Kabul by the insurgents or because the growing influence of Pakistan and Saudi Arabia over the mujahideen accentuated the radical Islamic flavor of the resistance.

Most important of all to Kabul's survival was aid from the Soviet Union. The Soviets were indeed leaving the territory of Afghanistan. But unlike the Americans in South Viet Nam, they were not simply abandoning their allies to their fate. The Soviets left behind $1 billion worth of equipment and supplies, while "substantial deliveries of military equipment—including tanks, armored personnel carriers, and aircraft—continued unabated through 1988."[172] American aid to the mujahideen for all of 1989 amounted to about $600 million, an amount matched by Saudi Arabia.[173] In comparison, the Soviets were giving the Kabul regime $250 million a month.[174] "The flow of Soviet food, fuel and weapons has played a determining role in sustaining the Afghan economy."[175] Soviet military advisers and Soviet-supplied aircraft played a crucial role in the defense of Kabul.

AFGHANISTAN AND VIET NAM

By the mid-1980s it had become fashionable to refer to Afghanistan as "Russia's Viet Nam." There is a sense in which such a comparison is valid: "The Soviet forces in Afghanistan repeated the U.S. experience in Viet Nam, in that they did not lose but could not win at a politically acceptable cost."[176]

No two wars can ever be exactly the same, clearly. But there are contrasts between the circumstances of the American and the Soviet conflicts in Asia so major that one should be especially skeptical of sweeping comparisons. Among the principal differences between the Vietnamese and Afghan conflicts are the following.

First, Afghanistan is right over the border from the Soviet Union, just like Czechoslovakia or Hungary. In contrast, Washington is closer to the South Pole than to South Viet Nam. It would therefore be less misleading to compare the Soviet withdrawal from Afghanistan to an American withdrawal not from Viet Nam but from northern Mexico.

Second, the nature of the Soviet polity was much better suited to suppressing a foreign insurgency. Like the French before them, American forces in Viet Nam only occasionally and in violation of their own laws committed the kinds of acts that for the Soviet forces in Afghanistan were standing policy.

Third, the Americans and the Soviets faced far different opponents. If American casualties in Viet Nam were incomparably higher than Soviet casualties in Afghanistan, this disparity was by no means solely due to the much smaller Soviet troop commitment. The mujahideen were brave and resilient, but in Viet Nam the Americans faced opponents much better trained, organized, and equipped than the Soviets ever dreamed of in Afghanistan. The Politburo in Hanoi, having developed its military and political techniques during long years of struggle against the French, gave the Viet Cong unity, discipline, and direction. Hanoi also sent into the south a constant and increasing flow of well-trained combatants and effective weapons. The mujahideen had nothing like this; thus the Afghan struggle had neither a Tet nor an Easter offensive.

Fourth, the Soviets withdrew their ground forces from Afghanistan, as the Americans had done in Viet Nam. But shortly after completing their military withdrawal, the Americans slashed their assistance to their erstwhile allies, even medical supplies. In contrast, the Soviets poured food, weapons, and ammunition into Kabul, supplies that enabled the regime to go on fighting. The Soviets had pursued a more conservative military strategy than the Americans in Viet Nam and had decided to get out before the strains of the war had become too severe; their leaders were nevertheless determined that their investment in Afghanistan should not be allowed simply to go down the drain.

THE MEANING OF THE AFGHAN WAR

During the decade of the 1980s the Soviets unleashed upon the poor and simple people of Afghanistan the full horror of a deliberate campaign of annihilation. By 1988, roughly 1.25 million Afghans "had died as a result of aerial bombing raids, shootings, artillery shelling, antipersonnel mines, exhaustion and other war-related conditions."[177] Yet the fearsome technology of the Soviet armed forces, wielded with utter indifference to questions of legality or humanity, proved insufficient for victory. At a truly frightful price and with good help from their well-wishers in the outside world, the Afghan people fought to a stalemate the forces of a superpower on their very border. And Afghanistan provides an exceedingly rare example of a struggle in which guerrillas were successful by themselves, unsupported by the proximity of conventional armed forces.

But the Afghan struggle was more than an embarrassing colonial reverse for the world's last multinational empire. By successfully refusing to be made into a Central Asian imitation of Ceausescu's Romania, the Afghan freedom fighters inflicted the first (but not the last) indisputable reverse on the "historical inevitability of Marxism-Leninism" in which Brezhnev had so devoutly believed. This double defeat helped stimulate profound forces of change inside the Soviet empire, hastening its process of decomposition. The configuration and consequences of these changes are not yet entirely clear. But one thing is quite clear: the brave, sad, martyred people of Afghanistan have helped to alter the course of world politics.

Thus Trotsky's aphorism about the connection between Central Asia and Europe has received a supremely ironic vindication: the cries of battle in the Afghan mountains found an echo in the shouts of freedom on the Berlin Wall.

NOTES

1. David C. Isby, "Soviet Strategy and Tactics in Low Intensity Conflict," in *Guerrilla Warfare and Counterinsurgency: U.S.-Soviet Policy in the Third World*, ed. Richard H. Shultz, Jr., et al. (Lexington, MA: Lexington Books, 1989).

2. Louis Dupree, "Post-Withdrawal Afghanistan: Light at the End of the Tunnel," in *The Soviet Withdrawal from Afghanistan*, ed. Amin Saikal and William Maley, (Cambridge: Cambridge University Press, 1989), p. 31.

3. Arnold Fletcher, *Afghanistan: Highway of Conquest* (Ithaca, NY: Cornell University Press, 1965), p. 25.

4. Leon B. Poullada, "The Road to Crisis: 1919–1980," in *Afghanistan: The Great Game Revisited*, ed. Rosanne Klass (New York: Freedom House, 1987), p. 54.

5. J. Bruce Amstutz, *Afghanistan: The First Five Years of Soviet Occupation* (Washington, DC: National Defense University, 1986), p. 103.

6. Joseph J. Collins, *The Soviet Invasion of Afghanistan: A Study in the Use of Force in Soviet Foreign Policy* (Lexington, MA: Lexington Books, 1986), p. 50.

7. Henry S. Bradsher, *Afghanistan and the Soviet Union* (Durham, NC: Duke University, 1985), p. 80.

8. Thomas T. Hammond, *Red Flag over Afghanistan: The Communist Coup, the Soviet Invasion, and the Consequences* (Boulder, CO: Westview, 1984), p. 63.

9. Anthony Arnold and Rosanne Klass, "Afghanistan's Divided Communist Party," in Klass, ed., *Afghanistan: Game*, p. 141.

10. Amin Saikal and William Maley, Introduction to *The Soviet Withdrawal from Afghanistan*, ed. Saikal and Maley, p. 5.

11. Henry S. Bradsher, *Afghanistan and the Soviet Union*, Chapter 5.

12. Elie Krakowski, "Afghanistan and Soviet Global Interests," in Klass, ed., *Afghanistan: Game*, p. 164.

13. Tahir Amin, "Afghan Resistance: Past, Present and Future," *Asian Survey*, vol. 24 (April 1984), p. 380.

14. Like the traitor Kadar in Hungary. Mark Urban, *War in Afghanistan* (New York: St. Martin's, 1988), p. 47.

15. Anthony Arnold, *Afghanistan: The Soviet Invasion in Perspective*, (Stanford, CA: Hoover Institution, 1985), p. 95.

16. Collins, *Soviet Invasion of Afghanistan*, p. 100; A. Rosul Amin, "The Sovietization of Afghanistan," in Klass, ed., *Afghanistan: Game*, p. 306.

17. Edward N. Luttwak, *The Grand Strategy of the Soviet Union* (New York: St. Martin's Press, 1983), p. 58.

18. Arnold, *Afghanistan: Soviet Invasion*, p. 133.

19. On the planned incorporation of northern Afghanistan into the Soviet Union, see Yossef Bodansky, "Soviet Military Operations in Afghanistan," in Klass, ed., *Afghanistan: Game*.

20. Collins, *Soviet Invasion of Afghanistan*, p. 26.

21. Krakowski, "Soviet Global Interests," in Klass, ed., *Afghanistan: Game*, p. 162.

22. Bradsher, *Afghanistan and Soviet Union*, p. 156.

23. Krakowski, "Soviet Global Interests," in Klass, ed., *Afghanistan: Game*, p. 167.

24. Luttwak, *Grand Strategy*, p. 60.

25. Dupree, "Post-Withdrawal," in Saikal and Maley, ed., *Soviet Withdrawal*, p. 31.

26. David C. Isby, *War in a Distant Country: Afghanistan; Invasion and Resistance* (London: Arms and Armour Press, 1989), p. 93.

27. Craig Karp, "Afghanistan: Seven Years of Soviet Occupation" (Washington, DC: U.S. Department of State, 1986), p. 9.

28. Andre Brigot and Olivier Roy, *The War in Afghanistan* (New York: Harvester-Wheatsheaf, 1988), p. 74; Isby, *War in a Distant Country*, p. 62.

29. Bradsher, *Afghanistan and Soviet Union*, p. 294.

30. Edward Girardet, *Afghanistan: The Soviet War* (New York: St. Martin's, 1985), p. 201.

31. Amstutz, *Afghanistan: First Five Years*, p. 122.

32. Craig Karp, "Afghanistan: Eight Years of Soviet Occupation" (Washington, DC: U.S. Department of State, 1987), p. 8.

33. U.S. Department of State, *Afghanistan: Soviet Occupation and Withdrawal* (Washington, DC: U.S. Department of State, 1988).

34. Amstutz, *Afghanistan: First Five Years*, p. 204.

35. Paul Trottier and Craig Karp, *Afghanistan: Five Years of Occupation*, Special Report no. 120 (Washington, DC: U.S. Department of State, 1984), p. 6.

36. Amin, "Sovietization," in Klass, ed., *Afghanistan: Game*, p. 325.

37. Gérard Chaliand, "The Bargain War in Afghanistan," in *Guerrilla Strategies*, ed. Gérard Chaliand (Berkeley: University of California Press, 1982), p. 330.

38. Amstutz, *Afghanistan: First Five Years*, p. 152.

39. Arnold, *Afghanistan: Soviet Invasion*, p. 98.

40. Claude Malhuret, "Report from Afghanistan," *Foreign Affairs*, vol. 62 (Winter 1984).

41. David Busby Edwards, "Origins of the Anti-Soviet Jihad," in Grant M. Farr and John G. Merriam, eds., *Afghan Resistance: The Politics of Survival* (Boulder: Westview, 1987), p. 24.

42. Amstutz, *Afghanistan: First Five Years*, p. 142.

43. Girardet, *Afghanistan: Soviet War*, p. 125.

44. Barnet R. Rubin, "Human Rights in Afghanistan," in Klass, ed., *Afghanistan: Game*, p. 345.

45. Girardet, *Afghanistan: Soviet War*, p. 63.

46. Paul Trottier and Craig Karp, *Afghanistan: Five Years of Occupation*, p. 5.

47. M. Siddieq Noorzoy, "Long-Term Soviet Economic Interests and Policies in Afghanistan," in Klass, ed., *Afghanistan: Game*, p. 91.

48. Amstutz, *Afghanistan: First Five Years*, p. 145.

49. Ibid., p. 150.

50. Eliza van Hollen, *Afghanistan: Three Years of Occupation*, (Washington, DC: U.S. Department of State, 1982), p. 5.

51. Amstutz, *Afghanistan: First Five Years*, p. 124.

52. Ibid., pp. 186–87; Urban, *War in Afghanistan*, p. 69.

53. Craig Karp, *Afghanistan: Six Years of Soviet Occupation*, (Washington, DC: U.S. Department of State, 1985), p. 7.

54. Chaliand, "Bargain War," p. 335.

55. Amstutz, *Afghanistan: First Five Years*, p. 166.

56. Ibid., p. 184.

57. Van Hollen, *Three Years*, p. 5.

58. Amstutz, *Afghanistan: First Five Years*, pp. 183, 189.

59. Girardet, *Afghanistan: Soviet War*, p. 141.

60. *New York Times*, March 21, 1984, p. 7.

61. Karp, *Seven Years*, p. 9.

62. Arnold, *Afghanistan: Soviet Invasion*, p. 102.

63. Van Hollen, *Three Years*, p. 7.

64. John F. Baddeley, *The Russian Conquest of the Caucasus* (New York: Russell and Russell, 1969 [first published 1908]), p. xxxvi.

65. Bodansky, "Soviet Military Operations," in Klass, ed., *Afghanistan: Game*, p. 234.

66. W. E. D. Allen and Paul Muratoff, *Caucasian Battlefields* (Cambridge: Cambridge University Press, 1953), Chapter 3.

67. Ibid., Chapter 3.

68. Geoffrey Jukes, "The Soviet Armed Forces and the Afghan War," in Saikal and Maley, eds., *Soviet Withdrawal*, p. 88.

69. Karp, *Eight Years*, p. 2. "Most Western estimates put Soviet troop strength at about 120,000 men." From U.S. Department of State, *Afghanistan: Soviet Occupation and Withdrawal*, p. 5.

70. Amstutz, *Afghanistan: First Five Years*, p. 168.

71. Ibid., p. 196.

72. Karp, *Six Years*, p. 7.

73. Collins, *Soviet Invasion*, p. 90.

74. Urban, *War in Afghanistan*, p. 176.

75. Bradsher, *Afghanistan and Soviet Union*, p. 210.

76. Jukes, "Soviet Armed Forces," in Saikal and Maley, eds., *Soviet Withdrawal*, p. 84.

77. Karp, *Seven Years*, p. 10.

78. Stephen T. Hosmer, "How Successful Has the Soviet Union Been in Third World Protracted Conflict?" in Shultz, et al., eds., *Guerrilla Warfare and Counterinsurgency: U.S.-Soviet Policy in the Third World*.

79. Bodansky, "Soviet Military Operations," in Klass, ed., *Afghanistan: Game*, p. 259 and passim.

80. *New York Times*, December 17, 1984, p. 1. See also report by Amnesty International, *Afghanistan: Torture of Prisoners* (London: 1986).

81. Girardet, *Afghanistan: Soviet War*, passim. This method, "perfected" in Afghanistan, has been used also in Ethiopia and Cambodia. See Malhuret, "Report from Afghanistan," pp. 427 ff.

82. Girardet, *Afghanistan: Soviet War*, p. 228.

83. Amstutz, *Afghanistan: First Five Years*, pp. 175–76.

84. Ibid., p. 188.

85. *Christian Science Monitor*, October 26, 1988, p. 11; Girardet, *Afghanistan: Soviet War*, pp. 219–20; Malhuret, "Report from Afghanistan."

86. Malhuret, "Report from Afghanistan," p. 430; on this revolting topic of toy bombs, see also Girardet, *Afghanistan: Soviet War*, p. 213; Amstutz, *Afghanistan: First Five Years*, p. 145; Arnold, *Afghanistan: Soviet Invasion*, p. 99; Bradsher, *Afghanistan and Soviet Union*, p. 211; *New York Times*, Editorial, December 10, 1985, p. 30.

87. Bradsher, *Afghanistan and Soviet Union*, p. 279.

88. Malhuret, "Report from Afghanistan," p. 430; see also the reports to the United Nations Commission on Human Rights by Felix Ermacora: "Report on the Situation of Human Rights in Afghanistan": U.N. Document No. E/CN.4/1985/21 (Feb. 19, 1985); U.N. Document No. A/40/843 (Nov. 5, 1985); U.N. Document E/CN.4/1986/24 (Feb. 17, 1986).

89. Karp, *Eight Years*, p. 9.

90. Urban, *War in Afghanistan*, p. 129.

91. Ibid., p. 127.

92. Karp, *Six Years*, p. 8.

93. Karp, *Seven Years*, p. 11.

94. Collins, *Soviet Invasion*, p. 85.

95. Girardet, *Afghanistan: Soviet War*, p. 42; Amstutz, *Afghanistan: First Five Years*, p. 149.

96. Urban, *War in Afghanistan*, p. 68.

97. Van Hollen, *Three Years*, p. 9.

98. Brigot and Roy, *War in Afghanistan*, p. 151.

99. *Afghanistan: Soviet Occupation and Withdrawal*, p. 5.

100. Collins, *Soviet Invasion*, p. 59.

101. Amstutz, *Afghanistan: First Five Years*, p. 132.

102. Ibid., p. 132.

103. Ibid., p. 135.

104. Bureau of Intelligence and Research, "Afghanistan: Four Years of Occupation" (Washington, DC: U.S. Department of State, 1983), p. 2.

105. Amstutz, *Afghanistan: First Five Years*, pp. 128, 181.

106. Trottier and Karp, *Five Years*, p. 4.

107. *New York Times*, October 24, 1984, p. 1.

108. Amstutz, *Afghanistan: First Five Years*, p. 140.

109. Arnold, *Afghanistan: Soviet Invasion*, p. 98.

110. Trottier and Karp, *Five Years*, p. 2.

111. Karp, *Six Years*, p. 2.

112. Karp, *Eight Years*, p. 12.

113. Bodansky, "Soviet Military Operations," in Klass, ed., *Afghanistan: Game*, p. 261.

114. Urban, *War in Afghanistan*, p. 200.

115. Karp, *Seven Years*, p. 1.

116. Karp, *Eight Years*, p. 6.

117. Ibid., p. 3.

118. Ibid., p. 5.

119. See, for example, *New York Times*, January 25, 1984, p. 1.

120. Bradsher, *Afghanistan and Soviet Union*, p. 276.

121. *Christian Science Monitor*, October 24, 1988.

122. *Washington Post*, December 15, 1985.

123. Van Hollen, *Three Years*, p. 11.

124. Girardet, *Afghanistan: Soviet War*, p. 248.

125. Malhuret, "Report from Afghanistan." In his article "Afghanistan: Postmortem" in the April 1989 *Atlantic*, Robert D. Kaplan wrote that foreign newsmen gave poor coverage to the Afghan war partly because there were no modern cities with good hotels close at hand.

126. Girardet, *Afghanistan: Soviet War*, p. 67.

127. Grant M. Farr and John G. Merriam, *Afghan Resistance: The Politics of Survival* (Boulder, CO: Westview, 1987), p. xii.

128. Amin Saikal, "The Regional Politics of the Afghan Crisis," in Saikal and Maley, eds., *Soviet Withdrawal*, p. 54.

129. Collins, *Soviet Invasion*, p. 153; on continuation of bombings of villages inside Pakistan, see, for example, *New York Times*, January 29, 1984, p. 1; and *New York Times*, March 25, 1987, p. 1.

130. Bradsher, *Afghanistan and Soviet Union*, p. 222.

131. Karp, *Eight Years*, p. 22.

132. Urban, *War in Afghanistan*, p. 97.

133. See Yaacov Vertzberger, "Afghanistan in China's Policy," *Problems of Communism*, vol. 31 (May–June 1982), pp. 1–24; Leslie Holmes, "Afghanistan and Sino-Soviet Relations," in Saikal and Maley, eds., *Soviet Withdrawal*, pp. 122–142.

134. Amstutz, *Afghanistan: First Five Years*, p. 216.

135. Amin, "Sovietization," in Klass, ed., *Afghanistan: Game*, p. 322.

136. Poullada, "Road to Crisis," in Klass, ed., *Afghanistan: Game*, p. 48.

137. Collins, *Soviet Invasion*, p. 19.

138. Hammond, *Red Flag*, pp. 26–28.

139. Collins, *Soviet Invasion*, p. 20.

140. Poullada, "Road to Crisis," in Klass, ed., *Afghanistan: Game*, p. 44.

141. Arnold, *Afghanistan: Soviet Invasion*, p. xii.

142. Collins, *Soviet Invasion*, p. 134.

143. Jimmy Carter, *Keeping Faith: Memoirs of a President* (New York: Bantam, 1982), p. 473.

144. Ibid., pp. 471–89; Cyrus Vance, *Hard Choices* (New York: Simon and Schuster, 1982), pp. 386–96; Zbigniew Brzezinski, *Power and Principle: Memoirs of the National Security Adviser* (New York: Farrar, Straus and Giroux, 1983), Chapter 12.

145. Carter, *Keeping Faith*, p. 483.

146. Collins, *Soviet Invasion*, p. 145.

147. On the Reagan Doctrine, see William R. Bode, "The Reagan Doctrine in Outline," and Angelo Codevilla, "The Reagan Doctrine: It Awaits Implementation," both in *Central America and the Reagan Doctrine*, ed. Walter F. Hahn (Boston: University Press of America, 1987); Secretary of State George Shultz, "America

and the Struggle for Freedom," *State Department Current Policy*, no. 659 (February 1985).

148. Arnold, *Afghanistan: Soviet Invasion*, p. 118; see *New York Times*, May 3, 1983, and November 28, 1984; *Wall Street Journal*, April 9, 1984; *Washington Post*, January 13, 1985; *Economist*, January 19, 1985; Anthony H. Cordesman and Abraham R. Wagner, *The Lessons of Modern War*, vol. 3, *The Afghan and Falklands Conflicts* (Boulder, CO: Westview, 1990), p. 20.

149. John Ranelagh, *The Agency: The Rise and Decline of the CIA* (New York: Simon and Schuster, 1986), p. 681; Amstutz, *Afghanistan: First Five Years*, p. 210.

150. Bradsher, *Afghanistan and Soviet Union*, p. 278; Amstutz, *Afghanistan: First Five Years*, p. 210.

151. Cordesman and Wagner, *Afghan and Falklands Conflicts*, p. 83.

152. U.S. Department of State, *Afghanistan: Soviet Occupation and Withdrawal*, p. 1.

153. Cordesman and Wagner, *Afghan and Falklands Conflicts*; Jukes, "Soviet Armed Forces," in Saikal and Maley, eds., *Soviet Withdrawal*, p. 83.

154. Isby, *War in a Distant Country*, p. 65; William Maley, "The Geneva Accords of 1988" in Saikal and Maley, eds., *Soviet Withdrawal*, p. 16.

155. Girardet, *Afghanistan: Soviet War*, p. 234.

156. John F. Shroder and Abdul Tawab Assifi, "Afghan Mineral Resources and Soviet Exploitation," in Klass, ed., *Afghanistan: Game*, p. 128.

157. Ibid., p. 101.

158. Alexandre Bennigsen, "The Impact of the Afghan War on Soviet Central Asia," in Klass, ed., *Afghanistan: Game*, p. 295.

159. Alexandre Bennigsen, "Mullahs, Mujahidin and Soviet Muslims," *Problems of Communism*, vol. 33 (November–December 1984), pp. 28–45; and the review article by Kemal Karpat, "Moscow and the 'Muslim Question,' " *Problems of Communism*, vol. 32 (November–December 1983), pp. 71–80. See also Graham E. Fuller, "The Emergence of Central Asia," *Foreign Affairs*, vol. 69, no. 2 (Spring 1990).

160. Cordesman and Wagner, *Afghan and Falklands Conflicts*, p. 95.

161. T. Daley, "Afghanistan and Gorbachev's Global Foreign Policy," *Asian Survey*, vol. 29 (May 1989), pp. 496–513.

162. An enlightening treatment of nonmilitary aspects of Soviet counterinsurgency in Afghanistan is James S. Robbins, "Soviet Counterinsurgency in Afghanistan, 1979–1989" (Ph.D. diss., Tufts University, 1991).

163. U.S. Department of State, *Afghanistan: Soviet Occupation and Withdrawal*, p. 2.

164. Ibid., p. 5.

165. Ibid., p. 1.

166. The resistance parties opposed the accords, for at least two reasons: first, the illegitimate and illegal Kabul regime could not enter into any agreement with any state; second, they feared that the accords might foreshadow a lessening of world interest in Afghanistan's struggle, leaving the insurgents without further assistance.

167. The State Department's *Afghanistan: Soviet Occupation and Withdrawal* contained these prognostications: "Most observers believe that the Najibullah regime will not long survive the Soviet departure." "Most experts agree that it [the Kabul

army] probably can survive no more than a matter of months after a complete Soviet withdrawal" (pp. 1 and 7).

168. Barnett R. Rubin, "The Fragmentation of Afghanistan," *Foreign Affairs*, vol. 68 (Winter 1989/90), p. 163.

169. U.S. State Department, *Afghanistan: Soviet Occupation and Withdrawal*, p. 7; Rubin, "Fragmentation of Afghanistan," p. 161.

170. Ahmed Rashid, "A Bloody Stalemate," *Far Eastern Economic Review*, June 8, 1989, p. 42.

171. Rubin, "Fragmentation of Afghanistan," p. 158.

172. *Afghanistan: Soviet Occupation and Withdrawal*, p. 4.

173. Sophie Quinn-Judge, "Splitting the Faithful," *Far Eastern Economic Review*, July 13, 1989, p. 21.

174. Ahmed Rashid, "Highway Lifeline," *Far Eastern Economic Review*, October 26, 1989, p. 22.

175. Ibid.

176. Jukes, "Soviet Armed Forces," in Saikal and Maley, eds., *Soviet Withdrawal*, p. 83.

177. William Maley, "The Geneva Accords of April 1988," in Saikal and Maley, eds., *Soviet Withdrawal*, p. 13.

Conclusion

Guerrilla Insurgency and American Policy

War is mainly a catalogue of blunders.

Carl von Clausewitz

Many years ago a seasoned student of guerrilla conflict observed that "the art of war must be modified to suit the circumstances of each particular case."[1] All insurgencies have important similarities. Each one also has features that make it unique in some important way. Consider some of the peculiar characteristics of merely those cases examined in this book.

• In Greece, the insurgents were associated in the public mind with unpopular groups at home and abroad. At the same time, American economic assistance to the Athens government undermined the insurgents' strategy of destroying the Greek economy. But the insurgents also threw away the very important cards they held: they antagonized the rural population upon whom they ultimately relied for their survival; they made the transition from guerrilla war to conventional war at the wrong time; and they alienated the rulers of their most vital sanctuary.

• In French Viet Nam, on the other hand, the government made all the big mistakes. During World War II the Japanese had broken the power and prestige of the French. In attempting to reassert their control by force, the French underestimated their opponents from start to finish. They refused both to match their ends to their means and to take steps that could have increased those means. Communist Chinese arms and instructors greatly assisted the insurgents, especially at Dien Bien Phu; but the French themselves had arranged that battle. Many like to deplore American naiveté and ignorance of foreign cultures; the French, in contrast, had long experience with colonial problems all over the globe. Yet it is very difficult to see that this experience was of much value to them against the Viet Minh.

• In the Philippines, a poor country with a tradition of guerrilla war, both Aguinaldo and the Huks met clear defeat. In each of those conflicts, the government of the day eventually came up with a close-to-foolproof formula for victory over the insurgents: restrained behavior by government troops, social and political reform, security for the civil population. Just to make it all perfect, the Pacific Ocean and the U.S. Navy on and later under it made foreign assistance to the insurgents close to impossible.

• In South Viet Nam, after an unnecessarily massive and ill-conceived American intervention had blocked what had once seemed like an inevitable victory for the Viet Cong, the guerrillas sacrificed themselves (or were sacrificed) in the debacle of the Tet Offensive. Then the United States pulled out its forces and allowed the country it had saved to be overrun in a conventional invasion.

• Afghanistan is often tagged "Russia's Viet Nam," but the many implied comparisons in this phrase obscure as much as they reveal. The mujahideen, poorly armed, ethnically fragmented, spontaneously rising in defense of their culture, confronted the world's most powerful totalitarian state, which unfortunately lay on their border. On the other hand, the Viet Cong, orchestrated and disciplined from Hanoi, organized into both guerrilla units and well-equipped conventional battalions, sustained by ever increasing numbers of North Vietnamese regulars, confronted a democratic society on the other side of the globe. The Americans committed many more troops to their war than the Soviets did to theirs, and took many more casualties. And clearly not the least of the contrasts, the Americans defeated the guerrillas in Viet Nam.

• Geography also exerts its always particular and often decisive effects. Geography worked mightily against Aguindaldo's followers and the Huks. But South Viet Nam—neither an archipelago like the Philippines, nor a peninsula like South Korea and Malaya, nor an island like Taiwan—succumbed finally not to insurgency but to invasion. The closing of the Yugoslavian frontier was not the decisive factor in the defeat of the Greek Communists, who mainly defeated themselves; yet if their sanctuaries had remained open to them, the war might have dragged on to an unpredictable end. If Afghanistan's eastern neighbor had been India instead of Pakistan, the insurgents might well have been broken by Soviet technobarbarism.

Clearly, in view of their diversities, an attempt to draw general lessons from a limited number of insurgencies is a journey through dangerous territory that one should undertake with trepidation. Nevertheless, it is apparent that the ability of a guerrilla movement to flourish depends to the greatest extent on the policies (mistakes) of the government. The following effort, therefore, to sketch out a basic counterguerrilla strategy, one with which a government can reasonably hope to emerge victorious, or at least not to make victory unattainable, approaches guerrilla insurgency in its very essence.

TO DEFEAT THE GUERRILLAS

The cases analyzed in this book strongly suggest that for a government facing a guerrilla threat, the beginning of wisdom is to grasp and hold on tightly to the idea that insurgency is a profoundly political problem. To see the cogency of this, consider merely the very basic question: "Where are the guerrilla units getting their members?"

- If people are joining the guerrillas because they have an attractive program, then to whom are the government's programs so unattractive, and why?
- If the guerrillas are able to recruit because the people fear them, then where are the police? (The very appearance of guerrilla bands in a country is a dead giveaway that something is quite wrong with the government's intelligence and police systems, to say the least).
- If guerrilla recruitment is a reaction to extortion or brutality on the part of local officials, the police, and the army, how has the government permitted such conditions to exist and flourish?

Clearly, then, the defeat of a guerrilla insurgency will require that the government carry out certain political and economic changes and that time be allowed for these to take effect. But extensive areas of the country may be under the control of the guerrillas and hence beyond the reach of reforms for the time being. Thus an effective military response by the government is necessary to allow the political offensive to take hold. The military response should complement, rather than negate, other vital parts of the anti-insurgency program.

A successful counterguerrilla strategy therefore needs to be a true mixture, not a juxtaposition, of both political and military elements. It should aim not to destroy the insurgents but to end the insurgency by strengthening governmental legitimacy, effecting social reforms, and launching indirect as well as direct military attacks on the guerrillas. In practical terms a strategy that was consistent with the analysis of the cases in this book would include:

1. Two fundamental points, without which the government will invite a defeat it probably deserves:
   - Ensuring that the conduct of government troops toward the civilian population does not make recruits for the insurgency.
   - Mitigating some principal peasant grievance(s).

2. Immediate steps by which a government can inexpensively but effectively weaken the guerrillas while putting the above fundamental points into practice:

- Encouraging defections—for example, with a resettlement program.
- Offering big rewards for the capture of specific individuals, especially leadership and/or criminal elements, and paying bounties for turned-in weapons.
- Sending small, specialized guerrilla-hunter groups into insurgent-dominated territory, with particular attention to disrupting guerrilla food supplies.

3. Long-term policies for final victory:

- Restoring or creating a peaceful road to political change, through free elections where possible and appropriate, or through more traditional legitimate means (normally some sort of national convocation).
- Closing down or restricting the utility of the guerrillas' sanctuary, if they have one, through diplomatic and/or military efforts. The government that can reduce neither the internal (peasant grievances) nor the external (sanctuary) support of an insurgency is probably beyond help; on the other hand, if the government side is clearly winning, the sanctuary problem may solve itself.
- Establishing as the principal focus of the military effort the separation of the guerrillas from the civil population.

Some of these prescriptions are self-evident; others may benefit from the following elaboration.

THE BEHAVIOR OF GOVERNMENT TROOPS

Misconduct or brutality by government troops has traditionally been one of the most fruitful sources of recruits for an insurgency.[2] It will also almost certainly make impossible the construction of an effective intelligence network without which operations against the insurgents will be needlessly prolonged. A government that condones or ignores bad behavior by its military is heading for defeat. Maybe inadequacy of means or political divisions prevent the government from carrying out profound or rapid social reforms. But even a resource-poor government can see to it that the arrival of government troops in a province or a village does not resemble the descent of a plague of locusts. Steps a government can take toward this end include:

- Indoctrinating military commanders down to the lowest levels with the importance of this principle;
- Stationing soldiers in their home district or province;
- Forbidding the assignment, even implicitly, of any quotas for either apprehended or killed guerrillas;
- Carrying out unscheduled inspections of units in the field by high-ranking civil and military figures;
- Providing the troops with suitable pay and rations.

In regard to the last point, twenty-five centuries ago in his *Art of War* Sun Tsu said, "Take heed to nourishing the troops." A strictly enforced equality of rations for officers and soldiers should have beneficial effects here.

CONCILIATING THE PEASANTRY

The most effective strategy for bringing an insurgency under control is for the government to remove or mitigate the basic cause(s) of that insurgency. This will probably not work with the leaders of the guerrilla movement, because for them the basic cause may be simply that they want to get into power. But for the peasants who compose the bulk of the insurgency's fighting forces and sympathizers, reforms in government policy can be extremely effective. It may be possible to restore peace in the rural areas simply by returning to traditional practices of land tenure, rents, and taxation, or by adjusting some particularly galling racial, religious, linguistic, or tribal disability. Such an approach will be much cheaper than fighting a protracted war—especially a losing one.

INDUCING SURRENDER

The most humane way to defeat the guerrillas is to convince them to give up. If the government implements an intelligent military policy against the guerrillas, a number of processes will develop within the insurgency: (1) those who joined in the anticipation of a quick and easy victory will begin to repent their decision; (2) the proportion of the guerrilla forces composed of those who were in one way or another coerced into joining will increase; and (3) the hardships of guerrilla life will take their relentless toll. Therefore, along with correct treatment of the peasantry and clear-and-hold operations (discussed below), amnesty will be a most important government weapon. Clearly, for amnesty to be effective guerrillas need to be fairly certain that upon surrender they will not be killed or abused.[3]

SEPARATING THE GUERRILLAS FROM THE CIVILIANS

A common historical tactic against guerrillas has been to build fortified posts in order to impede their movements from one area to another. This method usually yields very disappointing results. Small outposts soon reveal their vulnerability to guerrilla attack, so the government consolidates them into larger posts. But these are too few to seriously impede guerrilla movements and are also vulnerable to mass attack by heavy-armed units. This was the experience of the Greek government in the early days of the struggle with ELAS.

Another standard technique is the so-called sweep operation: government forces move through a village or a larger area searching for guerrillas. Sweeps rarely catch anybody worthwhile, they invite misbehavior by frustrated troops, and they convince the peasantry that the government cannot reliably protect them from guerrilla reprisals. Sweeps were common in the wars in Viet Nam.

Capturing competent guerrillas is very difficult; so is killing them. Besides, the revolutionary infrastructure can find replacements for them. The best way to fight guerrillas is to take the fish out of the water: to drive the guerrillas away from the peasants in their villages. Cut off from the civilians, the guerrillas are also cut off from their best intelligence and food sources, and ultimately from recruits. A sound military response to a guerrilla insurgency will have this aim at its center.

A classic method for isolating guerrillas is the clear-and-hold strategy.[4] The objectives are to chase the guerrillas out of a specific area, not very hard to do, and to make sure they do not return, something much more difficult; the latter is in fact the heart of clear-and-hold.

During a clear-and-hold campaign, the country consists of three parts from the government's viewpoint:

- the government's base area, normally the main population centers plus previously cleared districts;
- area(s) currently being cleared; and
- "contested" areas, those regions temporarily conceded to the guerrillas, normally the more remote and lightly populated regions of the country.

The government's base area will be under the control of the police and perhaps militia and army units. In contested areas, the government should hold any large towns (provided they can be supplied; otherwise one will fall into the "French trap"). A decent air force can prevent the guerrillas from using a desert as their base area, but efforts to cordon off a large jungle area (especially along a border) will be largely wasted. Nevertheless, small, specially trained hunter units can penetrate a guerrilla-infested jungle and make life there stimulating.

To clear a contested area means first of all to saturate it with soldiers. This is the easy part, because no intelligent guerrillas will stand and fight aggressive regular troops. But after the troops leave the newly cleared area, the guerrillas will return unless the government accomplishes two tasks there. It must uproot the revolutionary infrastructure: that means identifying and arresting or chasing out of the district active sympathizers or agents who are the eyes and ears of the guerrillas. Normal police methods can accomplish this, provided everyone understands that it will take time. Simultaneously, the government must build up a self-defense force to keep the guerrillas from infiltrating back after the troops move out to clear another area.

Well-led guerrillas attack only in overwhelming strength. Thus the main purpose of self-defense forces in a village or rural district is to offer armed resistance to guerrilla bands just long enough for government troops to arrive and chase the guerrillas away. These self-defense forces need not be large, nor must they have the best weapons; what is essential is for them to know that if they are attacked by guerrillas and call for help, help will arrive, and in time.

Thus, for village self-defense to work, the government must maintain relief forces that are permanently on call, mobile, and linked with the different self-defense units in the district by some kind of quick communications network. For linkage, two-way radios are much safer, as well as cheaper, than telephone lines. Ensuring swift response may be a major problem: in Viet Nam, the Viet Cong would attack a self-defended village at night; the village would send out the alarm; and the truck-borne government troops coming to the rescue would suffer heavy casualties in a carefully prepared ambush. Helicopters might seem to be the answer here, but they are easy to hit from the ground and are not very effective at night, which is the best time for guerrilla activities.

In the most threatened villages, such as those close to an insecure border or areas currently being cleared, the government could station small units of well-trained regulars to bolster the local self-defense group, as in the little-studied but lesson-laden Marine CAPs program in Viet Nam.[5] When it comes to an actual fire engagement with guerrillas, without exception the training and discipline of the government troops are incomparably more important than their numbers.

In those districts officially declared under government control ("cleared"), the government may legitimately impose the severest penalties upon civilians who actively cooperate with the guerrillas. But in contested areas, where the government by definition is unable to guarantee the peasants' physical security, civilian cooperation with the insurgents must be treated as a natural or at least pardonable phenomenon.

CLOSING THE SANCTUARY

If the guerrillas are receiving systematic help, especially weapons, from across the border, this is probably because the terrain of the frontier area makes it too difficult for the government to close. In that case, to stop or reduce the flow of arms, the government will usually have only diplomacy to rely on. This presents a grave problem, because the neighboring state must either be hostile or else too weak to stop arms shipments coming through it from another hostile state (Pakistan in the Soviet-Afghan conflict is an example of the first case, Cambodia in the war for South Viet Nam an example of the second). If the government cannot impede the flow of arms, the implementation of correct political and military responses to the insurgency becomes all the more crucial.

In the worst-case scenario, in which the government has pursued stupid policies against the guerrillas and is thus threatened with military and/or moral collapse, it should pull all of its troops back into the most politically reliable or most easily defended area(s) of the country, start implementing an intelligent program, and hope for a break in the game.

THE HEART OF THE MATTER: U.S. INTERVENTION

Finally, we confront the question of questions: should the United States government ever again deploy ground troops against an insurgency?

Guerrillas fighting against a foreign enemy have the distinct advantage that they can detect the enemy much more easily than the enemy can detect them, as in the case of the Viet Minh fighting against the French. But clearly the most common and powerful argument against the use of foreign troops arises from the belief that they would trigger a volcanically powerful nationalist reaction. It is of course to the advantage of the insurgents to avail themselves of the issue of nationalism where possible. There may nevertheless be a tendency among Westerners to overestimate both the likelihood and the consequences of this. Consider the following points:

• The Franco-Viet Minh war is everyone's favorite classic example of the invincibility of nationalism, but such a characterization of that struggle is subject to serious challenge (see Chapter 4).[6]

• Sometimes both the government and the insurgents rely quite openly on outside help, as in the Greek conflict. There, the government had the support of popular foreign countries (Britain and the United States), the insurgents had the support of unpopular ones (Yugoslavia and Bulgaria).

• Foreign soldiers composing part or all of a garrison to protect a large city may appear as a source of prosperity and/or security, as did the British forces in Athens in 1944 and the Americans in Saigon in the 1960s.

• Peasant xenophobia is not nationalism. Where the insurgency is fueled by hatred between ethnic or religious groups within the same country, the presence of foreign troops per se might not be exacerbating; in Malaya in the 1950s, the ethnic Malays disliked the local Chinese insurgents much more than they did the British authorities.

• Sometimes what is called nationalism may in fact be a reaction against the government, not because it is foreign but because it is cruel or stupid. In Afghanistan, the Soviets foolishly permitted themselves to run afoul of the religious sentiments of the Afghans, not of their nationalist loyalties, which were weak before the mid-1980s. The anti-Soviet struggle was more a stimulus to than a result of Afghan nationalism. Indeed, the insurgency began before the Soviet invasion, as a revolt against a regime that was not so much foreign as crudely anti-Islamic; it continued to rage after the Soviets went home. And a significant number of mujahideen casualties have been the result of clashes between resistance groups.

• In dramatic contrast to the Soviets in Afghanistan, American occupation of the Philippines neither provoked a nationalist firestorm nor irrevocably alienated the inhabitants there (the same for the occupation, under incomparably more tense circumstances, of Japan); and the CAP program, where small numbers of U.S. Marines lived for long periods in South Vietnamese villages, proved extremely effective despite certain notable imperfections. Clearly, the Viet Cong and Hanoi employed the weapon of anti-American propaganda. How successful this effort was (inside Viet Nam) is debatable. What is beyond debate is the fact that millions of South Vietnamese preferred the short-term presence of Americans in their country to its permanent subjugation by the North.

The assertion, therefore, that the presence of American forces in a Third World country must inevitably provoke a nationalist fury in favor of the insurgents, which in turn will lead to an American failure, is misleading. And the weaknesses of this position would of course be multiplied in any instance where the United States intervened in cooperation with one or more regional allies.

Even so, American policymakers contemplating the dispatch of U.S. ground combat troops to assist a Third World government assailed by an insurgency will confront a number of difficult questions. What are the prospects for the success of the intervention? (This is a very tricky problem, because the practice of the United States has been to actively consider intervention only when the situation was already far gone.) Why does the indigenous government need foreign troops anyway? Why can't it construct a program to defeat or at least hold the guerrillas at bay, while receiving foreign economic help and perhaps the assistance of foreign military instructors and advisers? Will the introduction of American troops reduce the inability of the indigenous government to confront its guerrillas or aggravate it? And not least, can the United States avoid going in alone?

And even if the prospects of a successful intervention are favorable, is it all worth it? This question leads to an extremely important consideration: the effects of an American intervention not on the insurgency-torn country but on the United States.

The Third World used to be the arena in which the First and Second worlds struggled for advantage. With the political, economic, and moral collapse of Marxism-Leninism, there is at present no overall framework to guide U.S. policymakers. In the absence of Cold War imperatives, many will argue that no single Third World country (except Mexico) is of vital strategic significance to the United States.

Even if they reject this view, American policymakers must deal with the

American political system as it is, and above all with the reluctance of the electorate to distinguish in foreign policy between what is strategically effective and what is morally acceptable.

Many American citizens have always believed, like Confucius, Plato, and Aquinas, that there is a close relationship between political morality and political stability. The American propensity to explain U.S. foreign policy in terms of ethical values, often dismissed as naive or arrogant, may be neither: the toppling of the Eastern European quisling regimes has provided new evidence that the only truly stable governments are those that rest ultimately on popular consent, and not on indoctrinated armies, lupine police, prostituted journalists, judges, and teachers, all serving the interest of a "vanguard" party simultaneously utopian and cynical. In 1989 the collapse of Leninism from Berlin to Bucharest took us by surprise because we forgot how in 1956 the vaunted Communist dictatorship in Hungary crashed, quite literally overnight, like an empty suit of polished armor; we forget everything.[7]

In any event, this fundamental factor in American politics—the electorate's desire that foreign policy be consistent with publicly proclaimed national values—will almost certainly become a source of profound domestic division during a protracted United States intervention in a foreign insurgency, because while all violent struggles are shot through with moral ambiguities, these will be especially perplexing in Third World conflicts.

And so we conclude at the point where we began: as the somber clouds of the Cold War disperse, the lurid flames of guerrilla insurgency will appear all the brighter. The temptation to focus our eyes and our hearts on our own serious domestic problems will clash divisively with the temptation to intervene in various parts of the world in defense of democracy or self-determination or national credibility or access to vital materials or all of these. The Americans must prepare themselves for hard and often bitter choices as they confront the new world disorder.

NOTES

1. C. E. Callwell, *Small Wars: Their Principles and Practice* (Wakefield, England: EP Publishing, 1976 [orig. 1906]).

2. See Dennis J. Duncanson, *Government and Revolution in Viet Nam* (New York: Oxford University Press, 1968); Sir Robert Thompson, *Defeating Communist Insurgency: The Lessons of Malaya and Viet Nam* (New York: Praeger, 1966); Chalmers Johnson, *Peasant Nationalism and Communist Power* (Stanford, CA: Stanford University Press, 1961).

3. Amnesty is always controversial and will meet serious opposition from some government supporters. The South Vietnamese Army intensely disliked Communists who took advantage of amnesty, because they viewed them as traitors twice. In Greece, opponents of amnesty maintained that it prolonged the war, because the

insurgents could say to themselves: "If we win, we have Greece; if we are defeated, we have amnesty."

4. See especially the version of this approach in Thompson, *Defeating Communist Insurgency*.

5. See F. J. West, Jr., *The Village* (New York: Harper and Row, 1972).

6. Another classic example is China during the Japanese invasion. It seems, however, a debatable question whether the reaction of Chinese peasants and townsmen to the savage depredations of the Japanese troops is properly characterized as "nationalism." See Samuel F. Huntington, *Political Order in Changing Societies* (New Haven: Yale University Press, 1968) and Chalmers Johnson, *Peasant Nationalism and Communist Power: The Emergence of Revolutionary China, 1937–1945* (Stanford: Stanford University Press, 1962).

7. See Anthony James Joes, *From the Barrel of a Gun: Armies and Revolutions* (Washington: Pergamon-Brassey's, 1986), Chapter 3.

Selected Bibliography

Acheson, Dean. *Present at the Creation*. New York: Norton, 1969.

Aguinaldo, Emilio. *A Second Look at America*. New York: Robert Speller, 1957.

Allen, W. E. D., and Paul Muratoff. *Caucasian Battlefields*. Cambridge: Cambridge University Press, 1953.

Amstutz, J. Bruce. *Afghanistan: The First Five Years of Soviet Occupation*. Washington, DC: National Defense University, 1986.

Arnold, Anthony. *Afghanistan: The Soviet Invasion in Perspective*. Rev. ed. Stanford, CA: Hoover Institution, 1985.

Art, Robert J. "A Defensible Defense: America's Grand Strategy after the Cold War." *International Security*, vol. 15, no. 4 (Spring 1991).

Asprey, Robert. *War in the Shadows*. London: Macdonald, 1976.

Barker, Elisabeth. *Macedonia: Its Place in Balkan Power Politics*. London: Royal Institute of International Affairs, 1950.

Barry, Michael. "Afghanistan: Another Cambodia?" *Commentary*, August 1982.

Bashore, Boyd. "Dual Strategy for Limited War." *Military Review*, vol. 40 (May 1960).

Berman, Larry. *Planning a Tragedy: The Americanization of the War in Viet Nam*. New York: Norton, 1982.

Bernstein, Carl. "Arms for Afghanistan." *New Republic*, July 18, 1981.

Billings-Yun, Melanie. *Decision against War: Eisenhower and Dien Bien Phu*. New York: Columbia University Press, 1988.

Blaufarb, Douglas S. *The Counterinsurgency Era: U.S. Doctrine and Performance*. New York: Free Press, 1977.

Blount, James H. *The American Occupation of the Philippines 1898–1912*. New York: Putnam, 1913.

Bodansky, Yossef. "The Bear on the Chessboard: Soviet Military Gains in Afghanistan." *World Affairs*, vol. 5, no. 3 (Winter 1982–83).

Bodard, Lucien. *The Quicksand War: Prelude to Viet Nam.* Boston: Little, Brown, 1967.

Borkenau, Franz. *European Communism.* New York: Harper, 1953.

Boyer de Latour, Pierre. *Le Martyre de l'Armée Française.* Paris: Presses du Mail, 1962.

Bradsher, Henry. *Afghanistan and the Soviet Union.* Durham, NC: Duke University Press, 1985.

Braestrup, Peter. *Big Story.* Boulder, CO: Westview, 1977.

Brigot, Andre, and Olivier Roy. *The War in Afghanistan.* New York: Harvester-Wheatsheaf, 1988.

Browne, Malcolm W. *The New Face of War.* New York: Bobbs-Merrill, 1965.

Broxup, Marie. "The Soviets in Afghanistan: The Anatomy of a Takeover." *Central Asian Survey*, vol. 1, no. 4 (April 1983).

Bui Diem. *In the Jaws of History.* Boston: Houghton Mifflin, 1987.

Bureau of Intelligence and Research. *Afghanistan: Four Years of Occupation.* Washington, DC: U.S. Department of State, 1983.

Burks, R. V. "Statistical Profile of the Greek Communist." *Journal of Modern History*, vol. 27 (1955).

Buttinger, Joseph. *Viet Nam: A Political History.* New York: Praeger, 1968.

Cable, Larry E. *Conflict of Myths: The Development of American Counterinsurgency Doctrine and the Viet Nam War.* New York: Free Press, 1986.

Cady, John. *Roots of French Imperialism in Asia.* Ithaca, NY: Cornell University Press, 1954.

Callison, Charles Stuart. *Land to the Tiller in the Mekong Delta.* Lanham, MD: University Press of America, 1983.

Callwell, C. E. *Small Wars: Their Principles and Practice.* Wakefield, England: EP Publishing, 1976 (original 1906).

Cao Van Vien. *The Final Collapse.* Washington, DC: U.S. Army Center of Military History, 1983.

Cao Van Vien and Dong Van Khuyen. *Reflections on the Viet Nam War.* Washington, DC: U.S. Army Center of Military History, 1980.

Carter, Jimmy. *Keeping Faith: Memoirs of a President.* New York: Bantam, 1982.

Chaliand, Gérard. *Report from Afghanistan.* New York: Viking, 1982.

———. "The Bargain War in Afghanistan." In *Guerrilla Strategies*, ed. Gérard Chaliand. Berkeley: University of California, 1982.

Charters, David. "Coup and Consolidation: The Soviet Seizure of Afghanistan." *Conflict Quarterly* (Spring 1981).

Churchill, Winston. *Triumph and Tragedy.* Vol. 6 of *The Second World War.* Boston: Houghton Mifflin, 1953.

Clodfelter, Mark. *The Limits of Air Power: The American Bombing of North Viet Nam.* New York: Free Press, 1989.

Clutterbuck, Richard L. *The Long, Long War: Counterinsurgency in Malaya and Viet Nam.* New York: Praeger, 1966.

Colby, William. *Lost Victory.* Chicago: Contemporary Books, 1989.

Collins, Joseph J. "The Soviet Invasion of Afghanistan: Methods, Motives and Ramifications." *Naval War College Review* (November 1980).

———. "Soviet Military Performance in Afghanistan: A Preliminary Assessment." *Comparative Strategy*, vol. 4 (Spring 1983).

————. *The Soviet Invasion of Afghanistan: A Study in the Use of Force in Soviet Foreign Policy*. Lexington, MA: Lexington Books, 1985.

Condit, D. M. *Case Study in Guerrilla War: Greece during World War II*. Washington, DC: Department of the Army, 1961.

Cooper, Chester L. *The Lost Crusade: America in Viet Nam*. New York: Dodd, Mead, 1970.

Cordesman, Anthony H., and Abraham R. Wagner. *The Lessons of Modern War*. Vol. 3, *The Afghan and Falkland Conflicts*. Boulder, CO: Westview, 1990.

Cross, James Eliot. *Conflict in the Shadows: The Nature and Politics of Guerrilla War*. Garden City, NY: Doubleday, 1963.

Daley, T. "Afghanistan and Gorbachev's Global Foreign Policy." *Asian Survey*, vol. 29 (May 1989).

Davidson, Phillip B. *Viet Nam at War: The History, 1946–1975*. Novato, CA: Presidio Press, 1988.

Dawson, Alan. *Fifty-Five Days: The Fall of South Viet Nam*. Englewood Cliffs, NJ: Prentice-Hall, 1977.

Dedijer, Vladimir. *Tito*. New York: Simon and Schuster, 1953.

Devillers, Philippe. *Histoire du Viet-Nam de 1940 à 1952*. 3d ed. Paris: Editions du Seuil, 1952.

Director of Operations, Malaya. *The Conduct of Anti-Terrorist Operations*. 3d ed. Malaya: 1958.

Djilas, Milovan. *Conversations with Stalin*. New York: Harcourt, Brace and World, 1962.

Dong Van Khuyen. *The RVNAF*. Washington, DC: U.S. Army Center of Military History, 1980.

Donnell, John C. *Viet Cong Recruitment: Why and How Men Join*. Santa Monica, CA: Rand Corporation, 1975.

Duiker, William J. *The Rise of Nationalism in Viet Nam, 1920–1941*. Ithaca, NY: Cornell University Press, 1976.

————. *The Communist Road to Power in Viet Nam*. Boulder, CO: Westview, 1981.

Duncanson, Dennis J. *Government and Revolution in Viet Nam*. New York: Oxford University Press, 1968.

Dunn, Peter M. "The American Army: The Viet Nam War." In *Armed Forces and Modern Counterinsurgency*, ed. Ian F. W. Beckett and John Pimlott. New York: St. Martin's Press, 1985.

————. *The First Viet Nam War*. New York: St. Martin's Press, 1985.

Dupree, Louis. *Afghanistan*. Princeton, NJ: Princeton University Press, 1973.

Ely, Paul. *L'Indochine dans la tourmente*. Paris: Plon, 1964.

————. *Lessons of the War in Indochina*, vol. 2 (translation). Santa Monica, CA: Rand Corporation, 1967.

Fall, Bernard. *Street without Joy*. Harrisburg, PA: Stackpole, 1964.

————. *The Two Viet Nams: A Political and Military Analysis*. 2d ed., rev. New York: Praeger, 1967.

————. *Hell in a Very Small Place*. Philadelphia: Lippincott, 1967.

Farr, Grant M., and John G. Merriem. *Afghan Resistance: The Politics of Survival*. Boulder, CO: Westview, 1987.

Fishel, Wesley. *Viet Nam: Anatomy of a Conflict*. Itasca, IL: Peacock, 1968.

Fletcher, Arnold. *Afghanistan: Highway of Conquest*. Ithaca, NY: Cornell University Press, 1965.

Foreign Relations of the United States. Washington, DC: U.S. Government Printing Office, 1961–1977.

Fuller, Graham E. "The Emergence of Central Asia." *Foreign Affairs*, vol. 69, no. 2 (Spring 1990).

Gallucci, Robert L. *Neither Peace nor Honor*. Baltimore: Johns Hopkins University Press, 1975.

Galula, David. *Counterinsurgency Warfare: Theory and Practice*. New York: Praeger, 1964.

Gardner, Hugh. *Guerrilla and Counterguerrilla Warfare in Greece, 1941–1945*. Washington, DC: Department of the Army, 1962.

Gates, John Morgan. *Schoolbooks and Krags: The United States Army in the Philippines, 1898–1902*. Westport, CT: Greenwood, 1973.

Gelb, Leslie, and R. K. Betts. *The Irony of Viet Nam*. Washington, DC: Brookings Institution, 1979.

George, Alexander. *The Chinese Communist Army in Action*. New York: Columbia University Press, 1966.

Ghaus, Abdul Samad. *The Fall of Afghanistan: An Insider's Account*. London: Pergamon-Brassey's, 1988.

Giap, General. *See* Vo Nguyen.

Girardet, Edward. "Russia's War in Afghanistan." *Central Asian Survey*, vol. 2, no. 1 (July 1983).

———. *Afghanistan: The Soviet War*. New York: St. Martin's Press, 1985.

Goodman, Allan E. *An Institutional Profile of the South Vietnamese Officer Corps*. Santa Monica, CA: Rand Corporation, 1970.

———. *Politics in War: The Bases of Political Community in South Viet Nam*. Cambridge, MA: Harvard University Press, 1973.

———. *The Lost Peace: America's Search for a Negotiated Settlement of the Viet Nam War*. Stanford, CA: Hoover Institution, 1978.

Grant, J.A.C. "The Viet Nam Constitution of 1956." *American Political Science Review*, vol. 52 (June 1958).

Greene, Thomas. *Comparative Revolutionary Movements*. Englewood Cliffs, NJ: Prentice-Hall, 1984.

Guevara, Ernesto. *Guerrilla Warfare*. New York: Vintage, 1961.

Gurtov, Melvin. *The First Viet Nam Crisis: Chinese Communist Strategy and United States Involvement, 1953–1954*. New York: Greenwood, 1967.

Hammer, Ellen J. *The Struggle for Indochina, 1940–1955*, Stanford, CA: Stanford University Press, 1954.

———. "South Viet Nam: The Limits of Political Action." *Pacific Affairs*, vol. 35 (Spring 1962).

———. *A Death in November: America in Viet Nam, 1963*. New York: Dutton, 1987.

Hammer, Kenneth M. "Huks in the Philippines," in *Modern Guerrilla Warfare*, Franklin Mark Osantia, ed. (Glencoe, IL: Free Press, 1962).

Hammond, Thomas T. *Red Flag over Afghanistan: The Communist Coup, The Soviet Invasion, and the Consequences*. Boulder, CO: Westview, 1984.

Hannah, Norman B. *The Key to Failure: Laos and the Viet Nam War*. Lanham, MD: Madison Books, 1987.

Hanrahan, Gene. *The Communist Struggle in Malaya.* New York: Institute of Pacific Relations, 1954.

Harkavy, Robert E., and Stephanie Neuman. Vol. 1 of *The Lessons of Recent Wars in the Third World.* Lexington, MA: Lexington Books, 1985.

Heilbrunn, Otto. *Partisan Warfare.* New York: Praeger, 1962.

Henderson, Darryl. *Why the Viet Cong Fought: A Study of Motivation and Control in a Modern Army in Combat.* Westport, CT: Greenwood, 1979.

Herring, George C. *America's Longest War: The United States and Viet Nam, 1950–1975,* 2d. ed. New York: Knopf, 1986.

Herrington, Stuart A. *Silence Was a Weapon: The Viet Nam War in the Villages.* Novato, CA: Presidio, 1982.

———. *Peace With Honor?* Novato, CA: Presidio, 1983.

Hoang Ngoc Lung. *The General Offensives of 1968–1969.* Washington, DC: U.S. Army Center of Military History, 1981.

Hoang Van Chi. *From Colonialism to Communism: A Case History of North Viet Nam.* New York: Praeger, 1964.

Honey, P. J. *North Viet Nam Today: Profile of a Communist Satellite.* New York: Praeger, 1962.

Hosmer, Stephen T. *Constraints on U.S. Strategy in Third World Conflicts.* New York: Crane, Russak, 1988.

———. *The Army's Role in Counterinsurgency and Insurgency.* Santa Monica, CA: Rand Corporation, 1990.

———. Konrad Kellen, and Brian M. Jenkins. *The Fall of South Viet Nam.* New York: Crane, Russak, 1980.

———, and Thomas W. Wolfe. *Soviet Policy and Practice toward Third World Conflicts.* Lexington, MA: Lexington Books, 1983.

Hung P. Nguyen. "Communist Offensive Strategy and the Defense of South Viet Nam." In *Assessing the Viet Nam War,* ed. Lloyd J. Matthews and Dale E. Brown. McLean, VA: Pergamon-Brassey's, 1987.

Hunt, Richard A., and Richard H. Shultz, Jr., eds. *Lessons from an Unconventional War.* New York: Pergamon, 1982.

Huntington, Samuel P. "Patterns of Intervention: America and the Soviets in the Third World." *National Interest,* vol. 7 (Spring 1987).

Huynh Kim Khanh. *Vietnamese Communism, 1925–1945.* Ithaca, NY: Cornell University Press, 1982.

Issacs, Arnold R. *Without Honor: Defeat in Viet Nam and Cambodia.* New York: Vintage, 1984.

Isby, David C. *War in a Distant Country: Afghanistan, Invasion and Resistance.* London: Arms and Armour, 1989.

Johnson, Chalmers. *Peasant Nationalism and Communist Power.* Stanford, CA: Stanford University Press, 1961.

———. *Autopsy on People's War.* Berkeley, CA: University of California, 1973.

Joint Low Intensity Conflict Project. *Analytical Review of Low Intensity Conflict.* Washington, DC: U.S. Government Printing Office, 1986.

Jones, Howard. *"A New Kind of War": America's Global Strategy and the Truman Doctrine in Greece.* New York: Oxford University Press, 1989.

Jukes, Geoffrey. "The Soviet Armed Forces and the Afghan War." In *The Soviet*

Withdrawal from Afghanistan, ed. Amin Saikal and William Maley. Cambridge: Cambridge University Press, 1989.

Jumper, Roy, and Marjorie Weiner Normand. "Viet Nam." In *Government and Politics in Southeast Asia*, ed. George Kahin. Ithaca, NY: Cornell University, 1964.

Karp, Craig. *Afghanistan: Six Years of Soviet Occupation*. Washington, DC: U.S. Department of State, 1985.

———. *Afghanistan: Seven Years of Soviet Occupation*. Washington, DC: U.S. Department of State, 1986.

———. *Afghanistan: Eight Years of Soviet Occupation*. Washington, DC: U.S. Department of State, 1987.

Kennan, George F. *Memoirs, 1925–1950*. Boston: Little, Brown, 1967.

Kerkvliet, Benedict J. *The Huk Rebellion: A Study of Peasant Revolt in the Philippines*. Berkeley, CA: University of California, 1977.

Klass, Rosanne, ed. *Afghanistan: The Great Game Revisited*. New York: Freedom House, 1987.

Koenig, Louis W. *Bryan: A Political Biography of William Jennings Bryan*. New York: Putnam, 1971.

Komer, R. W. *The Malayan Emergency in Retrospect*. Santa Monica, CA: Rand Corporation, 1972.

Kousoulas, D. George. "The Guerrilla War the Communists Lost." *U.S. Naval Institute Proceedings*, vol. 89 (1963).

———. *Revolution and Defeat: The Story of the Greek Communist Party*. London: Oxford University Press, 1965.

———. *Modern Greece*. New York: Scribners, 1974.

Krakowski, Elie D. "Afghanistan: The Forgotten War." *Central Asian Survey*, vol. 4, no. 2 (October 1985).

Krepinevich, Andrew F., Jr. *The Army and Viet Nam*. Baltimore: Johns Hopkins University Press, 1986.

Lam Quang Thi. *Autopsy: The Death of South Viet Nam*. Phoenix: Sphinx, 1986.

Lancaster, Donald. *The Emancipation of French Indochina*. London: Oxford University Press, 1961.

Lansdale, Edward Geary. *In the Midst of Wars: An American's Mission to Southeast Asia*. New York: Harper and Row, 1972.

Laqueur, Walter. *Guerrilla: A Historical and Critical Study*. Boston: Little, Brown, 1976.

Leech, Margaret. *In the Days of McKinley*. New York: Harper and Row, 1959.

Leeper, Reginald. *When Greek Meets Greek*. London: Chatto and Windus, 1950.

Le Gro, William E. *Viet Nam from Cease-fire to Capitulation*. Washington, DC: U.S. Army Center of Military History, 1981.

Leites, Nathan. *The Viet Cong Style of Politics*. Santa Monica, CA: Rand Corporation, 1969.

Lessing, Doris. *The Wind Blows Away Our Words*. New York: Vintage, 1987.

Lessons from the Viet Nam War. London: Royal United Services Institute, 1969.

Lewy, Guenter, *America in Viet Nam*. New York: Oxford University Press, 1978.

———. "Some Political-Military Lessons of the Viet Nam War." In *Assessing the Viet Nam War*, ed. Lloyd Matthews and Dale E. Brown. McLean, VA: Pergamon-Brassey's, 1989.

Lindholm, Richard W., ed. *Viet Nam: The First Five Years.* East Lansing, MI: Michigan State University Press, 1959.

Linn, Brian McAlister. *The U.S. Army and Counterinsurgency in the Philippine War, 1899–1902.* Chapel Hill, NC: University of North Carolina, 1989.

Lomperis, Timothy J. *The War Everyone Lost—And Won: America's Intervention in Viet Nam's Twin Struggles.* Baton Rouge: Louisiana State University Press, 1984.

Low Intensity Conflict Field Manual, No. 100–20. Washington: Department of the Army, 1981.

Luttwak, Edward N. *The Pentagon and the Art of War.* New York: Simon and Schuster, 1984.

Malhuret, Claude, "Report from Afghanistan." *Foreign Affairs,* vol. 62 (Winter 1984).

Maneli, Mieczyslaw. *War of the Vanquished.* New York: Harper and Row, 1971.

Marc, Henri, and Pierre Cony. *Indochine française.* Paris: Editions France-Empire, 1946.

Marchand, Jean. *L'Indochine en guerre.* Paris: Pouzet, 1955.

Martin, Mike. *Afghanistan: Inside a Rebel Stronghold.* Dorset, England: Blandford, 1984.

Matthews, L. J., and D. E. Brown, eds. *Assessing the Viet Nam War.* Washington, DC: Pergamon-Brassey's, 1987.

McAlister, John T. *Viet Nam: The Origins of Revolution.* Garden City, NY: Doubleday-Anchor, 1971.

McNeill, William H. *Greece: American Aid in Action.* New York: Twentieth Century Fund, 1957.

Millett, A. R. *Semper Fidelis.* New York: Macmillan, 1980.

Morgan, H. W., ed. *Making Peace with Spain: The Diary of Whitelaw Reid.* Austin, TX: University of Texas, 1965.

Munholland, J. Kim. " 'Collaboration Strategy' and the French Pacification of Tonkin, 1885–1897." *Historical Journal,* vol. 24, no. 3 (1981).

Murray, J. C. "The Anti-Bandit War." Reprinted in *The Guerrilla—and How to Fight Him,* ed. Lt. Col. T. N. Greene. New York: Praeger, 1962.

Navarre, Henri. *Agonie de L'Indochine.* Paris: Plon, 1956.

Neuman, Stephania, and Robert Harkavy, eds. *The Lessons of Recent Wars in the Third World.* Lexington, MA: Lexington Books, 1987.

Ngo Quang Truong. *The Easter Offensive of 1972.* Washington, DC: U.S. Army Center of Military History, 1980.

———. *Territorial Forces.* Washington, DC: U.S. Army Center of Military History, 1981.

Nixon, Richard. *No More Viet Nams.* New York: Arbor House, 1985.

Nolan, Keith William. *Into Laos.* Novato, CA: Presidio, 1986.

Norris, J. A. *The First Afghan War.* Cambridge: Cambridge University Press, 1967.

O'Ballance, Edgar. *The Indochina War, 1945–1954.* London: Faber and Faber, 1964.

———. *The Greek Civil War, 1944–1949.* New York: Praeger, 1966.

———. *Malaya: The Communist Insurgent War, 1948–1960.* Hamden, CT: Archon, 1966.

Oberdorfer, Don. *Tet!* Garden City, NY: Doubleday, 1971.

O'Neill, Robert, J. *General Giap.* New York: Praeger, 1969.

Palmer, Bruce, Jr. *The Twenty-Five-Year War: America's Military Role in Viet Nam.* Lexington, KY: University Press of Kentucky, 1984.

Palmer, Dave Richard. *Summons of the Trumpet.* San Rafael, CA: Presidio, 1978.

Papagos, Alexander. "Guerrilla Warfare." In *Modern Guerrilla Warfare*, ed. F. M. Osanka. New York: Free Press, 1962.

Paret, Peter, and John Shy. *Guerrillas in the 1960s.* New York: Praeger, 1962.

Penniman, Howard R. *Elections in South Viet Nam.* Washington, DC: American Enterprise Institute, 1972.

Peterson, Michael E. *The Combined Action Platoons.* New York: Praeger, 1989.

Phelan, John Leddy. *The Hispanization of the Philippines.* Madison: University of Wisconsin Press, 1967.

Pierce, Richard A. *Russian Central Asia, 1867–1917: A Study in Colonial Rule.* Berkeley: University of California Press, 1960.

Pike, Douglas. *Viet Cong.* Cambridge, MA: MIT Press, 1966.

———. *History of Vietnamese Communism, 1925–1976.* Stanford, CA: Hoover Institution, 1978.

———. *PAVN: People's Army of Viet Nam.* Novato, CA: Presidio, 1986.

Pimlott, John. "The French Army: From Indochina to Chad." In *Armed Forces and Modern Counter-Insurgency*, ed. Ian F. W. Beckett and John Pimlott. New York: St. Martin's Press, 1985.

Popkin, Samuel. *The Rational Peasant.* Berkeley: University of California Press, 1979.

Poullada, Leon B. "Afghanistan and the United States: The Crucial Years." *Middle East Journal*, vol. 35, no. 2 (Spring 1981).

Pratt, Julius. *Expansionists of 1898.* New York: P. Smith, 1949.

Pye, Lucian. *Guerrilla Communism in Malaya.* Princeton, NJ: Princeton University Press, 1956.

Race, Jeffrey. *War Comes to Long An: Revolutionary Conflict in a Vietnamese Province.* Berkeley: University of California Press, 1972.

Regional Conflict Working Group. *Commitment to Freedom: Security Assistance as a U.S. Policy Instrument in the Third World.* Washington, DC: Government Printing Office, 1988.

———. *Supporting U.S. Strategy for Third World Conflict.* Washington, DC: Government Printing Office, 1988.

Rice, Edward E. *Wars of the Third Kind.* Berkeley: University of California Press, 1988.

Robbins, James S. *Soviet Counterinsurgency Strategy in Afghanistan, 1979–1989.* Ph.D. diss. Tufts University, 1991.

Rolph, Hammond. "Vietnamese Communism and the Protracted War." *Asian Survey*, vol. 12 (September 1972).

Romulo, Carlos P. *Crusade in Asia.* New York: John Day, 1955.

Roy, Jules. *The Battle of Dien Bien Phu*, trans. Robert Baldick. New York: Harper and Row, 1965.

Roy, Olivier. *Islam and Resistance in Afghanistan.* New York: Cambridge University Press, 1985.

Rubin, Barnett R. *To Die in Afghanistan.* New York: Helsinki Watch and Asia Watch, 1985.

————. "The Fragmentation of Afghanistan." *Foreign Affairs*, vol. 68 (Winter 1989–90).

Rubin, Barnett R., and Jeri Laber. *A Nation Is Dying: Afghanistan under the Soviets, 1979–1987*. Chicago: Northwestern University Press, 1988.

Rubinstein, Alvin Z. *The Great Game: Rivalry in the Persian Gulf and South Asia*. New York: Praeger, 1983.

Russett, Bruce, and James S. Sutterlin. "The U.N. in a New World Order." *Foreign Affairs*, vol. 70, no. 2 (Spring 1991).

Ryan, Nigel. *A Hitch or Two in Afghanistan*. London: Weidenfeld and Nicolson, 1983.

Rywkin, Michael. *Russia in Central Asia*. New York: Collier, 1963.

Saikal, Amin, and William Maley, eds. *The Soviet Withdrawal from Afghanistan*. Cambridge: Cambridge University Press, 1989.

Sarkesian, Sam. *America's Forgotten Wars: The Counterrevolutionary Past and Lessons for the Future*. Westport, CT: Greenwood, 1984.

Schwartzstein, Stuart J. D. "Chemical Warfare in Afghanistan." *World Affairs*, vol. 145, no. 3 (Winter 1982–83).

Scigliano, Robert. *South Viet Nam: Nation under Stress*. Boston: Houghton Mifflin, 1964.

Scott, Harriet, and William Scott. *The Soviet Art of War*. Boulder, CO: Westview, 1982.

Seton-Watson, Hugh. *Eastern Europe between the Wars, 1918–1941*. New York: Harper, 1967.

Shafer, D. Michael. *Deadly Paradigms: The Failure of U.S. Counterinsurgency Policy*. Princeton, NJ: Princeton University Press, 1988.

Shahrani, M. Nazif, and Robert L. Canfield, eds. *Revolutions and Rebellions in Afghanistan*. Berkeley: University of California Press, 1986.

Shaplen, Robert. *The Lost Revolution: The U.S. in Viet Nam, 1946–1966*. New York: Harper and Row, 1966.

Sharp, U.S. Grant. *Strategy for Defeat: Viet Nam in Retrospect*. San Rafael, CA: Presidio, 1978.

Sheikh, Ali T. "Not the Whole Truth: Media Coverage of the Afghan Conflict." *Conflict Quarterly*, vol. 10, no. 4 (Fall 1990).

Shultz, Richard H., Jr., et al., eds. *Guerrilla Warfare and Counterinsurgency: U.S.-Soviet Policy in the Third World*. Lexington, MA: Lexington Books, 1989.

Social Science Research Bureau of Michigan State University. *Problems of Freedom: South Viet Nam since Independence*. Glencoe, IL: Free Press of Glencoe, 1961.

Spector, Ronald H. *Advice and Support: The Early Years, 1941–1960*. Washington, DC: U.S. Army Center of Military History.

Spencer, Floyd. *War and Postwar Greece*. Washington, DC: Library of Congress, 1952.

Stanley, Peter W., ed. *Reappraising an Empire: New Perspectives on Philippine-American History*. Cambridge, MA: Harvard University Press, 1984.

Stavrakis, Peter J. *Moscow and Greek Communism, 1944–1949*. Ithaca, NY: Cornell University Press, 1989.

Sturtevant, David. "Filipino Peasant Rebellions Examined: Lessons from the Past." *CALC Report*, vol. 12, no. 3, May–June 1986.

Tanham, George K. *Communist Revolutionary Warfare: From the Viet Minh to the Viet Cong.* Rev. ed. New York: Praeger, 1967.

Taruc, Luis. *He Who Rides the Tiger.* New York: Praeger, 1967.

———. *Born of the People.* Westport, CT: Greenwood, 1973 [original 1953].

Taylor, Maxwell D. *Swords and Ploughshares.* New York: Norton, 1972.

Thayer, Thomas C. *War without Fronts: The American Experience in Viet Nam.* Boulder, CO: Westview, 1986.

Thies, W. J. *When Governments Collide.* Berkeley: University of California Press, 1980.

Thompson, Sir Robert. *Defeating Communist Insurgency: The Lessons of Malaya and Viet Nam.* New York: Praeger, 1966.

———. *No Exit from Viet Nam.* New York: David McKay, 1969.

———. *Revolutionary War in World Strategy.* New York: Taplinger, 1970.

———. *Peace Is Not at Hand.* New York: David McKay, 1974.

Thompson, W. Scott, and Donaldon D. Frizzell, eds. *The Lessons of Viet Nam.* New York: Crane, Russak, 1977.

Thornton, Thomas P. "The Emergence of Communist Revolutionary Doctrine," in C. E. Black and T. P. Thornton, eds., *Communism and Revolution: The Strategic Uses of Political Violence.* Princeton: Princeton University Press, 1964.

Tran Van Don. *Our Endless War.* San Rafael, CA: Presidio, 1978.

Tran Van Tra. *Concluding the 30-Years War.* Foreign Broadcast Information Service, 1983.

Trinquier, Roger. *Modern Warfare: A French View of Counterinsurgency.* New York: Praeger, 1964 [French publication 1961].

Trottier, Paul, and Craig Karp. *Afghanistan: Five Years of Occupation.* Washington: U.S. State Department Special Report no. 120, 1984.

Truman, Harry S. *Memoirs.* Two Volumes. New York: Doubleday, 1955 and 1956.

Truong Chinh (pseud.). *Primer for Revolt.* New York: Praeger, 1963.

Truong Nhu Tang. *A Viet Cong Memoir.* New York: Harcourt, 1987.

Tsoucalas, Constantine. *The Greek Tragedy.* Baltimore: Penguin, 1969.

Turley, William S. *Vietnamese Communism in Comparative Perspective.* Boulder, CO: Westview, 1980.

Turley, G. H. *The Easter Offensive.* Novato, CA: Presidio, 1985.

Turner, Robert F. *Vietnamese Communism: Its Origins and Development.* Stanford, CA: Hoover Institution, 1975.

Urban, Mark. *War in Afghanistan.* New York: St. Martin's, 1988.

Valeriano, Napoleon, and C. T. P. Bohannan. *Counterguerrilla Operations: The Philippine Experience.* New York: Praeger, 1962.

Van Evera, Stephen. "Primed for Peace: Europe after the Cold War." *International Security*, vol. 15, no. 3 (Winter 1990–91).

Van Fleet, James A. "How We Won in Greece." *Balkan Studies*, vol. 8 (1967).

Van Hollen, Eliza. *Afghanistan: Three Years of Occupation.* Washington, DC: U.S. Department of State, 1982.

Van Tien Dung. *Our Great Spring Victory.* New York: Monthly Review Press, 1977.

Vo Nguyen Giap. *How We Won the War.* Philadelphia: Recon, 1976.

Wainhouse, E. R. "Guerrilla War in Greece, 1946–1949." In *Modern Guerrilla Warfare*, ed. Franklin Mark Osanka. New York: Free Press, 1962.

Warner, Denis. *The Last Confucian.* New York: Macmillan, 1963.

————. *Certain Victory: How Hanoi Won the War*. Kansas City: Sneed, Andrews and McMeel, 1978.

Welch, Richard E. *Response to Imperialism: The United States and the Philippine-American War*. Chapel Hill: University of North Carolina Press, 1979.

West, F. J., Jr. *The Village*. New York: Harper and Row, 1972.

Westmoreland, William. *A Soldier Reports*. Garden City, NY: Doubleday, 1976.

Wheeler, Geoffrey. *The Modern History of Soviet Central Asia*. London: Weidenfeld and Nicolson, 1964.

Wimbush, S. E., and A. Alexiev. "Soviet Central Asian Soldiers in Afghanistan." Santa Monica, CA: Rand Corporation, 1984.

Wittner, Lawrence S. *American Intervention in Greece, 1943–1949*. New York: Columbia University Press, 1982.

Wolff, Robert L. *The Balkans in Our Times*. Cambridge, MA: Harvard University Press, 1956.

Woodhouse, C. M. *The Struggle for Greece, 1941–1949*. London: Hart-Davis, MacGibbon, 1976.

Young, Kenneth. *The Greek Passion*. London: J. M. Dent, 1969.

Zimmerman, William, and Robert Axelrod. "The 'Lessons' of Viet Nam and Soviet Foreign Policy." *World Politics*, vol. 34, no. 1 (October 1981).

Zotos, S. *Greece: The Struggle for Freedom*. New York: Crowell, 1967.

Index

ABOUT THE AUTHOR

ANTHONY JAMES JOES is director of the international relations program at St. Joseph's University. He received his Ph.D. from the University of Pennsylvania in 1970. Among his previous writings are *Fascism in the Contemporary World*; *Mussolini*; *From the Barrel of a Gun: Armies and Revolutions*; and *The War for South Viet Nam* (Praeger, 1989).